Europe and the Cold War 1945–91 SECOND EDITION

David Williamson

HODDER
EDUCATION
AN HACHETTE UK COMPANY

To Luca David Mario Williamson

Study guides revised and updated, 2008, by Sally Waller (AQA), Angela Leonard (Edexcel) and Geoff Woodward (OCR).

Orders: please contact Bookpoint Ltd, 130 Milton Park, Abingdon, Oxon OX14 4SB. Telephone: (44) 01235 827720. Fax: (44) 01235 400454. Lines are open 9.00–5.00, Monday to Saturday, with a 24-hour message answering service. Visit our website at www.hoddereducation.co.uk

Impression number   11
Year   2013

Cover photo showing the nuclear explosion over Bikini Atoll © Corbis
Typeset in Baskerville 10/12pt and produced by Gray Publishing, Tunbridge Wells
Printed and bound by CPI Group (UK) Ltd, Croydon CR0 4YY

A catalogue record for this title is available from the British Library

ISBN: 978 0340 90700 9

Contents

Dedication

Keith Randell (1943–2002)

The *Access to History* series was conceived and developed by Keith, who created a series to 'cater for students as they are, not as we might wish them to be'. He leaves a living legacy of a series that for over 20 years has provided a trusted, stimulating and well-loved accompaniment to post-16 study. Our aim with these new editions is to continue to offer students the best possible support for their studies.

The publishers would like to thank the following individuals, institutions and companies for permission to reproduce copyright illustrations in this book: © CORBIS, pages 28, 38, 43, 48, 99 (top); © Bettmann/CORBIS, pages 3, 15, 17, 29, 70, 91 (bottom), 94, 109, 117, 121, 138; Courtesy of Richard and Alexander Marengo, page 37; © Owen Franken/CORBIS, page 144; Getty Images, page 112; © Hulton-Deutsch Collection/CORBIS, page 110; © Lester Cole/CORBIS, page 124; Press Office of the Government of Germany, pages 44, 68, 74, 91 (top), 97, 99 (bottom), 120, 147, 155; © Peter Turnley/CORBIS, page 152.
The publishers would like to acknowledge the following: British Broadcasting Corporation (BBC) for extracts from *The Unsettled Peace: A Study of the Cold War in Europe* by Roger Morgan, 1974 and *World Powers in the Twentieth Century* by Harriet Ward, 1985; Harvard University Press for an extract from *Inside the Kremlin's Cold War* by Vladislav Zubok and Constantine Pleshakov, 1996; Longman for an extract from *Russia, America and the Cold War, 1949–1991* by Martin McCauley, 1998; Penguin Press for extracts from *The Cold War: A New History* by John Lewis Gaddis, 2005 and *Colossus: The Rise and Fall of the American Empire* by Niall Ferguson, 2004; Routledge for extracts from *The Cold War 1945–1991* by John W. Mason, 1996 and *The Soviet Union in World Politics* by Geoffrey Roberts, 1999; Vintage UK for an extract from *The Cold War and the Making of the Modern World* by Martin Walker, 1994.
The publishers would like to thank the following for permission to reproduce copyright material in this book: Edexcel Limited for extracts used on pages 61, 133, 162.

1 The Cold War: An Introduction

POINTS TO CONSIDER
The point of this introductory chapter is to help you to understand the overall pattern of events before studying the various phases of the Cold War in Europe in greater detail. It introduces you to the main events and themes of the Cold War:

- How and why it started
- How it developed and changed between 1945 and 1989
- How historians have interpreted it

Key dates

1917	October	Russian Revolution
1918	April	Wilson's Fourteen Points
1945		End of the Second World War
1947	March	Truman Doctrine
	June	Marshall Plan
1948–9		Berlin Blockade
1949	April	Formation of NATO
1950	June	Start of the Korean War
1953	March 5	Death of Stalin
	July	Korean Armistice signed
1958		Second Berlin Crisis
1961	August 13	Construction of the Berlin Wall
1962		Cuban Missile Crisis
1968	August	Invasion of Czechoslovakia by Warsaw Pact forces
1971	September	Four Power Agreement on Berlin
1975		Helsinki Final Act
1979	December	USSR invaded Afghanistan
1983		Pershing and Cruise missiles installed in Western Europe
1989	November 9	Berlin Wall breached
1990	October	Germany reunited

1 | What Was the Cold War?

The term 'cold war' had been used before 1945 to describe periods of extreme tension between states stopping just short of war. In 1893 the German **socialist**, Eduard Bernstein, described the **arms race** between Germany and its neighbours as a kind of 'cold war' where 'there is no shooting but … bleeding'. In May 1945 when the USA and the USSR faced each other eyeball to eyeball in Germany this term rapidly came back into use. The British writer George Orwell, commenting on the significance of the dropping of the atom bomb, foresaw 'a peace that is no peace', in which the USA and USSR would be both 'unconquerable and in a permanent state of cold war' with each other. The Cold War was, however, more than just an arms race. It was also, as the historian, John Mason, has pointed out, 'a fundamental clash of ideologies and interests'. Essentially the USSR followed Lenin's and Marx's teaching that conflict between Communism (see page 3) and **capitalism** was unavoidable, while the USA and its allies for much of the time saw the USSR, in the words of President Reagan in 1983, as an 'evil empire', intent on the destruction of democracy and civil rights.

A US historian, Anders Stephanson, has defined the essence of the Cold War as follows:

- Both sides denied each other's legitimacy as a regime and attempted to attack each other by every means short of war.
- Increasingly this conflict became bipolar. There was an intense build up of both nuclear and conventional military weapons and a prolonged arms race between the USA and the USSR.
- Each side suppressed its internal dissidents.

Most historians would more or less accept this definition, although there is less agreement on the time-scale of the Cold War. The British historian, David Reynolds, whose chronology is for the most part followed in this book, argues that there were three cold wars:

- 1948–53
- 1958–63
- 1979–85.

These were 'punctured by periods of *détente*'. Two Russian historians, Vladislav Zubok and Constantine Pleshakov, however, provide a slightly different model: they define the Cold War as lasting from 1948 to the Cuban Crisis of 1962 and the subsequent 27 years as no more than a 'prolonged armistice' rather than actual peace. The problem with this interpretation is that it ignores the outbreak of the 'Third Cold War' in 1979.

While the chronology of the Cold War is open to debate, and the beginning of the 'Second Cold War' could as easily be dated from October 1956 as from November 1958, it is important to grasp that the years 1945–89 formed a 'Cold War era', in which

Key question
What were the main characteristics of the Cold War and how many cold wars were there?

Key dates

Germany was defeated and occupied by the USA, Britain and the USSR: May 1945

The war with Japan ended after the dropping of atom bombs on Hiroshima and Nagasaki: August 1945

Key terms

Socialist
A believer in socialism: the belief that the community as a whole, rather than individuals, should control the means of production, the exchange of goods and banking.

Arms race
A competition or race between nations to arm themselves with the most deadly and effective weapons available.

Capitalism
An economic system in which the production of goods and their distribution depend on the investment of private capital.

Détente
A state of lessened tension or growing relaxation between two states.

Profile: Karl Marx 1818–83

1818	– Born in Trier, Germany
1835–41	– Studied in Bonn and Berlin
1848	– Published the *Communist Manifesto*. Took part in the 1848 revolutions in Cologne
1849	– Fled to London when charged with high treason
1849–83	– Lived in London and formulated his theories of the class struggle and the economic laws determining the eventual collapse of capitalism and rise of Communism

Marx was a German philosopher of Jewish extraction, and the theoretical and philosophical system he constructed was the intellectual basis of Marxism–Leninism, the ideology of the USSR. Marx was convinced that capitalism would inevitably be overthrown by the workers or 'proletariat' in a revolution where they would seize control of the factories and banks. Initially they would create a 'dictatorship of the proletariat' in order to defend the revolution, but once the revolution was safe the new proletariat state would simply begin to 'wither away' and be replaced by a Communist society where economic production would be subordinated to human needs, or, as Marx put it: 'from each according to his ability, to each according to his need'.

Marx idealistically believed that once this stage was achieved, crime, envy and rivalry would become things of the past. Vladimir Ilych Lenin (1870–1924) both applied and adapted these ideas in Russia after the Revolution of 1917.

years of intense hostility alternated with periods of *détente*, but, even then, the arms race and ideological competition between the two sides continued. The US historian, John Gaddis, argues that the Cold War lasted for so long because of the nuclear balance. Soviet military, particularly nuclear, strength disguised the essential economic weakness of the USSR, which eventually caused its collapse (see page 141).

Key question
Did the Cold War pre-
date the end of the
Second World War?

2 | The Origins of the Cold War 1917–45

The simultaneous expansion of Russia and the USA until they dominated the world had been foreseen as early as 1835 by the French historian Alexis de Tocqueville, who observed:

> There are now two great nations in the world, which, starting from different points, seem to be advancing toward the same goal: the Russians and the Anglo-Americans. … [E]ach seems called by some secret design of Providence one day to hold in its hands the destinies of half the world.

It was, however, the First World War that brought these great states more closely into contact with each other. When the USA entered the war against Germany, they were briefly allies, but this changed dramatically once the **Bolsheviks** seized power in October 1917 and made peace with Germany.

The Russian Revolution and Allied intervention

One historian, Howard Roffmann, argued that the Cold War 'proceeded from the very moment the Bolsheviks triumphed in Russia in 1917'. There was certainly immediate hostility between Soviet Russia and the Western states, which initially tried to strangle Bolshevism at birth by intervening in the Russian civil war and backing its opponents. Ideologically, too, there was a clash between the ideas of the US President, Woodrow Wilson, and Lenin. Wilson, in his Fourteen Points of April 1918, presented an ambitious global programme for self-determination, free trade and collective security through a League of Nations, while Lenin preached world revolution and Communism.

The year 1917 was pivotal in the First World War. In Russia, a revolution broke out in February and in April the USA declared war on Germany. Then, in October, the Bolsheviks under Lenin's leadership seized power.

The USSR and the West 1924–45

The events of 1917–18 certainly marked the ideological origins of the Cold War, but if the meaning of a Cold War is interpreted along the lines of Stephanson's definition (see page 2), then there was not a proper Cold War during the 1920s and 1930s.

In 1920 the USA withdrew into **isolation**, and in the 1930s the USSR under Stalin increasingly concentrated on building up its military and industrial strength. This did not stop Moscow from attempting to undermine capitalism and the British and French colonial empires through the **Comintern**. In the late 1920s relations between Britain and the USSR were so poor that they have been described as the first Anglo-Soviet Cold War. Yet there was no bipolar line-up.

In the 1930s, for most of the time, the USSR and the USA were on the sidelines, while the growing divide was between the Axis powers, Germany and Italy, and the Western democracies, Britain and France. Shortly before war broke out in 1939, the USSR secured its neutrality on highly favourable conditions through the Nazi–Soviet Pact. Thus by the end of 1939 de Tocqueville's prophecy still seemed to be, as John Gaddis has put it, 'a wild improbability'.

It was Hitler who created the context for the Cold War, when he invaded Russia in June 1941 and then, just after the Japanese attack on Pearl Harbor in December, declared war on the USA. The subsequent defeat and occupation of Germany by the USSR and the Western Allies in 1945 at last brought the two superpowers, the USSR and the USA, face to face. A few days before he committed suicide in April 1945 Hitler predicted that:

Key dates
The Russian Revolution: October 1917
The Fourteen Points: April 1918

Key term
Bolsheviks Russian Communists. The term, which means majority, was originally given to Lenin's group within the Russian Social Democrat Party in 1903.

Key question
How did relations develop between the USSR and the main Western states, 1924–45?

Key terms
Isolation A situation in which a state has no alliances or contacts with other friendly states.

Comintern The Communist International was formed in 1919. Theoretically, in the words of its chairman, Zinoviev, it was 'a single foreign Communist Party with sections in different countries', but in reality it was controlled from Moscow.

Key date
War in Europe ended:
8 May 1945

With the defeat of the *Reich* [Germany] and pending the emergence of the Asiatic, the African, and perhaps the South American nationalisms, there will remain in the world only two Great Powers capable of confronting each other – the United States and Soviet Russia. The laws of history and geography will compel these two Powers to a trial of strength either military or in the fields of economics and ideology.

Key question
When did the Cold War start? Which of the two superpowers was more responsible for starting it?

3 | The Beginnings of the Cold War in Europe 1945–8

The years 1945–8 saw the beginning of the Cold War in Europe, but historians cannot agree on who started it or on whether it could have been avoided. Most, however, do not dispute that it was a consequence of Hitler's defeat. This created a vacuum not only in Germany but in most of continental Europe, which was filled by the armies of the wartime allies. The Soviets occupied the whole of Eastern Europe up to the river Elbe, while the Americans, British and French dominated Western Europe, Greece and the Mediterranean. Inevitably the interests of the Great Powers, particularly of the USA and USSR, collided with each other in this vacuum. Some historians see this as the key explanation of the Cold War. Louis Halle, for instance, has likened the Cold War to placing a 'scorpion and a tarantula together in a bottle'. The British historian S.R. Ashton calls this 'the centrist view', as it emphasises fundamental differences rather than stressing that the Cold War was the fault of one side or the other.

Key question
What are the interpretations of traditionalist historians of the Cold War?

Traditionalist interpretations

Traditionalist Western historians, such as Herbert Feiss, writing in the 1950s, and, more recently in 1995, R.C. Raack, firmly put the blame for starting the Cold War on Stalin. They argued that Stalin ignored promises given at the Yalta Conference in February 1945 (see pages 28–30), to support democratically elected governments. Instead, he proceeded over the next three years to put his own Communist stooges in power in the Eastern European states. Once it was clear that Britain and France were too weak to defend Western Europe, the Americans intervened and made the following key decisions, which in effect marked the beginning of the Cold War:

Traditionalist
In the sense of historians, someone who has a traditional view of historical events.

Bizonia
In 1945, war-defeated Germany was divided into four zones occupied by the Americans, British, French and Soviets. In January 1947 the British and American zones were amalgamated and called Bizonia.

- Rather then let Greece and Turkey go Communist, Truman offered them, in the spring of 1947, military and financial help to defend themselves from attack from Communist forces. This policy became known as the Truman Doctrine.
- The Marshall Plan, announced in mid-1947, helped to revive the Western economies through the injection of large sums of money and so block the spread of Communism.
- In Germany, the USA, in the absence of any agreement with the USSR, merged its zone of occupation with the British in January 1947, thereby creating **Bizonia**. In June 1948 the

Figure1.1: Central Europe in 1955.

Key term

Paranoia
Literally a mental condition characterised by an exaggerated fear of persecution. Here it means obsessive distrust.

Key question
What are the main arguments of the revisionist historians?

Key term

Revisionist
In the sense of historians, someone who revises the traditional or orthodox interpretation of events and often contradicts it.

Key question
How accurate is it to describe the early years of the Cold War as bipolar?

Key date

The Berlin Wall was built to stop East Germans fleeing to the West through the open frontier between East and West Berlin: 13 August 1961

Key question
Why did a Third World War not break out between 1948 and 1953?

Western Allies introduced a new currency into their zones and made the crucial decision to set up a separate West German state.

This interpretation of the start of the Cold War showed the USA responding defensively to aggressive Soviet moves. In the 1990s the historian John Gaddis gave a new slant to this interpretation by arguing that the Cold War was an unavoidable consequence of Stalin's **paranoia**, and was an extension of the way he dealt with opposition within the USSR.

Revisionist historians

Revisionist historians writing in the 1960s and 1970s, however, argued that the USA and, to a lesser extent, Britain, pursued policies that caused the Cold War in Europe. For instance, William Appleman Williams, writing as early as 1959, claimed that Washington was aiming to force the USSR to join the global economy and open its frontiers to both US imports and political ideas, which would almost certainly have undermined the Stalinist regime. Ten years later another historian, Gabriel Kolko, summed up US policy as aiming 'to restructure the world, so that American business could trade, operate, and profit without restrictions everywhere'.

The role of other European countries in influencing the course of the Cold War

Given the bipolar nature of the Cold War, historians initially concentrated on the USSR and the USA, yet in the early stages of the Cold War both Britain and France were still influential, although declining powers. Recent research has shown how Britain played a major role in the division of Germany and in turning the offer of Marshall Aid into a practical economic recovery plan. The Cold War ultimately divided Europe into two great blocs, yet within Western Europe, as we shall see, the individual states were, to quote Reynolds, not just 'blank slates on which America could write a new history'. Similarly, in Eastern Europe historians are beginning to discover that local Communist politicians were at times also able to influence events, as was seen particularly in the events leading up to the building of the Berlin Wall.

4 | The 'First Cold War' 1948–53

The years 1948–53 were a period of prolonged confrontation in Europe between the USA and the USSR. From 1948, at the latest, it became clear that the Cold War in Europe essentially revolved around the German question.

The Berlin Blockade

The Soviets were determined to stop the Americans and their Allies from building up a new and powerful state in West Germany. They therefore blockaded West Berlin, which was occupied by the three Western Allies, from June 1948 to May

1949, in the hope that they could force Washington to reverse this policy. They were thwarted because of the Anglo-American airlift, which managed to keep West Berlin supplied with food, clothing and raw materials right through the winter of 1948–9.

The Berlin Crisis was the first major confrontation between the Americans and Soviets. It reinforced the division of Germany and Europe and speeded up the arms race. In April 1949 the creation of **NATO** marked the foundation of a new Western alliance, while in July the Russians exploded their first atom bomb. The Federal Republic of Germany (FRG) was set up in September to be followed a month later by the Soviets establishing the German Democratic Republic (GDR).

The Korean War and its consequences

The outbreak of the Korean War led to demands for arming West Germany when a North Korean army invaded South Korea. The situation in Korea had disturbing parallels with divided Germany. Since 1945, when the Americans and Russians liberated Korea from the Japanese, North Korea had been within the Soviet sphere of influence, while South Korea had come under US control. There was considerable fear in Europe that the Korean situation might be the prelude to a similar attack on Germany. Military demands for West German rearmament and French fears of revived German power were reconciled through the Pleven Plan of October 1950, which proposed that West German soldiers should be integrated into the European Defence Community (**EDC**).

One of the consequences of the Korean War was that the former enemy states, Italy and (West) Germany, under US pressure, were gradually integrated both politically and economically into Western Europe. This was exactly what Stalin had hoped to avoid. In 1952 in an attempt to stop West German rearmament, Stalin proposed setting up a free neutral Germany with its own army, but he failed to overcome the suspicions of either the Western powers or the West Germans. During these years tension between the USSR and the Western powers was dangerously high. Why then did war not break out? Was it nuclear weapons that kept the peace or was Stalin in reality a cautious politician who was only too aware of the terrible losses the USSR had suffered in the Second World War?

5 | The 'Thaw' 1953–7

The death of Stalin marked a turning point in the Cold War in Europe. The Soviet leadership, absorbed in an internal power struggle, wanted to ease tension with the Western powers. It withdrew Soviet troops from Austria, but elsewhere the **Iron Curtain** remained firmly in place. When West Germany joined NATO in May 1955, the Russians responded by creating the Warsaw Pact, a military alliance composed of the USSR and the Eastern European satellite states.

Key dates

The Berlin Blockade: 1948–9

Formation of NATO: April 1949

Start of Korean War: 1950

Key terms

NATO
The North Atlantic Treaty Organisation was a military alliance which linked the USA and Canada to Western Europe. It became the cornerstone of the defence of Western Europe against Soviet threats.

EDC
The European Defence Community, the aim of which was to set up a Western European army jointly controlled by the Western European states.

Iron Curtain
A term used by Churchill to describe how Stalin had separated Eastern Europe from the West.

Key question
Why can it be argued that 1953 was the end of the 'First Cold War'?

Key date

Death of Stalin:
5 March 1953

The **thaw** confronted the Soviet leadership with a dilemma that it never solved. If it went too far down the line of destalinisation and liberalisation, it risked losing control of its satellites. Khrushchev's appeal for different 'national roads to Socialism' in 1956 fuelled demands for greater independence in both Poland and Hungary. In Poland these demands were partly satisfied, but in Hungary threats to withdraw from the Warsaw Pact and to end the domination of the Communist Party led to Soviet military intervention in 1956. The defeat of the Hungarian revolt showed both the limits to destalinisation, and that the Western Allies would not intervene in what was regarded as a Soviet sphere of interest.

6 | The 'Second Cold War' 1958–62

Second Berlin Crisis 1958–61

Key question
Why do some historians call this period the 'Second Cold War'?

Key dates

Second Berlin Crisis:
1958–61

Cuban Missile Crisis:
1962

Key terms

Thaw
A period of improved relations between East and West: a 'thaw' in the 'Cold War'.

Four power control
In 1945 it was agreed that Berlin should be divided into four zones and be administered jointly by the four occupying powers.

Free city
A city that enjoys self-government and is not part of a state.

Although Europe's division was a reality by 1958, the balance of power in Germany was still precarious. The government of the GDR was hated by its population and only kept in place by Soviet bayonets. The FRG, on the other hand, was rapidly becoming a major European power, and its growing prosperity exercised a magnet-like pull on the population of the GDR. Berlin was still under **four power control**. As it was possible to cross unhindered from the Soviet to the Western sectors of the city, between 1949 and 1958 well over 2.1 million East Germans out of a population of 17 million had escaped this way to the West. Inevitably this was a serious threat to the economic and social stability of the GDR.

The key to the dramatic increase in tension between 1958 and 1962 was Khrushchev's determination to use the impressive advances the USSR had made in missile technology to frighten the Western powers into making concessions in Germany. The Berlin Crisis began in November 1958, when Khrushchev demanded that West Berlin should become a '**free city**' and that all Western troops should withdraw from it. He threatened further that, if there was no agreement within six months, the USSR would sign a peace treaty with the GDR that would enable it to control the access routes to West Berlin. Khrushchev failed to carry out this threat, but he did allow the GDR to seal off East Berlin from the Western sectors on 13 August 1961 by the construction of what became known as the Berlin Wall.

The Cuban Missile Crisis 1962

Building the wall effectively ended the crisis, although global tension reached a new peak in October 1962 when Khrushchev installed nuclear missiles in Cuba in a bid to stop US attempts to overthrow the Communist regime of Fidel Castro. Only when he agreed to withdraw these, after the most dangerous confrontation between the USA and USSR in the whole of the Cold War, was a way open for *détente* between the superpowers in Europe.

7 | The Period of *Détente* 1963–79

In the 1960s both the USSR and USA wanted a relaxation of tension in Europe. The USA was distracted by the Vietnam War, while the USSR faced serious economic problems and a growing challenge from China. This resulted in the **Test Ban Treaty** of 1963 and the **Non-Proliferation Treaty** for nuclear weapons in 1969. The construction of the Berlin Wall had forced the FRG to rethink its relations with the GDR, as it now seemed that the latter would survive for the foreseeable future.

Despite the invasion of Czechoslovakia in August 1968 by Warsaw Pact forces to crush the 'Prague Spring', Willy Brandt, the new West German Social Democratic Chancellor, launched his Eastern Policy or *Ostpolitik* in October 1969. The FRG now recognised the GDR as a legal state and accepted the postwar frontiers of Poland and Czechoslovakia. Parallel to these negotiations the four victorious powers of 1945 negotiated an agreement guaranteeing West Berlin's links with the FRG.

Although these treaties, together with the agreement negotiated at Helsinki in 1975, the Helsinki Final Act, which recognised the division of Europe and the desirability of a peaceful settlement of disputes (see pages 146–7), did much to stabilise the situation in central and eastern Europe, Europe remained divided into two armed and potentially hostile blocs. By this date contemporaries believed that the division of Europe and the Cold War would last for an eternity, but in reality the strength of the USSR was less formidable than it seemed.

8 | The 'Third Cold War' and the Collapse of Communism 1979–91

What can be called a 'third' or the 'New Cold War' was started by the USSR's decision to deploy a second generation of medium-range nuclear missiles in Europe and to intervene in Afghanistan. The USA and the Western powers responded vigorously by deploying Cruise missiles in Western Europe. In 1983 President Reagan escalated the arms race in a dramatic way by announcing the Strategic Defence Initiative (SDI), which was a plan to enable the USA to destroy Soviet missiles launched into the atmosphere. Faced with this new and vastly expensive challenge, military defeat in Afghanistan, the flare-up of ethnic conflicts at home and national bankruptcy, Mikhail Gorbachev, who came to power in the USSR in 1985, had little option but to end the Cold War and seek Western loans to modernise the Soviet economy. Once it became clear in 1989 that the USSR would no longer prop up the satellite regimes in Eastern Europe, they collapsed. They failed to survive because they were kept in place by Soviet bayonets, were therefore by necessity police states and were unable to match Western Europe's prosperity.

Key question
To what extent had the Cold War in Europe changed its character by 1973?

Key terms

Test Ban Treaty
This prohibited the testing of nuclear weapons in the atmosphere, outer space and under water, but allowed them to be tested underground.

Non-Proliferation Treaty
Britain, the USA and the USSR pledged not to equip other countries with nuclear weapons.

Key question
Why did the Cold War end?

Key dates

Invasion of Czechoslovakia by Warsaw Pact forces: August 1968

Four Power Agreement on Berlin: September 1971

Helsinki Final Act: 1975

Soviet forces sent into Afghanistan to save a weak left-wing regime. They were unsuccessful and were pulled out in 1988: December 1979

Deployment of Pershing and Cruise missiles in West Germany and Britain: 1983

9 | The Nuclear Background

Key question
What role did nuclear weapons play in the Cold War?

Key terms

Hydrogen bombs
Thermonuclear devices, which explode at a very high temperature. Each one is capable of devastating 150 square miles by the blast and 800 square miles with radioactive fallout.

Intercontinental ballistic missile
A long-range missile that is powered initially, but falls on its target as a result of gravity and which can, for example, reach the USA from the USSR.

MIRVs
Multiple independently targeted re-entry vehicles. These were rockets that could fire well over 12 nuclear missiles on different targets.

Key dates

Berlin Wall breached: 9–10 November 1989

Germany reunited: October 1990

What prevented the Cold War from becoming a 'hot war' was the balance of terror created by nuclear weapons. When the USA dropped nuclear bombs on the Japanese cities of Hiroshima and Nagasaki, it was clear that, to quote the US historian John Gaddis, a 'quantum jump' in destructive weapons had been reached. Stalin responded by speeding up work on developing a Soviet atom bomb, which was tested on 20 August 1949.

Both powers then went on to develop **hydrogen bombs**, and to design long-range bombers that could carry them. Over the next decade bombers were replaced by rockets. With the assistance of German scientists, captured at the end of the Second World War, the Soviets successfully fired the world's first **intercontinental ballistic missile** (ICBM) in August 1957. Horrified by the apparent evidence of a missile gap, the USA first of all produced Thor and Jupiter missiles (see page 126), and then went on to develop a whole new generation of rockets, which included the Polaris missiles that could be fired from submarines. Steadily over the next 25 years these lethal systems were expanded and improved. In sheer quantity of missiles the USSR caught up with the USA by the early 1970s. Computerised guidance systems could now accurately guide ICBMs to their targets and the development of **MIRVs** meant that multiple missiles could be fired at the same time on different targets. In any nuclear conflict it was inconceivable that there could be a winner. In 1980 what President Dwight Eisenhower had told the South Korean leader, Syngman Rhee, in 1953 was even more relevant:

> There will be millions of people dead. War today is unthinkable with the weapons which we have at our command. If the Kremlin and Washington ever lock up in a war, the results are too horrible to contemplate.

Only in 1983 was this doctrine of Mutual Assured Destruction (or MAD) challenged when the US-pioneered Strategic Defence Initiative (SDI) achieved a revolutionary breakthrough. SDI or 'Star Wars' envisaged setting up a protective shield of lasers and particle-beam weapons in space aimed against ballistic missiles, and it seemed that the USA might eventually become safe from Soviet missile attacks. Whether this would really have been effective in the 1980s we do not know, but it certainly scared the Soviets into seeking a new *détente* and ultimately into ending the Cold War.

Summary diagram: The Cold War in Europe 1945–91

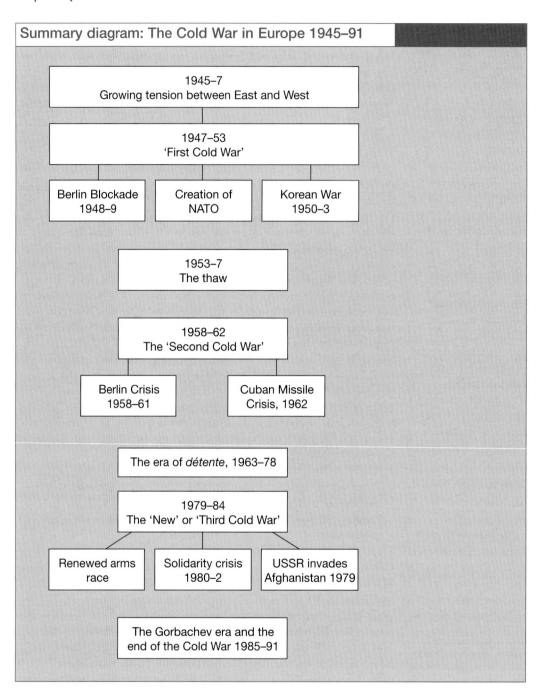

2

The Defeat of the Axis Powers 1943–5: Cold War Foreshadowed?

POINTS TO CONSIDER

The years 1943–5 saw the defeat and occupation of Nazi Germany, but also witnessed the growing rivalry between the USA and Britain on the one side and the USSR on the other. This chapter examines these issues through the following themes:

- The conflicting aims of the Big Three
- Inter-Allied negotiations 1943–4
- The liberation of Europe 1943–5
- The Yalta Conference, February 1945
- The end of the war in Europe

Key dates

1939	September	Hitler and Stalin partitioned Poland
	October	Polish government-in-exile set up in London
	November	Stalin attacked Finland and annexed territories along the Soviet border
1943	September 3	Italian Armistice
	November 28– December 1	Teheran Conference
1944	June 6	Allied forces invaded France
	July	Red Army entered central Poland; National Liberation Committee set up
	August 23	Formation of coalition government in Romania
	September 9	Communist *coup* in Bulgaria
	October 9	Anglo-Soviet 'percentages agreement'
	December	British suppressed Communist uprising in Greece
	December 10	Franco-Soviet Treaty
1945	February 4–11	Yalta Conference
	April	Liberation of Czechoslovakia
	May 8	Unconditional German surrender

1 | The Conflicting Aims of the Big Three

All three members of the **Grand Alliance** (the **Big Three**) were in agreement that Germany should never again be in a position to unleash a world war. They also hoped to continue the wartime alliance that had been so successful, and co-operate together in the new United Nations organisation, but as victory over the **Axis powers** became more certain, they began to develop their own often conflicting aims and agendas for postwar Europe.

Key question
On which issues were the Big Three powers in agreement?

The USSR

In the early 1950s, most Western observers assumed that Moscow's main aim was to destroy the Western powers and create global Communism, yet recent historical research, which the end of the Cold War has made possible, has shown that Stalin's policy was often more flexible and less ambitious than it appeared to be at the time. By the winter of 1944–5 his immediate priorities were clear. He wanted security for the USSR and reparations from Germany and its allies.

To protect the USSR against any future German attack Stalin was determined to hang on to the land annexed from Poland in 1939 and, as compensation, to give Poland the German territories that lay beyond the river Oder. He also aimed to reintegrate into the USSR the Baltic provinces of Estonia, Latvia and Lithuania, as well as the territory lost to Finland in 1941, to annex Bessarabia and to bring both Romania and Bulgaria within the Soviet orbit (see the map on page 6). In Eastern Europe, Stalin's first priority was to ensure that regimes friendly to the USSR were set up. In some states, such as Poland and Romania, this could only be guaranteed by a Communist government, but in others, such as Hungary and Czechoslovakia, Stalin was prepared to tolerate more broadly based governments in which the Communists formed a minority.

By 1944 Stalin seems to have envisaged a postwar Europe made up of three different areas:

- An area under direct Soviet control in Eastern Europe: Poland, Romania, Bulgaria and, for a time at least, the future Soviet zone in Germany.
- An 'intermediate zone', which was neither fully Communist nor fully capitalist, comprising Yugoslavia, Austria, Hungary, Czechoslovakia and Finland, in which the Communists would share power with the middle-class parties and form a bridge to the West.
- A non-communist Western Europe, which would also include Greece.

Key question
What were Stalin's aims in 1944–5?

Key terms

Grand Alliance
In 1941 Britain, the USSR and the USA allied to combat the Axis powers led by Germany, Japan and Italy.

Big Three
The major powers who formed the Grand Alliance: Britain, the USA and the USSR.

Axis powers
The major powers opposing the Allies: Germany, Japan and Italy.

Key dates

Hitler and Stalin partitioned Poland: September 1939

Stalin attacked Finland and annexed strategically important territories along the Soviet border. These were returned when Hitler invaded the USSR in 1941: November 1939

Profile: Josef Stalin 1879–1953

1879		– Born in Georgia, the son of a cobbler
1899		– Expelled from the seminary, where he was training to be a priest
1912		– Became the Bolshevik Party's expert on racial minorities
1917–22		– Appointed Commissar for the nationalities
1922		– Secretary of the Bolshevik Party
1928		– Defeated internal opposition and effectively became leader of the USSR
1928–34		– Introduced collectivisation of agriculture and the first Five Year Plan to industrialise the Soviet Union
1939	August	– The Nazi–Soviet Pact
1941	June	– Faced a German invasion despite believing it would not happen
1945		– Presided over the final defeat of Nazi Germany
1946		– Fourth Five Year Plan launched
	April 21	– Ordered formation of Social Unity Party (SED) in Germany
	September	– Reasserted state control over Soviet agriculture
1947	October 5	– Founded Cominform
1948	February 22	– Communist *coup* in Czechoslovakia
	June 24	– Berlin Blockade began
1949	May 12	– Lifted Berlin Blockade
	October 12	– GDR set up
1950	June 25	– Secretly approved North Korean plans to invade South Korea
1952	March 10	– Proposed a neutral united Germany
1953	January	– Doctors' Plot – accused his doctors of trying to kill him
	March 5	– Died

Key terms

Pragmatic
Practical, guided by events rather than by an ideology.

Marxist–Leninist
A combination of the doctrines of Marx and Lenin. Lenin adapted Karl Marx's teaching to the situation in Russia. Unlike Marx he advocated the creation of a party dictatorship, which would have absolute powers, even over the workers.

Stalin's character is important in any assessment of the causes of the Cold War. In many ways the record of his foreign policy before 1939 was cautious and **pragmatic**. He was ready to co-operate with Britain and France against Nazi Germany, but when he decided that they would not stand up against Hitler, he signed the Nazi–Soviet pact with the German government. On the other hand, he was also a **Marxist–Leninist**, who believed in the ultimate triumph of Communism, and was ruthless and brutal towards his opponents. Historians are divided as to whether he had ambitions to gain control of Germany and even of Western Europe after 1945. Some, like the US historian, R.C. Raack, believed that he pursued a revolutionary and expansionary policy until 1948, when he returned to a more defensive policy towards the USA and the West. Others point out that the USSR had suffered enormously in the war and was hardly in a position to challenge the West after 1945.

The USA

In the 1950s Western historians, such as Herbert Feiss, used to argue that the USA was too preoccupied with winning the struggle against Nazi Germany and Japan to give much thought to the shape of postwar Europe, since it assumed that all problems would in due course be solved in co-operation with Britain and the USSR. Yet this view of the USA was sharply criticised by revisionist historians in the 1960s and 1970s, who argue that the USSR in fact responded to aggressive policies of the USA.

More recently Melvyn Leffler, an American historian, has shown that the surprise Japanese attack on Pearl Harbor in 1941 and the dramatic developments in air technology during the war had made the Americans feel vulnerable to potential threats from foreign powers. Consequently, as early as 1943–4, US officials began to draw up plans for a chain of bases which would give the USA control of both the Pacific and Atlantic Oceans and guarantee that US industry and trade would have access to the raw materials and markets of most of Western Europe and Asia. Leffler argues that the steps the USA took to ensure its own security worried Stalin and so created a 'spiral of distrust'.

Much of President Roosevelt's policy was inspired by the ideas of his predecessor Woodrow Wilson, who in 1919 had hoped eventually to turn the world into one large **free trade area** composed of democratic states, where **tariffs** and **economic nationalism** would be abolished. Washington was determined that there should be no more attempts by the Germans to create an **autarchic economy**, and that the British and French, too, would have to abolish tariffs and allow other states to trade freely with their empires.

These ideas were all embodied in the **Atlantic Charter**, which Churchill and Roosevelt drew up in August 1941. The new, liberal world order was to be underpinned by the United Nations Organisation. By late 1943 Roosevelt envisaged this as being composed of an assembly where all the nations of the world would be represented, although real power and influence would be wielded by an executive committee, or Security Council, which would be dominated by the Big Three and China. For all his talk about Wilsonian Liberalism, he realised that the future of the postwar world would be decided by the Great Powers.

Key question
What plans did the USA have for the postwar period?

Key terms

Free trade area A region where states can trade freely with each other.

Tariffs Taxes placed on imported goods to protect the home economy.

Economic nationalism An economy in which every effort is made to keep out foreign goods.

Autarchic economy An economy that is self-sufficient and protected from outside competition.

Atlantic Charter A statement of fundamental principles for the postwar world. The most important of these were: free trade, no more territorial annexation by Britain or the USA, and the right of people to choose their own governments.

Profile: Franklin D. Roosevelt 1882–1945

1882		– Born in New York
1911		– Elected Democratic Senator
1913–20		– Assistant Secretary to the Navy
1932–45		– President
1932		– Introduced the New Deal
1933		– Afforded diplomatic recognition to the USSR
1941	August	– Issued the Atlantic Charter
1945	April	– Died

Roosevelt was criticised for believing that he could establish a personal link with Stalin, which would be able to continue the wartime Grand Alliance even when the war was over. He saw Stalin as a realist with whom the West could co-operate. Roosevelt was a man of great charm, but it is doubtful that his good relationship with Stalin would have survived the postwar disagreements over Germany and Poland.

Key question
What were Britain's postwar aims?

Britain

The British government's main aim in 1944 was to ensure the survival of Great Britain as an independent Great Power on friendly terms with both the USA and the USSR, but it was alarmed by the prospect of Soviet influence spreading into Central Europe and the Eastern Mediterranean where Britain had vital strategic and economic interests. As Britain had gone to war over Poland, Churchill also wanted to see a democratic government in Warsaw, even though he conceded that its Eastern frontiers would have to be altered in favour of the USSR.

Summary diagram: The conflicting aims of the 'Big Three'

USA	USSR	Britain
• Access to raw materials and the freedom to trade and export throughout the world • The creation of a United Nations • Continue into the postwar period the alliance with the USSR and Britain	• Security from further attack • Reparations from Germany • Territorial gains from Poland, Finland and Romania • Creation of friendly pro-Soviet regimes in Eastern Europe	• Preservation of British Empire • Remain on friendly terms with the USA and USSR • Block Soviet expansion in central and south-eastern Europe and the Middle East • Creation of an independent Poland with a democratic government

2 | Inter-Allied Negotiations 1943–4

In the autumn of 1943 the foreign ministers of the Big Three met for the first time in Moscow in an effort to reconcile their conflicting ambitions for postwar Europe. They agreed to set up the European Advisory Commission to finalise plans for the postwar Allied occupation of Germany and also to a joint Declaration on General Security, which proposed the creation of an international organisation (or United Nations) for maintaining global peace and security. This would be joined by all the 'peace-loving states'.

Publicly, the Americans argued that a United Nations organisation would make unnecessary any Soviet or British plans for creating spheres of influence to defend their interests. However, at the conference at Tehran in November 1943, attended by Churchill, Roosevelt and Stalin, the decision to land British and US troops in France rather than in the Balkans effectively ensured that the USSR would liberate both Eastern and Southeastern Europe by itself and hence be in a position to turn the whole region into a Soviet sphere of influence. It was this factor that left Churchill and Roosevelt with little option but to recognise the USSR's claims to Eastern Poland.

A year later, in an effort to protect British interests in the Eastern Mediterranean, Churchill flew to Moscow and proposed dividing south-eastern Europe up into distinct **spheres of interest**. This formed the basis of the notorious percentages agreement, which Churchill wrote out 'on a half sheet of paper'. This gave the USSR 90 and 75 per cent predominance in Romania and Bulgaria, respectively, and Britain 90 per cent in Greece, while Yugoslavia and Hungary were to be divided equally into British and Soviet zones of interest.

The agreement broadly corresponded to initial Soviet intentions in Eastern Europe, but it was rejected outright by Roosevelt, who informed Stalin that there was 'in this global war … no question, either military or political, in which the United States [was] not interested'. This may have been, as the revisionist US historian Daniel Yergin has pointed out, 'a fundamental statement of the new global vision that would shape American policy in the postwar era', but, with the **Red Army** advancing steadily towards Berlin, there was little Roosevelt could do to stop Stalin from turning all of Eastern Europe into a Soviet sphere of interest.

3 | The Liberation of Europe 1943–5

At the end of the war countries that had been occupied by Germany, such as Poland and France, or had been allies, such as Italy, Romania and Bulgaria, were liberated by the Allies. This liberation of Eastern Europe by Soviet forces and Western Europe by predominantly Anglo-American forces created the context for the Cold War. To understand the complex political situation

Key question
How far had the Great Powers agreed on dividing up Europe into spheres of influence by the end of 1944?

Key dates

Teheran Conference: 28 November– 1 December 1943

Anglo-Soviet 'percentages agreement': 9 October 1944

Key terms

Spheres of interest Areas where one power is able to exercise the dominant influence and to influence local politics.

Red Army The army of the USSR.

Key question
In what ways was the future of continental Europe decided in 1944–5 by the way it was liberated?

Allied Control Commissions
These were set up in each occupied territory, including Germany. They initially administered a particular territory in the name of the Allies.

Partisan groups
These were resistance fighters or guerrillas, in German- and Italian-occupied Europe.

Peasant parties
Parties representing the small farmers or peasants.

Key question
Why was it so vital to Stalin that there should be a friendly government in Warsaw?

created by the liberation it is important to remember the following factors as you read through the next section:

- Bulgaria, Finland, Italy, Hungary and Romania were Axis states, that is allies of Germany. Although they were allowed their own governments after their occupation, real power rested with the **Allied Control Commissions** (ACC). The first ACC was set up in southern Italy in 1943 by the British and Americans after the collapse of Fascism. As the USSR had no troops in Italy, it was not represented on the ACC. Similarly, as it was the USSR that had liberated Eastern Europe, Soviet officials dominated the ACCs in Romania, Bulgaria, Finland and Hungary. In this respect Soviet policy was the mirror image of Anglo-American policy in Italy.
- In the states actually occupied by the Germans and Italians in eastern and south-eastern Europe (Poland, Czechoslovakia, Greece and Yugoslavia) governments-in-exile were set up in London during the war. They were made up mainly of politicians, who had managed to escape the German occupation; yet, being in London, they lost control of the **partisan groups** fighting in the occupied territories. Except for Poland, the Communist partisan groups emerged as the strongest local forces and their leaders were not ready to take orders from their governments-in-exile. Sometimes this suited Stalin, and sometimes, as in Greece (see page 23), it did not.
- In the liberated territories, Stalin advised the local Communist parties to form popular fronts or alliances with the Liberal, Socialist and **peasant parties**. Eventually these fronts became the means by which Communism seized power in Eastern Europe.

The Polish question

The Polish question was one of the most complex problems facing the Allies. Britain and France had gone to war, in the first instance, to preserve Polish independence, while the USSR in 1939 had profited from the German rape of Poland to annex its eastern territories (see box overleaf). It was determined not only to regain these lands, but also to ensure that there was a friendly government in Warsaw. Inevitably this aim made the Soviet Union 'enemy number two' to all Poles, except for the Communists, and in turn ensured that Stalin initially treated Poland as an enemy-occupied territory. He liquidated the non-Communist resistance groups, which had been fighting the Germans, because of their hostility towards Communism.

Consequently, long before the Soviet 'liberation' of Poland, Stalin took the necessary precautions to ensure that no independent government hostile to the USSR would ever gain power in Warsaw. In 1940 in an attempt to eliminate potential opposition to Soviet influence in eastern Poland, Stalin ordered 4000 Polish officers to be shot at Katyn, near Smolensk. A few months later the Russian Secret Police, the NKVD, began training Polish volunteers to form a similar service in Poland.

> **Poland's frontiers**
> In 1919, when modern Poland was set up by the Versailles
> Settlement, the British Foreign Minister, Lord Curzon,
> proposed that its frontier with Russia should run about 100
> miles to the east of Warsaw (the so-called Curzon line), but the
> Poles rejected this, and in early 1920, exploiting the chaos of
> the Russian civil war, they invaded the Ukraine. By the Treaty
> of Riga in 1921 they annexed a considerable amount of the
> western Russian border territories (see the map on page 6). In
> 1939, as a result of the Nazi–Soviet Pact, the USSR regained
> these territories when Hitler defeated Poland in September,
> but lost them again after the German invasion of the Soviet
> Union in June 1941. Stalin remained determined to reclaim
> them at the end of the war.

The Soviet advance into Poland

Once the Red Army had crossed the Polish frontier in early
January 1944, Stalin systematically destroyed the non-Communist
resistance, the Polish Home Army, but did not allow the Polish
Communists to seize power straightaway for fear of antagonising
the Western powers.

In July, Stalin fatally undermined the authority of the Polish
government-in-exile by setting up the Committee of National
Liberation, which he considered to be the core of a future Polish
administration. Its role was to camouflage the extent of
Communist control in Poland by appealing to a wide cross-section
of society that wanted social reform. It had to reassure both the
Western governments and the Poles themselves that the USSR
had no immediate intention of creating a Communist Poland.
Stalin continued this dual strategy with some success. The
Western powers clung to the hope that Stalin would not insist on
a Communist regime provided he received territorial concessions
in Eastern Poland.

Key dates

Polish government-in-exile was set up in London, once Poland was occupied by the Germans: October 1939

Red Army reached central Poland and Committee of national Liberation set up: July 1944

The Warsaw uprising

The Soviet Union's real policy was revealed when the
underground Polish Home Army, the non-Communist resistance
to the German occupation of Poland, rose up in revolt against the
Germans in Warsaw in August 1944 and made a desperate
attempt to seize the initiative before the Red Army could overrun
the whole of Poland. By gaining control of Warsaw, the Home
Army hoped that it would win the backing of the Western Allies
and so thwart Stalin's policy in Poland. Although Soviet troops
penetrated to within 12 miles of Warsaw, the Polish insurgents
were left to fight it out alone with the Germans, who finally
defeated them on 2 October. Stalin refused to grant US requests
for permission to land behind the Soviet lines and refuel planes
carrying supplies for the rebels until mid-September, by which
time it was too late for them to make any difference.

By these means, Stalin managed to ensure that the most active political opponents of Communism were eliminated, and inevitably this made it easier for him to enforce his policy in Poland. As Soviet troops moved farther west towards the Oder river in the remaining months of 1944, the NKVD, assisted by Polish Communists, shot or imprisoned thousands of partisans from the Home Army.

Britain, the USA and Poland

Despite all that had happened, Roosevelt still clung to the hope that, once the United Nations Organisation was set up, it would be possible to reach a compromise with Stalin about the future of Poland. He was determined to avoid a premature break with the USSR over the Polish question. Consequently, when the Soviets formally recognised in January 1945 the Communist-dominated Committee for National Liberation as the provisional government of Poland, Britain and the USA, even though they supported the Polish government-in-exile in London, played down the significance of what the Soviets had done in the interests of Great Power unity.

Key question
Why were Romania and Bulgaria important to Stalin?

Romania and Bulgaria

On 20 August 1944 the Soviets launched a major offensive to drive the German army out of the Balkans. The immediate consequences of this brought about the collapse of the pro-German regimes in both Romania and Bulgaria. Like Poland, both states were vital to the security of the USSR. Soviet control of Romania would open up the land routes into Yugoslavia, Bulgaria and Central Europe, and enable it to strengthen its position in the Black Sea, while control of Bulgaria would give the USSR a base from which to dominate the approaches to the Turkish Straits and the Greek frontier (see the map on page 6).

Key question
What were the Soviet aims in Romania?

Romania

Russia was also determined to re-annex the former Romanian territories of Bessarabia and northern Bukovina, which it had occupied in 1940, and launched an offensive against Romania on 20 August 1944. In a desperate attempt to seize the initiative before the Soviets arrived in Bucharest, on 23 August the Romanian king deposed the pro-Nazi dictator, Marshal Antonescu. He was supported by the Liberal and non-Socialist parties, who hoped that, like Italy (see page 26), Romania would be able to negotiate a ceasefire with the Western allies and form a government in which the Communists would be in a minority. This idea was an illusion based on the false assumption that the British would open up a second front in the Balkans. In reality the king had no alternative but to negotiate an armistice on 12 September with the Soviets, who had in the meantime occupied the country.

The British and US ambassadors already tacitly accepted that Romania was in the Soviet sphere of influence, and gave no help to the Romanian government, which was anxious to obtain a guarantee that Soviet troops would be withdrawn as soon as the war with Germany was over. An Allied Control Commission (ACC) was set up, which was dominated by Soviet officials. A coalition government composed of Communists, Socialists, Liberals and the left-wing peasants' party, the Ploughmen's Front, was formed, but, backed by Soviet officials on the ACC, the Communists and their allies made Romania ungovernable in the winter of 1944–5. They formed the National Democratic Front and incited the peasants to seize farms from the landowners and the workers to set up Communist-dominated production committees in the factories. In March 1945 Stalin, following the precedent set by the British, who had intervened in December 1945 in Greece (see page 23), orchestrated a *coup* which led to the creation of the Communist-dominated National Democratic Front Government.

Key dates

Formation of coalition government in Romania: 23 August 1944

Communist coup in Bulgaria: 9 September 1944

Bulgaria

Although Stalin did not want a break with the West, Western observers noted the anti-Western bias of Soviet policy in Romania and how Soviet officials actively supported the workers and peasant parties. The occupation of Romania gave Stalin the opportunity in the first week of September 1944 to occupy Bulgaria, which was technically at war with Britain and the USA, but not with the USSR.

Key question
What were the Soviet aims in Bulgaria?

The local Communists controlled several thousand armed partisans, and had set up a Patriotic Front, an alliance of anti-German left-wing forces, composed of the Social Democrats, left-wing Agrarians (farmers) and members of *Zveno*, a group of anti-royalist officers. The Front, with the Communists playing a key role, seized power and set up a government in Sofia shortly before the Red Army arrived. Inevitably this success strengthened the local Communists, who attempted immediately to implement a Communist revolution in Bulgaria. The country's former ruling class were purged and well over 10,000 people executed. The trade unions and police were infiltrated and the large farms were taken over by peasant co-operatives.

This enthusiasm for revolution did not, however, fit in with Stalin's overall strategy. Essentially he was determined to safeguard Soviet control over Bulgaria, yet not antagonise his Western allies any more than necessary while the war with Germany was still being fought, and at a time when Poland was becoming an increasingly divisive issue. Since the USSR's position was guaranteed through the key role of the Soviet chairman of the ACC, and the strong position of the local Communist party, Stalin attempted in the autumn of 1944 to persuade the Bulgarian Communists to pursue a more moderate policy. He wanted them to tolerate a certain degree of political opposition and to work within the Patriotic Front coalition, but this policy was not easy to carry out, as the local Communists, sometimes backed by Soviet officials on the ACC, were determined to gain complete power regardless of the diplomatic consequences.

Key question
Why was Tito so successful in setting up a Communist government in Yugoslavia?

Key terms

Yugoslavia
In 1918 the kingdom of Serbs, Croats and Slovenes was formed. In 1929 it officially became Yugoslavia. The Serbs were the strongest nationality within this state. In 1991 Yugoslavia ceased to exist when Croatia and Slovenia left the union.

Nationalists
Those who champion their nation or country. Mihailovic was aiming to restore Serbian domination of postwar Yugoslavia.

Key question
Why were the Communists unable to seize control in Greece?

Key date

British suppressed Communist uprising in Greece: December 1944

Yugoslavia

After the occupation of Bulgaria, Soviet troops linked up with partisan forces in **Yugoslavia** under the Communist leader, Joseph Tito, and launched an attack on Belgrade on 14 October. By this time Tito was a formidable ally. He had built up an effective partisan army, which not only fought the Germans but also waged civil war against non-Communist Serbs and Croats **Nationalists** led by Colonel Mihailovic. As soon as his partisans occupied an area, they formed Communist-dominated liberation committees, which took their orders from him rather than the Yugoslav government-in-exile in London. Tito's position was enormously strengthened when the British decided for military reasons in May 1944 to assist him rather than Mihailovic.

To the Soviets, the key to controlling the situation in Southeastern Europe was to build up a military and political alliance between Yugoslavia, Bulgaria and the USSR. Molotov, the Soviet Foreign Minister, told Tito in April 1944 that he wanted Yugoslavia to become 'our chief mainstay in southeast Europe'. Up to 1948 Tito was certainly a loyal ally of Stalin, but he still tried to carry out his own policies independently of the USSR. Despite Stalin's fear of provoking the Western powers, Tito did not abandon his plans for introducing Communist regimes into Yugoslavia and Albania, which his forces had also liberated in November 1944. Stalin was, however, able to exercise a firmer control over his foreign policy. In January 1945, he vetoed his scheme for a federation with Bulgaria, which would have turned the latter state into a mere province of Yugoslavia. He made it very clear that Yugoslavia would have to subordinate its local territorial ambitions to the overall foreign policy considerations determined by Moscow.

Greece

Tito and Stalin also clashed over the attempts by the Communist-controlled People's Liberation Army (*Elas*) in Greece to set up a National Liberation Government on the Yugoslav model. During the war *Elas* had emerged as the most effective resistance force in Greece and, like Tito's partisans, had fought the Germans, while also attempting to eliminate rival non-Communist guerrilla groups. A British historian, C.M. Woodhouse, has observed that in Greece 'as early as 1942 one of two consequences was already inevitable: either a civil war or an unopposed Communist take-over'. Yet, as Greece was an area regarded by Stalin as being well within the British sphere of influence, he urged *Elas* to join a moderate coalition government. When the British forces in Greece ordered *Elas* to disband its partisan forces, a revolt, encouraged by Tito, broke out in Athens on 3 December 1944. Stalin, true to his agreement with Churchill (see page 18), stopped Tito from helping the Greek Communists and raised no objection to their defeat by British troops.

Hungary and Czechoslovakia

In neither Czechoslovakia nor Hungary did Stalin have any immediate plans for a Communist seizure of power, as he was anxious to avoid provoking trouble with Britain and the USA, while he consolidated his position in Poland. The local Communist parties were consequently ordered to enter democratic coalition governments and to work from within to consolidate their position.

Hungary

In 1943 the Hungarians secretly attempted to negotiate an **armistice** with Britain and the USA, so that they could be spared a liberation that they feared might in reality be an occupation by Soviet troops, but the decision not to open up a **second front** in the Balkans ensured that Hungary's fate would be decided by the Red Army. When Soviet troops crossed the Hungarian frontier in September 1944, Admiral Horthy, the head of state, appealed to the Soviets for a ceasefire, but the Germans took Horthy prisoner and encouraged the Hungarian fascists, the Arrow Cross Party, to seize power in western Hungary.

It was not until early December 1944 that Red Army units reached the outskirts of Budapest. In the Soviet-occupied section of the country the Communist Party was at first too weak to play a dominant role in politics, and it therefore had little option but to co-operate with the Social Democrats, the smallholders, a peasants' party, and several other middle-class parties. In December 1945, when elections took place for the national assembly, the Communists, despite the presence of the Red Army, only gained some 17 per cent of the votes cast, but they were given three key posts in the Provisional national government. Throughout 1945 Stalin's immediate aim was to strip Hungary completely bare of anything that could be taken to the USSR as reparation (see page 39). In the longer term he was not sure whether to integrate Hungary into the Soviet bloc or allow it the necessary independence to act as a bridge between Eastern and Western Europe.

Czechoslovakia

Of all the Eastern European states Czechoslovakia was the most friendly to the USSR. The Czechs felt betrayed by Britain and France over the **Munich Agreement** of 1938, and looked to the USSR as the power that would restore their country's pre-1938 borders. In 1943 the Czech government-in-exile in London under Eduard Beneš, the former Czech president, negotiated an alliance with the USSR, although this still did not stop Stalin from annexing Ruthenia in the autumn of 1944 (see the map on page 6).

As the Soviet army occupied more and more of Czechoslovakia in the winter of 1944–5, the balance of power tilted steadily away from the democratic parties represented by the government-in-exile in London to the Czech Communist Party led by Klement Gottwald, who was in Moscow. Stalin nevertheless forced Gottwald

Key question
What was Stalin's policy in Hungary?

Key terms

Armistice
The termination of fighting between two or more powers by official agreement.

Second front
The 'first' front was in the USSR, where there was large-scale fighting between Soviet and German troops. A 'second' would be elsewhere, for example, in Europe, where the Germans could be directly engaged by the British and US allies.

Key question
Why was there considerable support for the Communists in Czechoslovakia?

Key term

Munich Agreement
In September 1938 this handed over the German-speaking Sudetenland, which had become part of the new Czech state in 1919, to Hitler's Germany.

Key date

Liberation of
Czechoslovakia:
April 1945

Key term

**Provisional
government**
A temporary
government, in
office until an
election can take
place.

Key question
Why did Stalin treat
Finland so leniently?

to accept Beneš as President and work within a coalition
government. In turn, Beneš followed a conciliatory policy and was
ready to co-operate with the Czech Communist Party, which
enabled Stalin to achieve a harmony that had been impossible to
reach in Poland.

In January 1945 the leaders of the Czech government in
London and the Communist political leaders met in Moscow. In
retrospect Rudolf Slansky, the Communist Party Secretary, wrote
that 'here for the first time there was joined the battle of two
political worlds', namely the West and the Soviet-dominated East.
Yet Beneš, as the future constitutional President of
Czechoslovakia, refused to take sides against the Communists.
When the **provisional government** was formed, the Communists
were able to demand eight seats in the cabinet including the
influential Ministries of the Interior and Information, although
Gottwald skilfully camouflaged their powerful position by not
claiming the premiership.

Finland

Finland had been part of the Russian Empire up to 1917. As a
result of the Russian Revolution in 1917 Finland became
independent. In reaction to Finland's refusal to hand over a key
naval base and agree to frontier alterations, the Red Army
invaded Finland on 30 November 1939. Far from gaining a quick
victory, the Finns held out until March 1940 and inflicted some
200,000 casualties on the Soviets. In early 1940 Finland had been
defeated by Soviet forces after the brief Winter War, and in 1941,
not surprisingly, supported the Nazi attack on the USSR. Yet
despite this record, in the summer of 1944, when Soviet troops
invaded Finland, the Finns were granted an armistice on
unexpectedly generous terms. They had to declare war on the
Germans, eventually cede part of the strategically important
Petsamo region (see the map on page 6) on the Arctic coast to the
USSR and pay reparations, but politically they were allowed a
considerable degree of freedom. Marshal Mannerheim, who had
co-operated closely with Hitler, remained president until 1946
and there was only one Communist in the first postwar cabinet.

Why did Stalin pursue such a moderate policy in Finland? To a
certain extent this fitted in with his policy of calling a halt to
propaganda campaigns against Britain and the USA, which he
had followed since the dissolution in 1943 of the Comintern. This
was a gesture aimed at Britain and the USA to convince them that
the USSR was no longer planning world revolution. At this stage
Stalin appeared to believe that each state would find its own way
to Socialism in its own time. The Finns, unlike the Hungarians,
were also lucky enough to be able to quit the war at the right
moment and were in a position to give the USSR such vitally
needed reparations as barges, rolling stock and manufactured
goods. A repressive occupation policy would have disrupted these
deliveries.

The liberation of Italy and France

Italy and France were liberated by the Western Allies. Italy was a leading Axis state, while France, until its defeat in 1940, had played the main part in the war against Germany. In both states resistance to the Germans and the Fascist authorities 'legitimised' or made respectable the Communist Party.

Armistice with Italy signed: 3 September 1943

Allied forces invaded France: 6 June 1944

Key dates

Italy

It took nearly two years to liberate Italy. After the Allied landings in Sicily in July 1943, Mussolini was overthrown and in September an armistice was signed, but Allied forces were unable to stop the Germans seizing Rome. They were then forced to fight their way up the peninsula, and it was only in April 1945 that northern Italy was finally liberated. Italy was the first enemy state to sign an armistice, and the way its occupied areas were administered set important precedents for the future. All Soviet requests to be involved were firmly rejected by the British and Americans, which later gave Stalin an excuse to exclude them from Eastern Europe.

Key question
How did the Italian Communist Party manage to legitimise itself?

An Italian government was set up, and gradually it was given responsibility for the liberated areas as the Allies captured them from the Germans. It was closely supervised by the Anglo-American ACC. Large areas behind the front continued to be under the direct control of the Allied commander-in-chief. Stalin had little option but to accept these arrangements, although he was determined that the Italian Communists should not be excluded from participating in government.

Ignoring the fact that Italy's external relations were controlled by the Western Allies, Stalin went ahead on 14 March 1944, and officially recognised the Italian government. A few days earlier he had given Palmiro Togliatti, the leader of the Italian Communist Party, a 'plan of action', according to which he was to form a coalition with the Socialists. He was to avoid any premature mass action, such as an uprising or a civil war, which would cause tension between the USSR and the West and so make it more difficult for Stalin to consolidate his position in Eastern Europe. He was also to draft a popular programme for reforming the Italian economy, which would prepare the way for later Communist electoral successes.

Togliatti carried out these instructions as well as he could. He joined the new government that was formed when Rome was occupied by the Allies in June 1944. In the north in the winter of 1944–5 the Communists played a key role in resistance against the Germans. Togliatti, only too aware of how the British had crushed the Greek revolt, managed to keep his more radical partisans in check. By the time the war had ended, the resistance had, as the British historian Martin Clark has written, 'legitimised the PCI (the Italian Communist Party) and made it an indispensable pillar of the new national unity'. This was seen when Togliatti himself became Minister of Justice in the Italian government, which was formed in April 1945. At this stage, then, Stalin's policy in Italy was to push the Italian Communist Party into joining a governing multi-party coalition.

France

When Paris was liberated in August 1944, General de Gaulle, the leader of the **Free French**, immediately established an independent government. His aim was to rebuild French power and to create a powerful French-led Western European **bloc**. To counter the predominance of the Anglo-Americans he looked to Russia, and in December 1944 signed the Franco-Soviet Treaty, which actually committed France to supporting the USSR, if in the future it should have to launch a **preventive war** against Germany.

As in Italy, the French Communist Party, having played a prominent part in the Resistance, became a major force in French politics. Its leader, Maurice Thorez, was instructed by Stalin to support the Soviet–French alliance and work towards creating a left-wing coalition with the Socialists, which, it was hoped, would eventually be able to form a government.

Key question
How did General de Gaulle manage to preserve French independence?

Key terms

Free French
The French who supported de Gaulle after the fall of France in June 1940, when he set up his headquarters in London.

Bloc
A group of allies or closely linked states.

Preventive war
A limited war fought to prevent the later outbreak of a much larger war.

Key date

Franco-Soviet Treaty signed: 10 December 1944

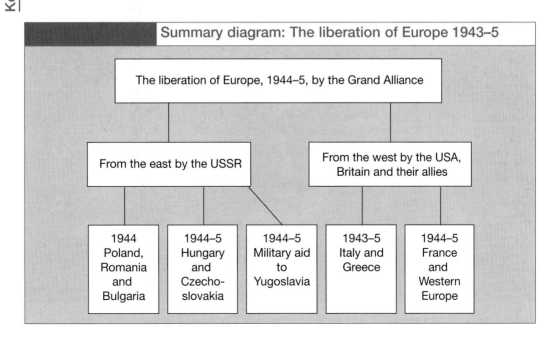

Summary diagram: The liberation of Europe 1943–5

The liberation of Europe, 1944–5, by the Grand Alliance

From the east by the USSR

From the west by the USA, Britain and their allies

1944 Poland, Romania and Bulgaria

1944–5 Hungary and Czecho-slovakia

1944–5 Military aid to Yugoslavia

1943–5 Italy and Greece

1944–5 France and Western Europe

4 | The Yalta Conference, February 1945

Key question
What was achieved at Yalta?

The Yalta Conference, attended by Stalin, Roosevelt and Churchill, was, to quote the British journalist and historian Martin Walker, 'the last of the wartime conferences ... [and] the first of the postwar **summits**'. Besides drawing up plans for finishing the war in Europe and the Far East, it also attempted to lay the foundations of the coming peace. Plans were finalised for the occupation of Germany by the victorious powers, amongst whom, on Churchill's insistence, France was to be included. Each power was allotted its own zone, including a section of Berlin, which was placed under four power control (see the map on page 42). The decision was taken to set up the United Nations.

Poland again proved to be the most difficult subject on the agenda, and the Allies were only able to reach agreement through a series of ambiguous compromises, which could be read differently by the USSR and the Western powers:

- Poland's eastern border would run along the Curzon line (see page 20), and as compensation for the land lost to the USSR, Poland would receive a substantial increase in territory in the north and west from land to be removed from Germany. The exact details of this were not stated.
- The decision was also taken to reorganise the provisional government by including democratic politicians from both Poland and the London government-in-exile.
- Elections would be held as soon as possible.

Key date
Yalta Conference:
4–11 February 1945

Key term
Summits
Conferences attended by the top political leaders.

The Big Three: Stalin, Roosevelt and Churchill (front row, left to right) at the Yalta Conference.

Profile: Winston Churchill 1874–1964

1874		– Born in Woodstock, near Oxford
1900		– Entered Parliament
1911–15		– First Lord of the Admiralty
1918–19		– Supported Allied intervention in Russia
1933–9		– Bitterly opposed Hitler
1940–5		– Prime Minister
1943	November– December	– Attended Tehran Conference
1944	October	– Visited Moscow and proposed 'percentages agreement'
1945	February	– Attended Yalta Conference
	July	– Attended Potsdam Conference until replaced by Clement Attlee
	July 26	– Defeated in the British general election by the Labour Party
1945–51		– Leader of the Opposition
1946	March 5	– Made Iron Curtain speech at Fulton, USA
1951–5		– Prime Minister
1953	May	– Proposed summit meeting after death of Stalin
1964		– Died

Churchill had the reputation of being a hardline anti-Bolshevik, but after the German invasion of the USSR in 1941 he welcomed Stalin as an ally. Nevertheless, as early as May 1945, he was becoming increasingly aware of the Soviet threat to Eastern and Central Europe, and in 1946 used the controversial phrase 'Iron Curtain' to describe what he perceived to be the division of Europe by Stalin. However, in 1953, as Prime Minister and after the death of Stalin, he attempted in vain to end the Cold War. He believed that, as the last surviving wartime leader, he would be able to negotiate successfully with the Soviets. He ran into opposition from the Americans and West Germans, who feared that he would make too many concessions over Germany. The summit did not meet until after his retirement in July 1955.

Superficially this seemed to be a success for the British and Americans, but in fact the terms were so vague that Stalin could easily manipulate them. First, the exact amount of land that Poland would receive at the cost of Germany was not fixed and secondly democracy meant very different things to Stalin on the one side, and Churchill and Roosevelt on the other. For the former it essentially meant the domination of the Communist Party, for the latter it meant effectively the domination of the non-Communist parties! In the words of the US **Chief of Staff**, Admiral Leahy, the Soviets could stretch the agreement 'all the way from Yalta to Washington without ever technically breaking it'.

Key term

Chief of Staff
The head of military planning.

To underpin the right of the liberated states to determine their own governments Roosevelt persuaded Stalin and Churchill to agree to the Declaration on Liberated Europe, which committed the three governments to carry out emergency measures to assist the liberated states and to set up democratically elected governments.

Once the Cold War started, this became, as Martin Walker observed, a key text 'upon which all future accusations of Soviet betrayal and bad faith were made'. Yet it completely ignored the reality of the situation in Eastern Europe. Stalin saw Poland as a corridor for an attack from Germany or Western Europe on the USSR. He was therefore going to ensure that a friendly government, which in Poland's case could only mean a Communist one, was in place.

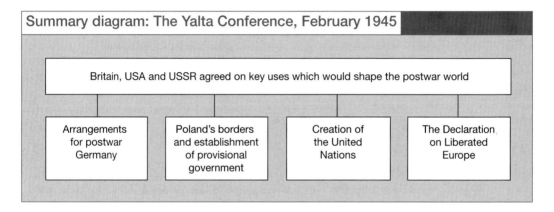

Summary diagram: The Yalta Conference, February 1945

Britain, USA and USSR agreed on key uses which would shape the postwar world

Arrangements for postwar Germany

Poland's borders and establishment of provisional government

Creation of the United Nations

The Declaration on Liberated Europe

5 | The End of the War in Europe

Key question
Why did Churchill view the USSR's advance westwards with suspicion?

Three months after the Yalta Conference the war in Europe ended, and East and West confronted each other in the vacuum caused by the defeat of the Axis powers. In the final weeks of the war there had been considerable jockeying for position by the Great Powers. British and US forces raced to Trieste in an attempt to stop Tito seizing the port, while the British army in northern Germany crossed the river Elbe and advanced into Mecklenburg to prevent the Soviets from occupying Denmark (see map on page 6). Churchill also urged the Americans to make special efforts to take Berlin and Prague.

But the US generals were not ready to see their soldiers killed for what they regarded as political reasons, and so both capitals fell to Soviet troops. Nevertheless when the war ended, with the surrender of Germany on 8 May 1945, Anglo-American forces occupied nearly half the area that was to become the Soviet zone in Germany (see the map on page 42). It was not until early July that these troops were withdrawn into the American and British zones.

Unconditional German surrender: 8 May 1945

Key date

Key question
Had the Cold War
already started by
1945?

Key term

Archives
Government
records which are
deposited in a
repository and later
open to historians.

6 | Conclusion

The collapse of Germany and its allies formed a vacuum in
Central Europe, which was filled by the advancing armies of the
Grand Alliance. This certainly created the context in which the
Cold War was waged, but did it make the struggle inevitable?

In many ways, as modern historians who have had access to the
Soviet **archives** have shown, Stalin had shown himself to be
pragmatic. He believed firmly in zones of influence. Provided that
Soviet power was secure in the key states of Poland, Romania and
Bulgaria, he was ready, at least for a time, to be flexible in
Hungary, Finland and Czechoslovakia and respect the interests of
his allies elsewhere, as his attitude to British intervention in
Greece showed. In Italy and France he kept his options open by
instructing the Communist parties to join democratic coalitions.

Roosevelt and Churchill privately conceded that Eastern
Europe was predominantly a Soviet sphere of interest, and in
practice treated Western Europe, particularly Italy, as an Anglo-
American sphere of interest from which Soviet influence was
excluded. They hoped that Stalin would eventually tolerate
democratic governments in Eastern Europe and respect the
Declaration on Liberated Europe. They accepted that the USSR
had special interests in Poland, but it was Stalin's ruthless defence
of these that already by the summer of 1945 had begun to
alienate the West and make the Declaration seem a mockery.

Study Guide: AS Question

In the style of OCR

To what extent did the liberation of Europe contribute to the start of the Cold War? Explain your answer.   (50 marks)

Exam tips

The cross-references are intended to take you straight to the material that will help you to answer the question.

This question asks you to analyse the liberation of Europe in light of the start of the Cold war. Your aim throughout should be to address the central question 'to what extent' was liberation a factor that contributed to the start of the Cold War. All your points have to relate to this. Remember that, on the one hand, you must flesh out your arguments with sufficient accurate evidence, but on the other hand you must not lapse into narrative and get bogged down in intricate explanations.

Your discussion of the liberation as a factor in contributing to the start of the Cold War should include the following factors:

- In 1945 the USA and its allies met the USSR in the middle of Germany. Inevitably this produced strains as the wartime allies had different aims, particularly in Poland (page 29).
- Both sides had very different ideologies, which were mutually hostile (page 2).
- Stalin was deeply suspicious of the West, despite his desire to co-operate with the USA and Britain in the United Nations.
- Stalin's treatment of Poland did much to alienate the West (pages 20–1).

However, you need to ask yourself whether a prolonged 'stand-off' on the scale of the Cold War was inevitable. After all, initially Stalin had shown himself to be quite pragmatic:

- Arguably his aims were limited to securing friendly governments in Poland, Bulgaria and Romania (pages 14–15 and 19–22).
- He appeared to be flexible in Czechoslovakia, Hungary and above all in Finland.
- In Italy and France he ordered the Communist parties to co-operate with the Liberal and moderate Socialist groups.

Your conclusion should reach a substantiated judgement as to the extent that the liberation of Europe contributed to the start of the Cold War. Was it more or less important than other factors?

Study Guide: Advanced Level Question

In the style of Edexcel

Study Sources 1–3 below.

Source 1

From: Geoffrey Roberts, The Soviet Union in World Politics, *published in 1999.*

The security perspective is the view that the driving force of Soviet foreign policy was the search for national security in what was perceived to be a hostile and threatening world. ...

This security perspective has much to commend it: ... [it] focuses attention on the very real national security issues and dilemmas confronting Moscow. ... The limitation of this perspective is that it underestimates the extent to which the USSR was a revolutionary state committed to a radical transformation of the international status quo. Such a commitment meant that in practice the USSR pursued political aims which went far beyond what was required for the sake of security. It meant continued adherence to a Marxist–Leninist view of international relations and world politics.

Source 2

From: Roger Morgan, The Unsettled Peace: A Study of the Cold War in Europe, *published in 1974.*

... Stalin's motive for incorporating the Baltic states, eastern Poland and Czechoslovakia and northern Romania into the Soviet Union, like his motive for installing obedient satellite governments as far westwards as his military power would reach, was the time-honoured motive for power politics: the wish to establish a security buffer between his country and its potential enemies. Russia had been invaded and devastated by Germany twice in thirty years, and Stalin wished to make any repetition of this impossible.

Source 3

From: John W. Mason, The Cold War, 1945–1991, *published in 1996.*

Poland was the country over which the Second World War had broken out when Germany invaded it in September 1939; likewise, Poland was at the centre of the origins of the Cold War after 1945. In October 1944 the Soviet Union allowed the pro-Western Warsaw uprising to be crushed by the Nazi occupation forces. It was now becoming clear that the Soviet idea of friendly governments in eastern Europe clashed with America's long-term interests.

To what extent do you accept the view that the USA and the USSR were already divided by irreconcilable differences by the end of the fighting in Europe in May 1945?

Explain your answer, using Sources 1, 2 and 3 and your own knowledge of the issues related to this controversy.   (40 marks)

Exam tips

The cross-references are intended to take you straight to the material that will help you to answer the question.

You are asked to use the sources and your own knowledge. The sources raise issues for you. You can use these as the core of your plan. They contain points for and against the stated claim. Make sure that you have identified all the issues raised by the sources, and then add in your own knowledge – both to make more of the issues in the sources (add depth to the coverage) and to add new points (extend the range covered).

The issues raised by the sources show that there were divisions between the USSR and the Western powers over ideology and security. You can show these differences and consider how serious they were – do they appear to have been 'irreconcilable'?

Your answers will be stronger if you cross-refer between the sources rather than treating each of them separately.

The issue of ideology can be raised by using Source 1. You can show that it argues that the USSR was a revolutionary Marxist–Leninist state, which was essentially hostile to the West.

The issue of security can be raised by using Source 2, which emphasises Stalin's wish for a 'security buffer' and sees Stalin's aims as essentially defensive. You can link this to Source 3 which focuses on one such buffer state, Poland, and shows its significance in making clear the differing interests of the USSR and the USA. In dealing with security, note the opportunity to link with Source 1, which also raises the security issue: the Soviet search for national security. However, Source 1 clearly gives security less weight than the USSR's political aims. It will be important for you to pick up on points where the sources seem to agree to an extent, but also to note where there are clear differences of emphasis.

You can expand on these issues using your own knowledge. You can show that Poland was a major source of friction, developing the points in Source 3 using material from pages 19–21 and 28–30. You can integrate a new issue into your argument: the USA's economic aims (page 16) and show that the defensive aims of the USSR (page 14) were at variance with the desires of the USA to open the world's markets to US money and products.

How serious were these disagreements? Stalin was ready to regard Greece as a British sphere of influence (page 18). His policies in Finland, Czechoslovakia and Hungary appeared to favour a compromise with the West (pages 24–5). You must ask yourself whether, in the light of this, it is accurate to talk of 'irreconcilable differences' in the period 1944 to May 1945.

3

The Break-up of the Grand Alliance 1945–7

POINTS TO CONSIDER

This chapter considers two interlocking questions:

- The reasons for the break-up of the Grand Alliance between 1945 and 1947
- The consequences of this for Germany and Europe as a whole

It is important not only to understand the impact of Stalin's policies on Eastern Europe and of British, US and French policies on Western Europe, but also how they interacted and increasingly began to tear Europe apart.

   This chapter examines these issues through the following sections:

- Early postwar tensions between the Great Powers, April–August 1945
- The peace treaties with Italy and the minor Axis powers
- Germany, June 1945–April 1947
- The Truman Doctrine of Containment
- The Marshall Plan
- The European states, June 1945–December 1947

Key dates

1945	July–August	Potsdam Conference
1946	March 5	Churchill's Iron Curtain speech
	April 21	Social Unity Party (SED) formed
	April–July	Paris Conference of Foreign Ministers
	May 3	General Clay halted reparation payments from Soviet zone
1947	January 1	Anglo-American Bizone formed
	February 10	Peace treaties signed with Italy, Romania, Bulgaria, Finland and Hungary
	March 12	Truman Doctrine announced
	March 10–April 24	Council of Foreign Ministers' Meeting in Moscow
	May	Communists excluded from government in France and Italy
	June 5	Marshall Aid Programme announced
	October 5	Cominform founded

Key question
What initial impact did Truman have on US policy towards the USSR?

Key term

Lend–lease aid programme
In March 1941 Roosevelt approved the Lend–Lease Act which enabled any country, whose defences were judged to be vital for the USA, to obtain war supplies. These would, however, have to be paid for later on. By 1945 over $50 billion had been spent on this scheme.

1 | Early Postwar Tensions between the Great Powers, April–August 1945

The impact of Harry Truman

All three Great Powers wished to continue the wartime alliance, yet for an alliance to survive there needs to be either a common danger or agreement between its members on key principles. In postwar Europe this was no longer the case. Roosevelt had privately recognised that the West had little option but to accept Soviet control over Eastern Europe, but on his death in April 1945 he was replaced by Harry Truman, who was at first determined not to write this area off as a Soviet sphere of interest and to pursue a much tougher policy towards the USSR. Not only did he strongly criticise Soviet policy in Poland, but in May he abruptly ended the **lend–lease aid programme**, which had made available food and armaments to the USSR during the war.

'Christmas Card' 1945 by the Egyptian-born cartoonist Kem (Kimon Evan Marengo). It shows Truman (as the Statue of Liberty) with Stalin, Attlee, de Gaulle and Chiang Kai-shek.

Profile: Harry S. Truman 1884–1972

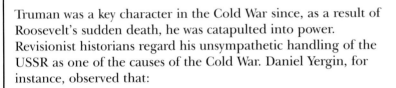

1884		– Born in Lamar, Missouri
1917–18		– Served in the US army in France
1922		– Joined the Democratic Party
1934		– Elected to the Senate to represent the state of Missouri
1944		– Became Vice-President
1945	April 12	– Became President of the USA on Roosevelt's death
1947	March 12	– Announced the Truman Doctrine
1948		– Elected President for a second term
1950		– Committed US forces to defend South Korea
1951		– Refused to extend the war to China
1952		– Retired
1972		– Died

Truman was a key character in the Cold War since, as a result of Roosevelt's sudden death, he was catapulted into power. Revisionist historians regard his unsympathetic handling of the USSR as one of the causes of the Cold War. Daniel Yergin, for instance, observed that:

Truman could not believe that Russia's quest for security had a rationality. When he was finally confronted with foreign policy questions, all he had as a background was a storybook view of history and a rousing Fourth of July patriotism. He tended to see clearly defined contests between right and wrong, black and white. Neither his personality nor his experience gave him the patience for subtleties and uncertainties.

On the other hand, John Gaddis argues that Roosevelt's death did not fundamentally change the course of history, as the Cold War was principally fuelled by Stalin's distrust of the West, which long pre-dated Roosevelt's death.

The Potsdam Conference

The interlinked questions of Germany and Poland dominated the agenda of the Conference. Stalin was determined to move Poland's frontiers westwards at the expense of Germany to compensate Poland for the loss of the Polish territory he was seizing in the east for the USSR. Failure was only avoided by ambiguous compromises on all the most difficult issues. While Britain, the USA and USSR could agree on the necessary measures for German demilitarisation, denazification and the punishment of war criminals, they were only able to draw up the following minimal political and economic guidelines for the future of Germany:

Key question
To what extent did the Potsdam Conference reveal fundamental disagreements between the wartime allies?

Potsdam Conference: July–August 1945

Key date

- As there was no central German government, an Allied Control Council (ACC) was set up on which the commanders-in-chief of the armies of the four occupying powers would sit. To avoid being outvoted by the three Western powers, the Russians insisted that each commander should have complete responsibility for his own zone. This decision effectively stopped the ACC from exercising any real power in Germany.
- A limited number of central German offices dealing with finance, transport, trade and industry, which were to deal with Germany as a whole, were to be formed at some point in the future.

Key terms

Reparations
Materials, equipment or money taken from a defeated power to make good the damage of war.

Oder–Neisse line
The line formed by the Oder and Neisse rivers. The Neisse had both a western and an eastern branch.

- There was no agreement on how much **reparations** the USSR should be paid. The Soviets had already begun to strip their zone of industrial plant and raw materials, but the British and Americans were convinced that the German economy must be left sufficiently strong to pay for imported food and raw materials, and were not ready to subsidise the Soviet zone. The British were particularly concerned because they had the highest population density within their zone, which would starve unless food was imported. A compromise was negotiated whereby both the USSR and the Western powers would take reparations from their own zones. In addition to this, the British and Americans would grant 10 per cent of these to the Soviets and a further 15 per cent in exchange for the supply of food and raw materials from the Soviet zone. The lack of a common reparation policy was a major step in the later partition of Germany, as it made agreement on a joint four power economic policy much more difficult to achieve.

The USSR had already handed to Poland all of Lower Silesia up to the western **Oder–Neisse line**. At first London and Washington insisted that the Polish border lay along the eastern Neisse, but then on second thoughts they decided to recognise the western Neisse line in the unrealistic hope that this concession would persuade Stalin to adopt a more liberal policy in Poland (see map on page 42).

The impact of the atom bomb

Churchill had hoped that the Big Three would meet as soon as possible after the end of the war in Europe, but it was not until 16 July that the Potsdam Conference opened. It was delayed because Truman wished to wait until the atom bomb had been tested at Alamogordo in New Mexico. When this took place successfully on 16 July, he was told that the bomb had a much greater destructive potential than was expected and was ready for immediate use against Japan. The news produced some dramatic changes in US policy. The Americans no longer wanted the USSR to join in the war against Japan, as now, it seemed likely that they would quickly defeat Japan by themselves. US officials also thought that the possession of the bomb would enable the USA to force Stalin to make concessions in Eastern Europe.

Arguably, the two atom bombs, which were dropped on Hiroshima and Nagasaki in early August, were primarily intended to impress the USSR. Thanks to the teams of highly skilled codebreakers at Bletchley Park in Britain and elsewhere, who cracked the secret Axis codes with the help of the world's first programmable computer, Colossus, the Allies already knew that Japan was ready to surrender. Stalin, however, refused to be intimidated. On the contrary, the news about the bomb made him both more suspicious of the USA and determined to make the USSR a nuclear power as soon as possible.

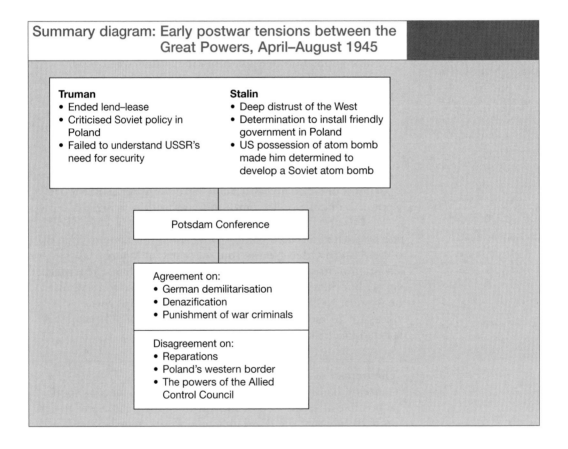

Summary diagram: Early postwar tensions between the Great Powers, April–August 1945

Truman
- Ended lend–lease
- Criticised Soviet policy in Poland
- Failed to understand USSR's need for security

Stalin
- Deep distrust of the West
- Determination to install friendly government in Poland
- US possession of atom bomb made him determined to develop a Soviet atom bomb

Potsdam Conference

Agreement on:
- German demilitarisation
- Denazification
- Punishment of war criminals

Disagreement on:
- Reparations
- Poland's western border
- The powers of the Allied Control Council

2 | The Peace Treaties with Italy and the Minor Axis Powers

Key question
Why, despite worsening relations between the USSR and Britain and the USA, was it possible to negotiate the peace treaties with Italy and the minor Axis powers?

At Potsdam it had been agreed that the **Council of Foreign Ministers** would draw up the peace treaties with Germany's allies. Arguments broke out almost immediately at the first session of the Council in September 1945. The Soviets pressed for a harsh peace with Italy, while the British and Americans argued that Italy, having broken with Germany in September 1944, deserved more lenient treatment. The USSR also insisted that its armistice agreements with Bulgaria, Finland, Hungary and Romania should form the basis of the subsequent peace treaties.

To save the negotiations from a complete breakdown, James Byrnes, the US **Secretary of State**, went to Moscow, where after some hard bargaining a compromise was reached whereby the Eastern European and the Italian peace treaties would be negotiated simultaneously. Negotiations dragged on for over a year and were frequently threatened by the escalating tension between the USSR and the West. Nevertheless in the final analysis both sides wanted the peace treaties concluded, and were able to make compromises. As a concession to the USSR, the treaty with Italy was harsh; it lost both Trieste, which became a self-governing 'free territory', and its colonies, as well as having to pay reparations. In Eastern Europe the USSR gained what it wanted, particularly in the question of keeping troops in Romania to guard its lines of communication with Austria.

The peace treaties with Italy and the minor Axis states were signed on 10 February 1947, but disagreements about the value of former German property to be handed over to the USSR delayed the Austrian treaty until 1955 (see page 100), and no treaty could be signed with Germany until an independent central German government had been restored.

Key date
Peace treaties signed with Italy, Romania, Bulgaria, Finland and Hungary: 10 February 1947

Key question
Why did the four occupying powers fail to work out a joint programme for Germany's future?

Key terms

Council of Foreign Ministers
Composed of the foreign ministers of Britain, France, the USA and the USSR. Its role was to sort out the German problems and prepare the peace treaties.

Secretary of State
The US Foreign Minister.

National federation of trade unions
A national organisation representing all the trade unions.

3 | Germany, June 1945–April 1947

Germany's position in the middle of Europe and its potential wealth and military and economic strength ensured that neither the USSR nor the Western Allies could allow the other to dominate it. Indeed, as tension rose, both sides began to wonder whether Germany itself could not perhaps be enlisted as a future ally in a possible East–West conflict.

Germany under four power control, June 1945–November 1946

In June 1945 Stalin told a group of German Communists that there would be 'two Germanies', implying that Germany would be divided into a Soviet-dominated part and a Western-dominated part. Nine months later, however, he informed the Yugoslavs that 'all Germany must be ours'. For a time, however, he seemed ready to co-operate with the Western powers in creating a new democratic Germany, in which the Communist Party, as in France and Italy (see pages 26–7), would play an important though not dominating role. This may well have been the reason why in June 1945 the USSR was the first occupying power to allow democratic parties in its zone. At first, the USSR was also a more co-operative partner on the ACC than France. In the autumn of 1945 the Russians were ready to agree to setting up a central German transport authority and a **national federation of trade unions**, but both these proposals were defeated by French opposition to restoring a united Germany, which might again dominate Europe.

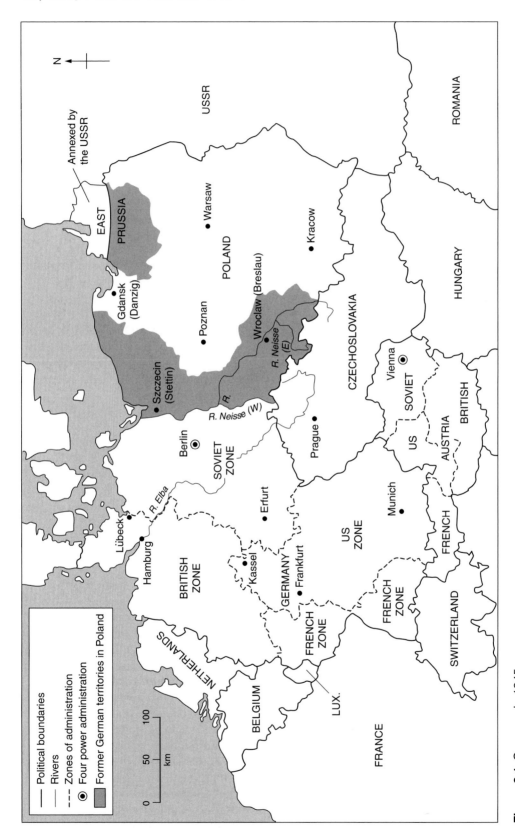

Figure 3.1 Germany in 1945.

Latent fear
Concealed (latent) or indirect terror and pressure.

Central Executive
Central organising committee.

Why, then, was this co-operation not maintained? In the first place there were many high-ranking British and US officials, as well as West German politicians, such as Konrad Adenauer, the future West German Chancellor, who were convinced that the Soviet zone was lost to the rest of Germany. The historian Willy Loth has also argued that Stalin's approach was not fully grasped by his officials in the Soviet zone, who tended naturally to rely on local German Communists and to see middle-class Germans as the class enemy. As in Poland, the NKVD and the Soviet army did not hesitate to arrest anybody who got in their way, which inevitably created a climate of '**latent fear**'.

Profile: Konrad Adenauer 1876–1967

1876	– Born in Cologne
1917–33	– *Oberbürgermeister* (Lord Mayor) of Cologne
1946–9	– Head of the German Christian Democrat Party in the British zone
1949	– Chairman of the German parliamentary council, which drafted the West German constitution
1949–63	– Chancellor of the Federal Republic of Germany
1967	– Died

Adenauer was a key figure in the early Cold War history. As Chancellor he refused point blank to negotiate with the Communist East Germany and took every chance to integrate West Germany into a US-dominated Western Europe. Some historians, such as the revisionist Willy Loth, argue that his refusal to contemplate a neutral united Germany perpetuated the division of Germany. Others, like the more orthodox Hans-Peter Schwarz, however, stress that Adenauer was simply a realist, who saw that the only way of unifying Germany was to wait until East Germany collapsed as a result of its own economic weaknesses.

It was this atmosphere that made a voluntary amalgamation in the Soviet zone of the revived German Social Democratic (SPD) and Communist (KPD) parties impossible to achieve without the use of force. After the poor showing of the Communist Party in the Hungarian elections of November 1945, Stalin realised that only a union between the SPD and KPD could create a strong, friendly party in Germany. In these elections, which were held in November, the non-Communist smallholders or peasants' party gained well over 50 per cent of the vote, while the Socialists and Communists each gained only 25 per cent.

In an effort to win over the SPD the Soviets did force the KPD to make considerable concessions, but the threats and violence used by the Soviet Military Administration effectively disguised their extent, and alienated many SPD members. In the end, after 20,000 Social Democrats had been interrogated, imprisoned and in some cases even murdered, the **Central Executive** of the SPD in the Soviet zone agreed to the formation of a new united party,

The historic handshake between Otto Grotewohl (right), leader of the SPD in the Eastern Zone and Wilhelm Pieck, leader of the KPD (left). Looking on is the future leader of East Germany, Walter Ulbricht.

the Socialist Unity Party (SED), by a vote of 8 to 3 in February 1946. The Russians were then embarrassed when a month later a **referendum** on the decision was held in Berlin for members of both parties. In East Berlin they managed to close down the polling stations, but in the West voting went ahead and 82 per cent of the SPD members opposed the union. Inevitably, as with the USSR's actions in Poland, this only served to confirm the West's suspicions of Soviet policy.

At the end of April 1946 Stalin took stock of the situation in Germany, and in an important directive to his officials in the Soviet zone he announced:

> from the standpoint of the Soviet Union, it is not yet time to establish central authorities nor in general to continue with a policy of centralisation in Germany. The first goal, organising the Soviet occupation zone under effective Soviet control, has been more or less achieved. The moment has thus now come to reach into the Western zones. The instrument is the United Socialist–Communist Party. Some time will have to elapse before the party is organised in an orderly fashion in Greater Berlin itself, and this process will take even longer in the Western zones. Only when the Soviet vision has been realised and the Unity Party has established itself in the Western zones, will the time have come to address once again the question of central Administrations and of effective Soviet support for a policy of centralisation in Germany.

The reason why Stalin wanted to delay setting up a central administration in Germany was probably that he suspected that

Key date

Social Unity Party (SED) formed: 21 April 1946

Key term

Referendum
The referring of a political question to the electorate for a vote. In this case the electorate was limited to members of the SPD and KPD.

the Americans and British were aiming to end the occupation of Germany as soon as possible because of the heavy financial burden it imposed on them. If that happened, he feared that the guarantees agreed on at Potsdam would be abandoned and that an aggressive and capitalist Germany would re-emerge.

The problem of reparations

Key question
Why could the occupying powers not agree on the reparation question?

Key date
General Clay halted reparation payments from the Soviet zone: 3 May 1946

By the spring of 1946 the compromise over reparations, which had been negotiated in Potsdam, was already breaking down. As the Western zones, particularly the heavily populated British zone, were taking the majority of the German refugees, who had been expelled by the Poles and Czechs from the former German territories that had been ceded to them at the end of the war (see map on page 42). Britain and the USA were anxious to encourage a moderate German economic recovery so that their zones could at least pay for their own food imports. Consequently, until that point was reached they wished to delay delivering to the USSR the quotas from their own zones of machinery and raw materials, which had been agreed at Potsdam (see pages 38–40). There was even talk that the Soviet zone would have to deliver food to the hard-pressed Western zones.

In May, General Clay, the military governor of the US zone, in an attempt to bring the French into line and to force the Soviets to agree to treat Germany as an economic unity with its economy organised on a national rather than a zonal level, announced that no further reparation deliveries would be made until there was an overall plan for the German economy. To the Soviets it seemed that the Americans were bringing pressure to bear on them to agree to a reconstructed German economy within an international capitalist system. They feared that a united German capitalist economy would play a key part in a US-dominated global capitalist trading system. In June they responded to this threat by increasing production in their zone and transforming 213 German firms into special Soviet-controlled companies, the total production of which was to go straight to the USSR.

The creation of Bizonia

Key question
Why was Bizonia formed?

Key dates
Paris Conference of Foreign Ministers: April–July 1946

Anglo-US Bizonia formed: 1 January 1947

Key term
Trade surplus
A surplus of exports over imports.

When the Conference of Foreign Ministers returned to the question of Germany in July, Molotov, the Soviet Foreign Minister, insisted that the Germans should pay the USSR the equivalent of $10 billion in reparations. Byrnes again argued that reparations could only be paid once Germany had a **trade surplus** that would cover the cost of food and raw material imports. He then offered to unify the US zone economically with the other three zones (see map on page 42). Only Britain, which was finding its zone a major drain on its fragile economy, accepted.

In retrospect this was a major step in the division of Germany between East and West, although its significance was played down initially. When the British and US zones were merged economically in January 1947 to form what became called Bizonia, the Americans argued that, far from breaking the Potsdam Agreement, the amalgamation would serve as an economic magnet and so create the economic preconditions for fulfilling the Potsdam Agreement. It was hoped that Bizonia would become so prosperous that through inter-zonal trade it would gradually attract and knit the French and Russian zones in a united national German economy. A more prosperous Germany would then be able to pay the reparations, which had been demanded at Potsdam (see page 39). In an attempt to convince the USSR that Bizonia was not an **embryonic state** the offices responsible for food, finance and transport were deliberately located in different cities.

Embryonic state
Organisation that has some of the powers of a proper state, and is likely to grow into a fully fledged state.

Key term

The Moscow Conference of Foreign Ministers, March–April 1947

Key question
Why did the Moscow Conference fail?

The Moscow Conference was one of the turning points in early postwar history. The Soviets made a determined effort to destroy Bizonia by demanding that a new central German administration under four power control should be immediately set up. They ran into strong opposition from the British Foreign Secretary, Ernest Bevin, who feared that this would slow up the economic recovery of the British zone. In London his officials had skilfully drawn up a plan for revising the Potsdam Agreement, which Bevin knew the Soviets could not accept. The USSR would, for instance, have to return some of the reparations that it had seized in its zone to help balance the budgets in the Western zones, and it would receive no coal or steel deliveries until the whole of Germany could pay for its own food and raw material imports. Bevin successfully managed to manoeuvre the USSR into a corner when he persuaded the Americans to agree that political unity could only come after economic unity. As this would mean a protracted delay in reparation deliveries, the Soviets had little option but to reject the proposal, which is exactly what the Western powers hoped they would do.

Moscow Conference: 10 March–24 April 1947

Key date

To the British and Americans the Moscow Conference was what Willy Loth called a 'successful failure' in that it enabled them to press on with building up Bizonia. Nothing, however, was decided on the divisive issues of reparations, and the future of Germany was left to dominate the agenda of the next conference scheduled to meet in London in November (see page 64).

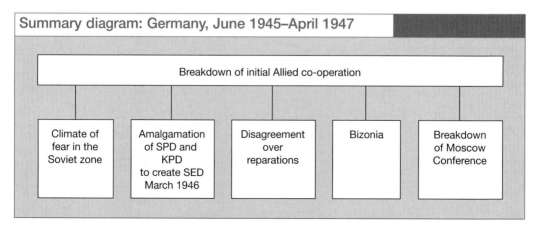

Summary diagram: Germany, June 1945–April 1947

Breakdown of initial Allied co-operation

| Climate of fear in the Soviet zone | Amalgamation of SPD and KPD to create SED March 1946 | Disagreement over reparations | Bizonia | Breakdown of Moscow Conference |

4 | The Truman Doctrine of Containment

Origins of the Truman Doctrine

Key question
What events led to the formulation of the Truman Doctrine?

In June 1945 the Americans had assumed that Britain would continue to play a major role in the eastern Mediterranean, but by January 1947 Britain faced a crippling economic crisis. As a result of political unrest in India, Palestine and Egypt and the long delay in completing the postwar peace treaties, Britain had to keep a large number of troops in Germany, Italy, the Middle East and Asia. This was, of course, enormously expensive, and by January 1947 the postwar US loan of £3.75 billion had nearly been used up. The situation was made worse by the heavy blizzards and exceptionally cold weather that had brought transport, industry and coal mining virtually to a halt for several weeks. On 21 February the British, in desperation, informed the Americans that their financial and military aid to both Greece and Turkey would have to cease on 31 March.

This was very unwelcome news to Washington, as civil war had broken out again in Greece in September 1946 when Stalin, contrary to his earlier policy in 1944 (see page 23), had asked the Yugoslavs to assist the Greek Communists against the British-backed Greek government. Truman feared above all that the Communists might launch a similar uprising in Italy once Allied troops had left after the signing of the peace treaty (see page 41). He felt therefore that he had to act quickly to strengthen non-Communist forces in areas that were vulnerable to Soviet pressure, but to do this he required money, which could only be found by persuading **Congress** to vote the necessary funds.

Key terms

Congress
The US parliament.

Totalitarian regimes
Regimes such as those in Soviet Russia or Nazi Germany, which sought to control every aspect of their people's lives.

The announcement of the Doctrine

Key question
What were the main points of the Truman Doctrine?

On 12 March, in a deliberately dramatic speech designed to appeal to Congress, Truman stressed the seriousness of the international situation and how Europe was increasingly becoming divided into two mutually hostile blocs:

Key date
Truman Doctrine announced: 12 March 1947

One way of life is based upon the will of the majority, and is distinguished by free institutions, representative government, free elections, guarantees of individual liberty, freedom of speech and religion, and freedom from political oppression. The second way of life is based upon the will of a minority forcibly imposed upon the majority. It relies upon terror and oppression, a controlled press and radio, fixed elections and the suppression of personal freedoms.

I believe that it must be the policy of the United States to support free peoples who are resisting attempted subjugation by armed minorities or by outside pressures. I believe that we must assist free peoples to work out their own destinies in their own way. … The seeds of **totalitarian regimes** are nurtured by misery and want. They spread and grow in the evil soil of poverty and strife. They reach their full growth when the hope of a people for a better life has died.

Initially Stalin dismissed this speech as an exercise in propaganda, but it soon became clear that it marked a new and important US policy initiative, which was to lead to what became called the Marshall Plan.

5 | The Marshall Plan
The origins of the Plan

Since 1945 the Americans had been pumping money into Western Europe in an attempt to prevent famine and total economic collapse. In 1947 influential US journalists and politicians were beginning to argue that only through political and economic integration could Western Europe solve the whole complex of problems facing it. This would create a large and potentially prosperous market, which would act as a barrier to the further spread of Communism and perhaps in time even pull the Eastern European states out of the Soviet bloc. It would also build a political structure into which West Germany, or indeed the whole of Germany, could be integrated and so contained.

Key question
What were the aims of the Marshall Plan and why did the USSR reject it?

General Marshall's offer

In June 1947, after extensive consultations in Washington, General George Marshall, the new US Secretary of State, made his historic offer of an aid package for Europe. The key to it was that:

Marshall Plan announced: 5 June 1947

Key date

> … there must be some agreement among the countries of Europe as to the requirements of the situation and the part those countries themselves will take in order to give proper effect to whatever action might be undertaken by this Government.

Profile: George C. Marshall 1880–1959

1880		– Born in Pittsburg, Pennsylvania
1939–45		– Chief of Staff of the US army
1946–7		– US ambassador to China
1947–9		– Secretary of State
1947	June 5	– Announced the Marshall Plan at Harvard University
1950–2		– Defence minister
1953		– Awarded Nobel Peace Prize
1959		– Died

At the time the Russians, and later some revisionist historians, such as Thomas Paterson and J. Garry Clifford, claimed that the Marshall Plan was inspired by the US desire to build up Europe as a market for US goods. Its prime purpose, however, was to use US economic power to halt Soviet expansion by creating a prosperous Western Europe.

Key question
Why were the Americans disappointed by the way the West Europeans organised the carrying out of the Marshall Plan?

The Paris negotiations

Stalin suspected that the offer masked an attempt by the USA to interfere in the domestic affairs of the European states, but he sent Molotov to Paris to discuss further details with the British and French. The Soviets certainly wanted financial aid from the USA but without any conditions attached. Britain and France, however, argued that the European states should draw up a joint programme for spending the aid, rather than each individual state sending in a separate list of requests. On Stalin's orders Molotov rejected this and left the Conference. Stalin feared that a joint programme would enable US economic power to undermine Soviet influence in Eastern Europe. Bevin, who had done much to engineer this break, as he did not want to run the risk of the USSR obstructing talks with the Americans, observed that Molotov's departure marked the beginning of the formation of a **Western bloc**.

On 16 July detailed negotiations on the Marshall Plan began in Paris, where 16 Western European nations, including Turkey and Greece, were represented. Relevant information on Bizonia was provided by the occupation authorities. The Eastern European states were invited but were stopped by Stalin from attending. For the Western powers this simplified the negotiations, but even so, agreement was difficult to arrive at. Each Western European state had its own agenda. The French, for instance, wanted to ensure that their own economy had preference in receiving US aid over the economic needs of Bizonia. They were, however, ready to consider the formation of a **customs union**, as long as it enabled France to control the West German economy. The British on the other hand wished to safeguard their **sovereignty** and were opposed to creating powerful **supranational** organisations.

By mid-August the Americans were disappointed to find that the Western Europeans had not come up with any radical plans for economic integration, and had only produced a series of national 'shopping lists'. Each country had merely drawn up a list of requests with its own needs in mind, rather than thinking supranationally. Jefferson Caffery, the US Ambassador in Paris, complained that this simply re-created prewar economic conditions with all the 'low labor productivity and maldistribution of effort which derive from segregating 270,000,000 people into 17 uneconomic principalities' or 17 small countries with their own separate economies. As a US citizen he was dismissive of small historical countries fiercely proud of their independence.

The Western European states also asked for $29 billion, far more than Congress was ready to grant. To avoid the conference ending in failure, Bevin called an emergency meeting in Paris, which decided to let the Americans themselves propose where cuts in this sum could be made. The US officials immediately set up an **Advisory Steering Committee**, which attempted to bring

Key terms

Western bloc
An alliance of Western European states and the USA.

Customs union
An area of free trade unhindered by national tariffs.

Sovereignty
Independence. A sovereign state possesses the power to make its own decisions.

Supranational
Transcending national limits.

Advisory Steering Committee
A committee that would advise on priorities and the key decisions to be taken.

the Europeans into line with essential US requirements, but by late September Washington had achieved only a limited success:

- Although the 16 states promised to liberalise trade and France promised to start negotiations for a customs union, these commitments were hedged around with qualifications aimed at protecting national independence.
- Germany's economic revival was declared essential, although it was to be carefully controlled to protect its neighbours.
- There was to be co-operation on the development of **hydroelectric sources**, pooling of railway wagons and the setting up of production targets for coal, agriculture, refined oil and steel. But there were to be no supranational authorities that could force the individual states to carry out these policies. At most the 16 states promised to set up a joint organisation to review how much progress was being made.

Hydroelectric sources
Power stations that generate electricity through water power.

Key term

The Soviet response

Stalin's decision to put pressure on the Eastern European states to boycott the Paris Conference marked the end of his attempts to co-operate with the USA and maintain the Grand Alliance. In September 1946 he invited the leaders of the Eastern European, French and Italian Communist parties to a conference at Szklarska Poreba in Poland to discuss setting up the Communist Information Bureau (Cominform), which would co-ordinate the policies and tactics of the Communist parties in both the satellite states and in Western Europe. Andrei Zhdanov, Stalin's representative, told the delegates that the world was now divided into two hostile camps: the imperialist bloc led by the USA, intent on 'the enslavement of Europe', and the 'anti-imperialist and democratic camp' led by the USSR. From this it followed that the whole policy of co-operating with moderate socialist and liberal parties would have to be abandoned and, where possible, Communist parties would have to take over power themselves and create societies whose economy and social system would be modelled on the Soviet system. From now on, as Martin McCauley has put it, 'there was to be only one road to socialism'.

Key question
What was the Soviet response?

Cominform founded: 5 October 1947

Key date

Summary diagram: The Truman Doctrine of containment, the Marshall Plan and the Soviet response

Truman Doctrine, March 1947

Reasons for its announcement

- Britain unable to defend eastern Mediterranean
- Yugoslavs assisting Greek Communists

The Doctrine

- Truman offers US support to countries resisting Communist subversion
- Stresses need to improve economic conditions in Europe

The Marshall Plan

- Offer of aid package
- Funds to be distributed by supranational organisation

- Accepted by Western European states
- Rejected by USSR, which sets up Cominform

---

6 | The European States, June 1945–December 1947

The 'Iron Curtain'

Key question
How correct was Churchill's assessment that an Iron Curtain had descended across Europe?

Churchill's 'Iron Curtain' speech: 5 March 1946

In a famous speech at Fulton in the USA on 5 March 1946, Churchill observed that 'from Stettin in the Baltic, to Trieste, in the Adriatic, an iron curtain has descended across the continent'.

How accurate was this analysis? Up to the spring of 1947 it can be argued, to quote the British historians, G. and N. Swain, that 'diversity rather than uniformity' still characterised the situation in Europe. Yugoslavia and Albania had their own Communist regimes whose aggressive plans for a Balkan union and meddling in Greek domestic affairs Stalin at first attempted to control. Poland and Romania, both vital to the USSR's security, underwent Socialist revolutions and were in effect already Soviet satellites. In Hungary, Czechoslovakia, Finland and even Bulgaria, Stalin pursued a more moderate policy of influence rather than direct control. Yet with the escalation of the Cold War brought about by the Marshall Plan discussions and the creation of the Cominform, Stalin began to impose a much more uniform pattern on Eastern Europe. In Western Europe the intensifying Cold War **polarised** domestic politics with the

Polarised
Divided into extremes (polar opposites).

Communists on one side and non-Communists on the other. Communist parties were forced out of coalitions in France and Italy. Only in Finland did the situation remain unchanged.

Poland

To deflect Western criticism from his Polish policy, Stalin had set up a provisional Government of National Unity in June 1945, which had been joined by Stanislaw Mikolajczyk, the former leader of the government-in-exile in London. Stalin could not risk genuinely free elections as the Communist Party would inevitably suffer defeat. Mikolajczyk therefore resigned in protest from the provisional cabinet in August 1945, and in October 1946 he refused to allow his party, the Polish Peasants' Party, to join the Communist-dominated **electoral bloc**, which would present the electors with a single list of candidates who would all support a Communist-dominated government. He hoped that this boycott would trigger a political crisis that would force Britain and the USA to intervene.

In fact the new **doctrine of containment** being worked out by Truman accepted unofficially that Poland was within the USSR's sphere of interest and that the USA would not intervene in its domestic affairs. Thus, when Mikolajczyk suggested that Britain and the USA should send officials to monitor the election in January 1947, both declined in the knowledge that there was little they could do to influence events in Poland. The results were a foregone conclusion. The bloc, which used terror and falsified electoral results with impunity, officially gained 394 seats, while the Peasants' Party gained a mere 28.

Although Wladyslaw Gomulka, the leader of the Polish Communist Party, was dependent on Soviet assistance, he believed passionately that Poland had a unique history and could not just follow unquestioningly the Soviet example. He therefore viewed with dismay the creation of the Cominform, as he feared that it would force the Eastern European Communist parties to follow down to the last detail the Moscow model of socialism. Only under considerable pressure did he reluctantly accept it, and a year later Stalin had him removed from the leadership (see page 66).

Romania

The Soviet Union's claim that Romania was a vital security zone continued to meet with considerable understanding from the Western powers. There was no strong opposition leader there like Mikolajczyk in Poland and consequently the Soviets were able to consolidate their position more quickly than they did in Poland. In March 1946 the Socialist Party agreed to amalgamate with the Communists and in November the voters were presented with an electoral bloc which even the opposition joined. Not surprisingly it won 80 per cent of the vote.

Key question
Why did Britain and the USA not intervene in Poland to stop the Communists from seizing power?

Key terms

Electoral bloc
An electoral alliance by a group of parties.

Doctrine of containment
A policy of halting the USSR's advance into Western Europe. It did not envisage actually 'rolling back' Soviet power from Eastern Europe.

Key question
How did the USSR tighten its control of Romania?

Key question
How did the USSR
tighten its control of
Bulgaria?

Bulgaria

Soviet techniques and policy were similar in Bulgaria, although Stalin hoped to avoid unnecessary friction with the Western powers until the peace treaty had been signed. In December 1945 he therefore forced the Communist-dominated Bulgarian government to include two members of the opposition, but when these began to demand changes in policy Stalin advised the Communists to adopt a series of well-planned measures to smother the opposition. Yet with an eye on the still unfinished peace treaties (see page 41) he remained anxious to mask the party's dictatorship. He even urged the sceptical Bulgarian Communists in September 1946 to set up a 'Labour Party' which would have 'a broader base and a better mask for the present period'.

In October elections took place for a national assembly. The opposition parties managed to win over one-third of the total votes, but Western hopes that this would form the basis of an effective parliamentary opposition were soon dashed. The Truman Doctrine and increasing US involvement in Greece meant that Bulgaria became a frontline state in the defence of Communism. Consequently, Stalin allowed the Communists to liquidate the opposition. The Bulgarian Communist Party also took the creation of the Cominform as a cue for pressing on with its radical programme for nationalising industry, **collectivising agriculture** and creating a one-party state.

Key term

Collectivising agriculture
Abolishing private farms in favour of large units run collectively by the peasantry along the lines of Soviet agriculture.

Key question
How did the political question in Yugoslavia differ from elsewhere in Eastern Europe?

Yugoslavia

Yugoslavia occupied a unique position among the Soviet-dominated states in Eastern and Southeastern Europe, as the Communist Party had effectively won power independently of the Soviet forces. The People's Front, a bloc of parties dominated by the Yugoslav Communist Party, won 90 per cent of the votes in the election of November 1945, and Tito was then able smoothly to implement a revolution based on the Stalinist model in the USSR. Tito had his own plans for making Yugoslavia the major regional power in Southeast Europe. Only the continued presence of British and US troops stopped him from annexing Trieste in the period 1945–8, when he was perceived by the West, not entirely accurately, to be acting as the proxy of the USSR. Yet his dramatic break with Stalin in 1948 was to change this assessment (see pages 66–8).

Key question
Why were Hungary and Czechoslovakia not able to remain 'bridges' between Eastern and Western Europe?

Czechoslovakia and Hungary

Up to the autumn of 1947 Stalin appeared to be interested primarily in preserving a strong Communist influence in Czechoslovakia and Hungary rather than in complete domination.

Czechoslovakia

In Czechoslovakia, the postwar social revolution had been carried out by an alliance of socialists and Communists under the direction of President Beneš. Soviet troops had been withdrawn as early as December 1945. The elections in May 1946, in which the Communists won some 38 per cent of the vote, were carried out without any violence or efforts by the Communist Party to manipulate the vote. Although Gottwald had established a tight grip on the Czech security forces, he had no plans for a *coup* and appeared to pin his hope on winning the 1948 election. Without the intensifying Cold War Czechoslovakia might perhaps have remained a bridge between East and West, as Beneš had hoped, but the Marshall Plan and the subsequent creation of the Cominform effectively created a climate where this was impossible. The Czech cabinet voted unanimously in July to attend the Paris Conference on the Plan (see page 49), but the Soviet government insisted that the Americans under cover of offering a loan were trying to form a Western bloc and isolate the Soviet Union.

Czech proposals for compromise were ruthlessly dismissed. Jan Masaryk, the Foreign Minister, later told the British Ambassador: 'I went to Moscow as the Foreign Minister of an independent sovereign state; I returned as a **lackey** of the Soviet government'. What this implied became clearer at Szklarska Poreba in September when the Secretary-General of the Czech Communist Party, Rudolf Slansky, told the conference that the reactionary forces would have to be expelled from the National Front.

Key terms

Lackey
An uncritical follower, a servant, who cannot answer back.

Liberation
The freeing of a country from foreign occupation.

Hungary

It seemed in the autumn of 1945 that Hungary, like Czechoslovakia, was treated as a special case by Stalin. The elections of November 1945 were free, even though the Soviets could have influenced them easily. Two years later the press was still free as was debate in parliament, the borders with the West were open and most small- and medium-sized businesses were in private hands. Yet, until the signing of the peace treaty, Soviet influence was guaranteed through its dominating position on the Allied Control Commission, which was the real governing force in Hungary (see page 19), and Stalin was able to insist on the Communist Party participating in the coalition government and controlling the vital Ministry of the Interior.

In the spring of 1947 the most powerful opposition to the Communists was shattered, when the leader of the Smallholders' Party, Bela Kovacs, was arrested by Soviet troops for conspiring against the occupation. Yet even this did not lead to an overwhelming Communist success in the August elections when the left-wing bloc only won 45 per cent of the vote. As late as the autumn of 1947, it still seemed possible that Hungary might retain some independence, but it was increasingly being drawn into the Soviet bloc. On 8 December a Treaty of Friendship and co-operation was signed with Yugoslavia and, a month later, a mutual aid treaty with the USSR.

France and Italy
France

After the **liberation**, the French government initially attempted to balance between the USSR and the Western powers. Indeed many historians argue that France did not really join the Cold War on

Key question
What role did the Communist parties play in France and Italy?

the side of Britain and the USA until the Moscow Conference of March 1947. However, a French historian, Annie Lacroix Riz, has shown that long before then Paris had unofficially aligned itself with Britain and the USA. As early as October 1945 General de Gaulle was thinking of a Western European Defence Organisation with a US and possibly even a German contribution, but when he fell from power, the new government, a Communist, Socialist and Christian Democrat coalition, attempted to act as a bridge between East and West. Even then, though, to quote the French historian Georges-Henri Soutou, 'behind the scenes and in the utmost secrecy' the Christian Democrats and some of the Socialists attempted to draw nearer to the USA.

In March 1946 the French Socialist leader, Leon Blum, went to Washington to negotiate an American loan, and quite voluntarily accepted the US arguments for free international trade, which effectively meant France's inclusion in the capitalist Western world. At the Moscow Conference in March 1947 France openly aligned itself with the British and Americans, and two months later the Communists were expelled from the governing coalition. Initially they remained allied with the Socialists, but in the autumn Stalin ordered them to stage a series of violent strikes against the Marshall Plan. This finally persuaded the Socialists to distance themselves from them and to accept the pro-US policy of the Christian Democrats.

Italy

There was a similar pattern of events in Italy. The Communists joined the coalition government in April 1945, and some Italian statesmen argued that Italy should try to balance between the USSR and the Western powers. Yet essentially, Italy, as Stalin himself conceded, had little option but to support the latter group, since it had been liberated and occupied by them. In December 1945 a new coalition government was created under de Gasperi, a Christian Democrat, who rapidly won US support for his economic policies. As East–West tension grew in 1946–7, the Italian government moved to the right, and in May 1947 the Communists were dismissed from the cabinet. This cleared the way for the government to accept the Marshall Plan and to align itself unambiguously with the West.

Key date
Communists excluded from government in France and Italy: May 1947

Key question
Why was Finland able to retain its neutrality in 1946–7?

Finland

Finland again remained the exception to the pattern developing in the other Eastern European states. Its weak Communist Party received little help from the USSR. Why was this so? The British historian Adam Ulam argues that Finland escaped being integrated into the Soviet bloc merely by chance, as Zhdanov, the Soviet chairman of the Allied Control Commission, was away most of the time in Moscow. Yet Jukka Nevakivi, who has studied the relevant Soviet sources, argues that Stalin simply wanted to neutralise Finland, and once the Finns had signed the Treaty of Friendship, Co-operation and Mutual Assistance in 1948, he was ready to leave them alone.

Summary diagram: The division widens – the European states, June 1945–December 1947

Eastern Europe

Poland	Romania	Bulgaria	Yugoslavia	Hungary and Czechoslovakia
Communist-dominated electoral bloc won January 1947 elections	Communists in control by March 1946	Enemies of Communist Party liquidated	Communist Party dominant under Tito	By December 1947 ceased to be a 'bridge' to the West

Finland: remained neutral but not under Communist control

Western Europe

France	Italy
Communists joined coalition and worked with the Socialists and Christian Democrats, but expelled May 1947	Communists expelled from government, May 1947

7 | Conclusion

How likely was the break-up of the Grand Alliance by the autumn of 1947? We have seen that its real glue was Hitler. Once Nazi Germany and Imperial Japan were defeated, it was always more realistic to suppose that it would disintegrate than remain intact. Stalin was quite determined to turn Poland, Romania and Bulgaria into satellite states regardless of what the liberal West might think about the violation of democracy or human rights. On the other hand, he did have a **'differentiated' policy**, which for two years allowed Hungary and Czechoslovakia to be 'bridges' to the West.

Is it an exaggeration to say that Stalin pursued a relatively moderate line in Eastern Europe up to 1947, and that his German policy, rather than a result of deep-laid plans to take over the former *Reich*, was more a clumsy attempt to neutralise it and gain the vital reparations needed by the USSR? Michael MccGwire has argued that Stalin was actively seeking to preserve the 'remaining shreds of the collaborative wartime relationship', and as a consequence of this, had by 1947 lost his chance to control Greece and allow Yugoslavia to seize Trieste. By the spring and summer of 1947 Stalin was thrown on the defensive first by the Truman Doctrine and then by the Marshall Plan.

Does this mean that Truman in fact started the Cold War? The Truman Doctrine and the Marshall Plan were certainly important

Key question
Was the break-up of the Grand Alliance in the period 1945–7 more a result of Soviet or US policies?

'Differentiated' policy
Stalin's policy to treat each Soviet-occupied country differently.

thresholds or stages reached in the escalation of the Cold War, but the context in which the Americans acted is also important. The seismic events of early 1947 – Britain's near bankruptcy and withdrawal from the eastern Mediterranean, growing economic paralysis in Germany and the strength of the Communist parties in Italy and France – galvanised the Americans into announcing first the Truman Doctrine and then the Marshall Plan. This was the turning point in the immediate postwar period and provoked the USSR into tightening its grip on Eastern Europe and creating the Cominform.

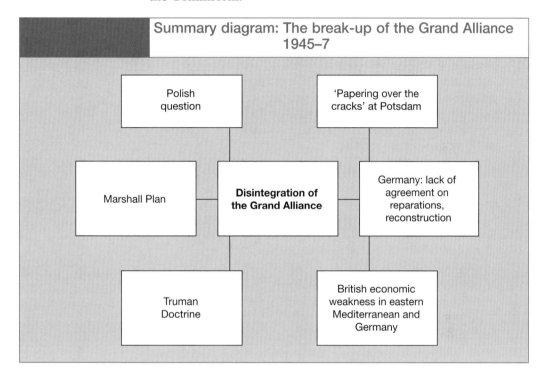

Summary diagram: The break-up of the Grand Alliance 1945–7

Study Guide: AS Questions

In the style of OCR

1. To what extent was disagreement on Germany the cause of the break-up of the Grand Alliance? (50 marks)
2. Was the Marshall Plan an act of pure generosity or of 'American imperialism'? (50 marks)

> ### Exam tips
>
> The cross-references are intended to take you straight to the material that will help you to answer the questions.
>
> 1. When preparing an essay first ask yourself what the question actually means and what information you need to draw on to answer it. Examiners often use the words 'to what extent'. This indicates that you must make some sort of judgement or evaluation. Thus, before you assess whether or not disagreement on Germany was the cause of the break-up of the Grand Alliance, you need to consider other factors that played a part in its destruction, such as:
>
>   *   Soviet policy in Poland (page 52), which did so much to alienate the West.
>   *   The emergence of the 'Iron Curtain' (page 51).
>   *   The vulnerability of an impoverished Europe to Communism and the perceived Soviet threat in Greece and Turkey, which provoked Truman to announce the Truman Doctrine (pages 47–8).
>   *   The lack of understanding in Washington of the USSR's desire to create a security belt in Eastern Europe.
>   *   The perception in Moscow of the Marshall Plan as an act of 'US imperialism'.
>
>   Within this context disagreement on Germany can be seen to be another, albeit key area of confrontation.
>
> 2. Question 2 is a deliberately provocative question and invites you to consider the revisionist case against the USA (page 48). The answer requires an analysis of the Marshall Plan (pages 48–51), but you will also need to ask yourself why the USA formulated it. You will need to view the Marshall Plan within the context of disagreements on Germany, Poland and the announcement of the Truman Doctrine. Was it a response to perceived Soviet threats or an example of US economic imperialism? Why did Stalin reject it?
>
>   When preparing essays of this sort it is wise to take the following steps:
>
>   *   Ask yourself what areas of knowledge the essay question is asking you to explore.
>   *   Then decide on the key themes of your answer and how you will effectively use them to answer the question.

- Remember that you are required to construct an *argument* backed up with relevant evidence. Do not just tell the story and allow the examiner to do the thinking!
- Before you start writing the essay, it is a good idea to draw up a plan.
- Your essay should have a short introductory paragraph in which you introduce the gist of your main arguments.
- Then in the main section of your essay you should develop these arguments further, backed up with well-chosen evidence.
- Most students find the final paragraph the most difficult. Just repeating points you have already made earlier in the essay in a more simplified form will not bring you any extra credit. It is better to end your essay with your strongest and most convincing argument, which reinforces those you have made elsewhere. Supported by a brief quotation or reference to a relevant historian, this can be a very effective way of rounding off your essay.

Study Guide: Advanced Level Questions

In the style of AQA

'Basic differences between the aims of the USSR and the USA in the period 1945–7 made the Cold War inevitable.' Assess the validity of this view. (45 marks)

> ### Exam tips
>
> *The cross-references are intended to take you straight to the material that will help you to answer the question.*
>
> You will need to analyse where the aims of the two powers conflicted and how this affected relations between them and whether there were other factors that are relevant. You need, for instance, to mention:
>
> - The different understanding of what the word democracy meant to both states (page 29).
> - The ambiguities in the Declaration on Liberated Europe (page 30).
> - Stalin's determination to create a ring of friendly states around his western frontiers (page 14).
> - The determination of Britain and the USA to minimise Soviet influence in Western Europe (pages 26–7).
> - The disagreements over the new government of Poland (pages 28–9).
> - The USA's determination to create a liberal world order (page 16).
>
> You will need to refer to the immediate post-war tensions (pages 37–9) and in particular how differences were exacerbated by the atom bomb. The situation in Germany, which had brought the two superpowers 'eyeball to eyeball', produced a context in which differences were magnified and the importance of this will need to be assessed. You might consider whether there was a point of 'no return' – perhaps with the issuing of the Truman Doctrine and/or the Marshall Plan and whether the Soviet response was because of basic 'aims' or merely a reaction to provocation.
>
> You will need to consider whether Cold War was ever 'inevitable' and if you think it was, you should be able to say at what point it became so and why. If you disagree, you again need to be able to justify your decision and assess whether the differences in aims between the two powers could have been reconciled. You should convey a judgement in your answer and back all your arguments with suitable factual detail.

In the style of Edexcel

Study Sources 1 and 2 below.

Source 1
From: Martin Walker, The Cold War, *published in 1994.*

The Soviet Union was not just another great power, defending its interests with a mixture of force and diplomacy in the classic manner of international affairs. Stalin's USSR was also seen in the West as something different and more menacing, a unique and unbending armed ideology threatening to expand.

In the course of one hundred days in late 1945 and early 1946, the West's view of the Soviet Union changed from an assumption that the Russian bear was up to its old tricks of dominating Eastern Europe into a conviction that the West was being conscripted into a new ideological crusade.

Source 2
From Vladislav Zubok and Constantine Pleshakov, Inside the Kremlin's Cold War, *published in 1996.*

Two events in early 1945 altered Stalin's view of the diplomatic landscape and let loose his demons of suspicion. The first was the death of Roosevelt; the second was America's dropping of the A-bomb on Hiroshima.

When Stalin had hoped to encourage London and Washington to resolve tensions by redistributing spheres of influence, his dream partner had been Franklin D. Roosevelt. Roosevelt was the only President whom Stalin accepted as a partner, even when he felt that FDR was scheming behind his back. In April 1945, when Soviet intelligence informed Stalin of Nazi attempts to conclude a separate peace with the Americans, his faith in the possibility of a partnership with the West was not shaken. As long as the two Western leaders did not 'gang up on him', there remained the chance for an international regime of co-operation. When Roosevelt died and Churchill was not re-elected, Stalin lost his two equals. There was no longer a common threat or a European war to forge a strong relationship of equals between Stalin and the new Western politicians.

It was the atomic bombardment of Japan and the abrupt end of the war in the Pacific that convinced Stalin that his dream of a post-war partnership was not to be fulfilled. The old demons of insecurity were back. The atomic bomb threw Stalin back into neurotic solitude.

Sample Assessment Materials © Edexcel Limited 2007, Edexcel GCE in History

How far do you agree with the view that the origins of the Cold War in 1945 and 1946 owed much to ideological differences and little to personalities and conflicting national interests?

Explain your answer, using the evidence of Sources 1 and 2 and your own knowledge of the issues related to this controversy.   (40 marks)

Exam tips

The cross-references are intended to take you straight to the material that will help you to answer the question.

Source 1 initially emphasises 'ideological differences' even ending with a reference to 'crusade'. The perspective is Western and it specifically challenges the view that the Soviet Union was 'just … defending its national interests'. Note too, the reference to 'armed ideology, threatening to expand'. In relating this to the question be careful to distinguish the first sentence of the source that gives Walker's own view from the remainder in which the views of the Western powers in 1945–6 are presented.

In contrast to Source 1, Source 2 concentrates on Eastern (specifically Stalin's) perspectives and concentrates on short-term events: the death of Roosevelt and the very different personality of Truman (page 37) and the dropping of the atom bomb (pages 39–40). This source suggests that Stalin was genuinely ready to co-operate in the 1945–6 period. The emphasis here on the impact of individuals and events would suggest that personalities and conflicting national interests played a significant part in the origins of the Cold War.

The sources provide clear differences of view that you can explore, expand upon and debate, using your own knowledge of 1945–6. In dealing with events and disputes in the period, be careful to relate them back to the question. Clearly all three of the factors stated in the question played their part. Which do you view as having most significance?

What was the significance of Yalta (pages 28–9), Potsdam (pages 38–40) and disagreements about Germany (pages 41–5)? What evidence is there of Western fears of what they saw as Soviet expansionism? Churchill's Fulton, Missouri, speech (page 51) could be used as evidence of the gulf between East and West, but keep in mind that this was not a foregone conclusion in 1945 (page 31) and what caused that belief is a matter of debate which this questions allows you to enter into.

4

The Division of Germany and Europe 1948–9

POINTS TO CONSIDER

This chapter covers the crucial two years from the collapse of the London Conference in December 1947 to the creation of the German Democratic Republic in October 1949. It is the period when not only Germany, but Europe, was divided into two blocs dominated by the USA and USSR. How this came about is studied under the following headings:

- The emergence of a Western bloc
- The consolidation of the Eastern bloc 1948–9
- The Yugoslav–Soviet split
- The decision to create a West German state
- The Soviet response: the Berlin Blockade
- The North Atlantic Treaty Organisation
- The division of Germany

Key dates

1947	December 15	Break-up of London Foreign Ministers' Conference
1948	February 22	Communist *coup* in Czechoslovakia
	March 17	Brussels Pact signed
	June 7	London Six Power Conference recommended calling of a West German Constituent Assembly
	June 20	Currency reform in Western zones
	June 24	Berlin Blockade began
	September 5	Parliamentary council met in Bonn
1949	April 4	NATO set up
	May 12	USSR lifted Berlin Blockade
	May 23	Basic Law approved in FRG
	May 30	People's Congress approved GDR Constitution
	September 22	Occupation Statute in force in FRG
	October 12	GDR set up

1 | The Emergence of a Western Bloc

The London Conference of Foreign Ministers, November–December 1947

By the time the conference opened in London the chances of any agreement on Germany seemed remote. The Americans vigorously supported the idea of **Western European integration** and had at least temporarily resigned themselves to the division of Germany. The USSR still wished to avoid the partition of Germany, as this would result in the great industrial complex of **the Ruhr** becoming a part of a US-dominated Western European bloc; but its attempts to disrupt the Marshall Plan (see pages 48–50) by orchestrating widespread strikes in Italy and France merely fuelled the mistrust of the Western powers of Soviet intentions in Germany and indeed throughout Europe.

The Soviets had also tried hard to rally public opinion right across Germany against the policy of the Western Allies. Walter Ulbricht, the leader of the SED (see page 44), was instructed to organise a 'German People's Congress for Unity and a Just Peace'. Representatives from all parties throughout Germany were invited to attend its meetings on 6–7 December 1947 in Berlin. The intention was then to send a delegation to the London Conference to back up the Soviet demand for the formation of a German central government. Roughly one-third of the 2225 delegates came from the West, but these were overwhelmingly Communists from areas like the Ruhr and the big industrial towns. The movement did not therefore genuinely reflect West German opinion and Bevin refused to allow its delegation permission to enter Britain.

The London Conference broke up on 15 December 1947 amid bitter recriminations. The Soviets accused Britain and the USA of violating the Potsdam Agreement and of denying the USSR its fair share of reparations, while the Western powers rejected Soviet proposals for forming a German government, which would govern a united Germany, as they feared that it would only fall under Soviet control. All hope of four power co-operation now disappeared, and instead the alternatives of a Western alliance, closer economic co-operation in Western Europe and the creation of a West German state appeared to be the only practical options. All three policies were interrelated and depended ultimately on the military and political integration of West Germany into a Western European defence system linked to the USA and directed against the USSR.

Key question
Why did the Western European and North Atlantic states begin to form a Western bloc?

Key question
Why was no agreement on the future of Germany achieved at the London Conference?

Key terms

Western European integration
The process of creating a Western Europe that was united politically, economically and militarily.

The Ruhr
The centre of the German coal and steel industries and at that time the greatest industrial region in Europe.

Key date

The London Conference broke up: 15 December 1947

Key question
What was the real intention of the Brussels Pact?

Key dates
Communist *coup* in Czechoslovakia: 22 February 1948

Signature of Brussels Pact: 17 March 1948

The Brussels Pact and 'Western Union'

The creation of a West German state was still viewed with deep mistrust and fear by the French. In an effort to calm their anxieties, the British came up with a plan for a defensive alliance against Germany, but which, in reality, as Paul-Henri Spaak, the Belgian Prime Minister, pointed out, 'was meant as a screen behind which to consider defences against Russia', as occupied Germany was hardly in a position to threaten its neighbours. The Communist seizure of power in Prague on 22 February (see page 67) was a powerful factor in persuading the French to join an alliance system directed primarily against the USSR rather than Germany. The French government was also reassured by the US decision to keep troops in West Germany for the foreseeable future.

On 17 March the Brussels Pact was signed by Belgium, Britain, France, Luxemburg and the Netherlands. It did not mention the USSR by name but simply promised mutual defence against an aggressor from any quarter. The treaty contained clauses on cultural and social co-operation and provision for setting up a **Consultative Council**. This reflected Bevin's wish to encourage general Western European co-operation as a further barrier to the spread of Communism. Bevin intended that the Brussels Pact should be underpinned by an Atlantic alliance in which the USA would be a key member. The Americans responded rapidly to this suggestion, and by the end of March the first of a series of secret meetings between British, Canadian and US officials began to explore the possibility of such an alliance. Eventually this was to lead to the signing of the North Atlantic Treaty (see pages 72–3).

Key term
Consultative Council
A council on which the member states were represented and where they could discuss mutual problems.

Key question
What did the Americans hope to achieve with the Marshall Plan?

The Marshall Plan and European integration

The Americans intended, as the revisionist historian Michael Hogan has said, to 'refashion' Western Europe 'in the image of the USA'. They hoped that a European political and economic union would create a United States of Europe, which would be very similar to the USA. They were convinced that once an economically integrated and politically united Western Europe existed, it would rapidly become as wealthy as the USA. It would deter the USSR, significantly boost world trade and provide valuable markets for US exports.

In the spring of 1948 the US Congress approved a programme for $5 billion as the first instalment of the Marshall Plan aid. Washington then attempted to persuade the Western European states to set up an international committee, which would be powerful enough to supervise the distribution of Marshall aid and enforce the integration of their economies. In response to this, the Organisation for European Economic Co-operation (OEEC) was set up, but each state still had its own national agenda, especially Britain, which was determined not to surrender any power to a supranational organisation. Effectively this defeated US attempts to use Marshall aid as a means to create an integrated Western Europe in the US image, although over the next three years the Europeans themselves were to develop their own path to integration.

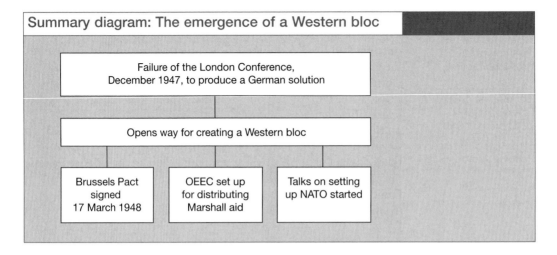

Summary diagram: The emergence of a Western bloc

Failure of the London Conference,
December 1947, to produce a German solution

Opens way for creating a Western bloc

Brussels Pact
signed
17 March 1948

OEEC set up
for distributing
Marshall aid

Talks on setting
up NATO started

2 | The Consolidation of the Eastern Bloc

By June 1948 the Cominform (see page 50) had become a
powerful instrument for controlling the Soviet bloc. Theoretically
each state in the bloc remained independent, but all had to adopt
identical cultural, military, economic and social policies. This
meant an end to the policy of diversity that had characterised
Eastern Europe for the first two years after the war (see
pages 51–4). In Czechoslovakia the Communists seized power at
the end of February, while in Hungary they steadily strengthened
their position throughout 1948. A Communist-dominated
People's **Independence Front** was set up there, and in the
elections in May 1949 only candidates approved by the Front
could stand. In Poland the Deputy Premier, Wladyslaw Gomulka,
who wished to create a socialist society that would reflect the
actual conditions in Poland rather than the USSR, was forced to
resign in August 1948 and then imprisoned.

Key question
How did the USSR
consolidate
Communism in the
Eastern bloc?

**Independence
Front**
A political bloc or
alliance of parties.

Key term

3 | The Yugoslav–Soviet Split

By the summer of 1948 not only was Europe divided into two
blocs, but within the Soviet bloc there ran a split between the
USSR and Yugoslavia that was every bit as deep and bitter.
Although Tito had been publicly praised at the Cominform
meeting (see page 50) in September 1947 as one of the USSR's
most loyal and effective allies, Stalin nevertheless had some
reservations about him. He was critical of Yugoslav attempts to
play an independent role in the Balkans and of 'certain
tendencies' among Yugoslav party leaders 'to overestimate their
achievements'. In the course of the winter 1947–8 the friction
between Moscow and Belgrade increased.

  Tito alarmed Stalin with talk about forming a South-eastern
European federation which would include Greece and Bulgaria.
He was also planning to set up a military base in Albania. Stalin
feared not only that this would make the Yugoslav Communist

Key question
What caused the
Yugoslav–Soviet
split?

The Communist seizure of power in Czechoslovakia

The Prague *coup* did not come as a surprise to the West. In practice, London, Washington and Paris had already written off Czechoslovakia and were not ready to intervene to save it from Communism. The Czech Communists, with nothing to fear from the West, were anxious to seize power as quickly as possible because their popularity was sharply declining and they were likely to suffer a severe defeat in the coming elections.

The crisis point was reached on 13 February 1948 when the cabinet protested against the unfair demotion of eight senior non-Communist police officers. A week later in protest against the Communist Minister of Interior's refusal to intervene, 12 ministers resigned from the cabinet, hoping to bring down the government, but this did not happen, as the Social Democrats and the two non-Party ministers, Jan Masaryk and Ludvik Svoboda, remained. The Communists were therefore able to use their control of the trade unions and the police to seize power and force Beneš to appoint a new cabinet which would follow loyally the policies laid down in Moscow. The elections of 30 May were held on the basis of a single National Front list which committed all candidates to a manifesto approved by Moscow.

Party the strongest force in the Balkans, but also that it would provoke the USA at a time of escalating tension over Germany.

As a result, party delegations from Bulgaria and Yugoslavia were summoned to Moscow and made to confess their 'mistakes'. Stalin specifically vetoed the stationing of Yugoslav troops in Albania and, instead of the wider federation favoured by Tito, proposed a smaller Bulgarian–Yugoslav union. The two states also had to commit themselves from now on to regular consultations with Soviet officials on foreign policy questions. Tito refused to subordinate his foreign policy to Moscow, and rejected union with Bulgaria, as he feared that, given Soviet influence there, it would merely be a way for Stalin to tighten his grip on Yugoslavia.

Stalin reacted to this open defiance of his leadership by turning the conflict into what has been called 'a head-on collision'. He withdrew his advisers from Yugoslavia and accused its leaders of a long list of political and ideological 'crimes'.

Stalin also put pressure on the other Eastern bloc states to support the Soviet line. By the time of the second Cominform meeting in June 1948 the whole Soviet bloc, as well as the Western European Communist leaders, were united against Tito, who was then formally expelled from the organisation. Although many privately doubted the truth of Stalin's accusations, they supported them because in the final analysis, at a time of acute tension with the West triggered by the Berlin Blockade (see page 69), they were dependent on Moscow for their own survival. Only in Yugoslavia did a Communist party have a base genuinely independent of the USSR.

On 1 July 1948 the three Western military governors handed over their permission to start drawing up a constitution for a West German state.

4 | The Decision to Create a West German State

The collapse of the London Foreign Ministers' Conference in December 1947 (see page 64) and the emergence of two rival power blocs in Europe strengthened the Western allies in their resolve to form a separate West German state. How this was to be done was then discussed by Britain, France, the USA and the **Benelux states** at another conference in London, which sat, except for a break of six weeks in the middle, from 23 February to 2 June 1948.

Anglo-American plans for creating a West German state met with considerable hostility from France, which dreaded the revival of German power. Neither the British nor the Americans were ready to compromise on this, but as the new West German state was to be subjected to tight controls and the Americans had already committed themselves to joining a North Atlantic Treaty Alliance, French fears were to a certain extent appeased (see page 65). The production of the great industrial centre of the Ruhr was to be regulated by the

Key question
How was French opposition to setting up West Germany overcome at the London Conference (February–June 1948)?

Benelux states
Belgium, the Netherlands and Luxemburg.

Key term

London Six Power Conference recommended creation of a West German state: 7 June 1948

Key date

Key question
Why did the Soviets think that they could exert pressure on the Western allies in Berlin?

Key question
Why did the Berlin Blockade fail?

Currency reform in West Germany: 20 June 1948

The Berlin Blockade began: 24 June 1948

Military Governor
The head of a zone of occupation in Germany.

International Ruhr Authority, which would be controlled by the Western allies. The West Germans would also have to accept the **Occupation Statute**, which would give Britain, France and the USA far-reaching powers over trade, foreign relations, economic questions and disarmament.

The West Germans were authorised on 7 June to draft a constitution for a democratic, federal West German state. On 20 June the Western allies introduced the new currency, the Deutschmark, into the Western zones and four days later the Soviets responded by introducing the new East German Mark (*ostmark*) into the their own zone. With the introduction of the currency reforms the outline of the two German states was beginning to take shape.

5 | The Soviet Response: The Berlin Blockade
Pressure on Berlin begins
The Six Power Conference in London and the Brussels Treaty had confronted the Soviets with a major challenge. Stalin, however, believed that he could force the Western allies to reconsider the whole German question by applying pressure to their position in West Berlin, which as a city deep in the Eastern zone (see the map on page 42) was vulnerable as it was dependent on rail and road links running through the Soviet zone for bulk supplies from the West.

Consequently, in March 1948 the Soviet occupying forces began to exercise an ever tighter control over the movement of people and freight from West Berlin to the Western zones. The introduction of the Deutschmark first into the Western zones and then into West Berlin on 23 June provided the Soviets with the necessary excuse to begin the full blockade of West Berlin. They argued that it was a defensive measure to stop the Soviet zone being swamped with the **devalued Reichsmarks**, which the new Deutschmark was replacing in West Germany. During the night of 23–24 June the blockade began. The rail and road links to the West as well as the supply of electricity from East Berlin to the Western sectors were all cut.

The Berlin Blockade, 24 June 1948–12 May 1949
The Western response was confused and unsure. The French were convinced that West Berlin could only hold out for a matter of weeks, while, to quote the British historian, Avi Schlaim, the US administration 'seemed almost paralysed by uncertainty and fear'. It was Bevin who again provided the initial leadership of the alliance, and suggested forceful counter-measures. Essentially he was determined to maintain the Western position in Berlin and press on with setting up a West German state, while at all costs avoiding war. He rejected suggestions by General Clay, the US **Military Governor**, that an armed convoy should force its way through to West Berlin, because this could easily have provoked a clash with Soviet forces. Instead he

convinced the Americans that West Berlin could be supplied by an **airlift** made possible by aircraft flying along the three 'corridors', or flight paths, allocated to the Western Allies by the Soviets in 1945 (see the diagram on page 72). He also responded enthusiastically to US requests to transfer 60 B-29 bombers to East Anglia. It was assumed at the time that these carried atomic bombs, but in fact this was a bluff, as the modified B-29s, which could carry them, only arrived in Britain in 1949. Nevertheless this gesture probably did deter the Soviets from trying to interfere with the airlift, although they, too, wanted to avoid war.

By the end of July British and US planes were managing to fly into West Berlin an average of 2000 tons of food and raw materials a day. Yet if stocks were to be built up for the coming winter, 5000 tons would have to be flown in on a regular daily basis.

As it was very uncertain whether these totals could be maintained, the three Western powers were ready to explore the possibility of reaching an agreement over Berlin. On 2 August their ambassadors met Stalin in Moscow. Interpreting their approach as a sign of weakness, he was uncompromising over his demands. According to the Soviet record of the meeting on 2 August:

> Comrade Stalin spoke of two factors – the special currency in Berlin and the decisions of the London Conference. He thought that it was those decisions which gave rise to the restrictive measures under discussion ... Comrade Stalin said that ... simultaneously with the rescinding of the restrictions on transport applied by the Soviet Military Administration, the special currency [the Deutschmark] ... introduced by the three powers into Berlin should be withdrawn and replaced by the currency circulating in the Soviet zone. ... That was the first point. Secondly, assurance should be given that application of the London Conference's decisions would be postponed until representatives of the four powers had met and negotiated on all the basic questions concerning Germany.

Airlift
The transport of food and supplies by air to a besieged area.

Key term

West Berlin children watch a US plane, loaded with food, come in to land in early August 1948.

The Western powers would not reverse their decision to create a West German state, but they were ready to agree to the circulation of the *ostmark* in the whole of Berlin, subject to four power financial control. Yet, as further discussions between the Military Governors of the four zones in September showed, the Soviets wanted total control of the currency. If they were to abandon the blockade, at the very least, they intended, as one Soviet official observed:

> to restore the economic unity of Berlin, to include all Berlin in the economic system of the Soviet zone and also to restore unified administration of the city. That would have served as a basis for winning over the population of West Berlin, and would have created the preconditions for completely ousting the Western powers from Berlin.

These talks broke down on 7 September because neither side would give way. As the Soviets were convinced that the airlift to West Berlin could not be sustained during the winter, they decided to play for time and avoid any compromise. Consequently all the efforts of the United Nations to mediate during the winter of 1948–9 failed.

End of the blockade

By the end of January 1949, however, it became clear that Stalin's gamble was failing. The winter of 1948–9 was exceptionally mild and, thanks to the effective deployment of the large American **C54s**, which flew to Berlin from bases in the British zone, the average daily tonnage for January was 5620. By April this had reached 8000 tons per day and about 1000 aircraft were able to use the air corridors to Berlin at any one time (see the diagram on page 72). In February, the Western powers also declared the Deutschmark to be the sole legal currency in West Berlin and stopped all Western exports to the Soviet zone, which increased the pressure on the zone's economy.

Stalin, who was not prepared to go to war over Berlin, had little option but to cut his losses. In an interview with a US journalist on 31 January he made a considerable concession, when he indicated that he would make the lifting of the blockade dependent only on calling another meeting of the Council of Foreign Ministers. The Americans responded to this and talks began between the Soviet and US representatives on the Security Council of the United Nations in New York. In early May they finally reached agreement that the blockade would be called off on 12 May and that 11 days later a Council of Foreign Ministers should meet in Paris to discuss both the future of Germany and the Berlin currency question. On neither issue did the Council produce a breakthrough, but the four powers approved the New York agreement on lifting the blockade and agreed to discuss how the situation in Berlin could be normalised.

Key term

C54s
Large US transport planes.

Key date

USSR lifted the Berlin Blockade: 12 May 1949

SCHLESWIGLAND
LUBECK
FUHLSBUTTEL
RUSSIAN ZONE
FASSBERG
BRITISH ZONE
WUNSTORF
CELLE
GATOW
TEGEL
TEMPELHOF
BUCKEBURG
VHF RANGE
WIESBADEN
RHEIN/MAIN
AMERICAN ZONE
LEGEND
USAF BASE
RAF BASE
COMBINED RAF/USAF BASE
M/F BEACON
VAR
M/F & EUREKA BEACON
EUREKA BEACON
TRACKS TO BERLIN
TRACKS FROM BERLIN

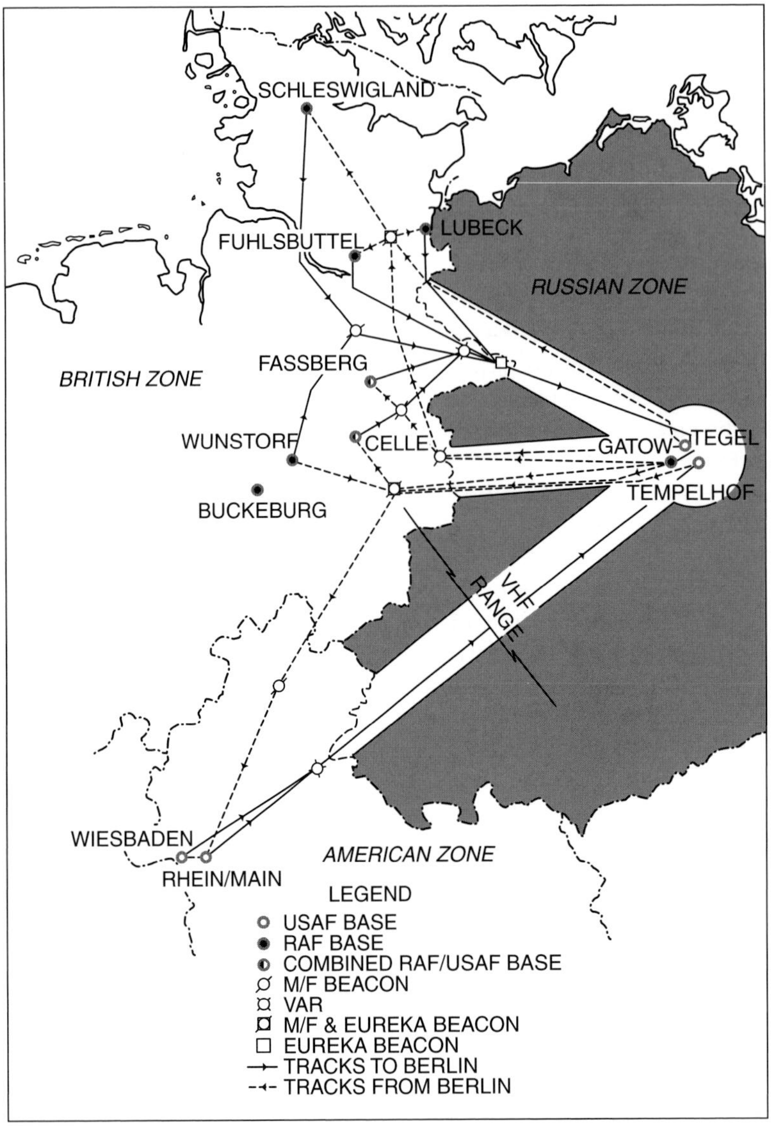

A diagram showing how the airlift worked. Radar beacons regulated the flow of aircraft before they entered the corridors to Berlin.

6 | The North Atlantic Treaty Organisation

Negotiating the Treaty

The Prague *coup* and the Berlin Blockade finally persuaded the Americans that there was no alternative to a formal commitment to defend Western Europe. From the spring of 1948 through to early 1949 the US government gradually worked out the framework for a North Atlantic–Western European military alliance with both **Congressional leaders** at home and its allies in Europe. Over the course of these negotiations it became increasingly clear that the proposed North Atlantic Treaty interlocked with the plans for setting up a West German state. Without this treaty it would have been very difficult, perhaps even

Key question
Why was the treaty signed and to what extent was it a compromise between European and US wishes?

Key term
Congressional leaders
Influential political leaders in the US Congress (parliament).

Key terms

NATO Council
NATO's decision-making committee on which each member state was represented.

High Commission
A civilian body charged with the task of defending the interests of the Western allies in Germany.

Key date

NATO Treaty: 4 April 1949

Key question
Why did the Western Allies persist with the setting up of the FRG?

Key dates

West Germans approved the Basic Law or West German Constitution: 23 May 1949

Occupation Statute approved in the FRG: 22 September 1949

impossible, to have persuaded the French to tolerate the creation of West Germany, whose potential military and industrial power they still feared.

The US government had to take a middle line between the West Europeans, who hoped for a military alliance, which would commit US troops to the defence of Western Europe, and Congress, which wanted to avoid any precise commitments. To win over Congress, President Truman had to stress that the treaty did not commit the USA to go to war without its consent and that it would help the West Europeans to defend themselves. In the end the key article 5 contained the rather imprecise wording that each treaty member 'will take such action as it deems necessary, including the use of armed force, to restore and maintain security in the North Atlantic area'. The West Europeans, particularly the French, found this too weak, but decided to use article 3, which called for 'continuous and effective self-help and mutual aid', to involve the Americans ever more closely in the defence of Western Europe.

The creation of NATO
The North Atlantic Treaty was signed on 4 April 1949 in Washington for an initial period of 20 years by Canada, the USA, the Brussels Pact Powers (page 65), Norway, Denmark, Iceland, Italy and Portugal. It came into force on 24 August 1949. When the **NATO Council** met for the first time in September, defence and military committees were set up and its members were divided into five regional groups to all of which the USA belonged. At the same time Congress approved a military assistance programme to help to build up Western Europe's armed forces. These actions ended, for the time being anyway, the fears that the Europeans still had that the USA might again retire back into isolation as it had done in 1919.

7 | The Division of Germany
The creation of the Federal Republic of Germany
The West German constitution was approved in the spring of 1949 by the three Western occupying powers, and elections for the new parliament (*Bundestag*) took place in August. A month later when parliament met, Konrad Adenauer (see page 43) became the first West German Chancellor.

The FRG was, however, far from being independent. The Occupation Statute, which came into force in September, replaced the military government in the former Western zones with a **High Commission**. This still gave Britain, France and the USA the final say on West German foreign policy, security questions, exports and many other matters that an independent state is free to decide on for itself.

Konrad Adenauer being sworn in as Chancellor of the Federal Republic of Germany, 15 September 1949.

The emergence of the German Democratic Republic

In the winter of 1948–9 the Soviets were reluctant to set up a separate East German state if there was still a chance of stopping British and US plans for West Germany and of one day creating a neutral pro-Soviet Germany. Stalin was prepared to give the Soviet zone a greater degree of independence, but for the moment this was just a temporary step that would not block eventual German unity. He feared that the creation of an East German state would make the division of Germany final.

Throughout the spring and summer of 1949 Walther Ulbricht and the other leaders of the SED claimed that only their party was working for national unity, in contrast to the **splitters** in the West, who he alleged were deliberately plotting to divide Germany. To emphasise this claim, in March 1948 the SED set up a 'German People's Council' (*Volksrat*) of 400 delegates, a quarter of whom were Communists from the Western zones, to draft a constitution for a united German state. If a unified Germany proved impossible to create, then this constitution would form the basis of a new East German state. In May, Wilhelm Pieck, the Chairman of the SED, pointed out that once a West German state was set up, the Soviet zone would inevitably have to 'develop its own independent state structure. It did not matter whether the Western Powers tore Germany apart … a month earlier or a month later. The important thing was to be prepared for every eventuality.'

By March 1949 the SED was ready for this 'eventuality'. The constitution of the future East German state had been drafted and approved by the People's Council. On paper at least, it did

Key question
To what extent was East Germany set up in response to the creation of the FRG?

Splitters
The SED accused the West Germans and the Western allies of splitting or dividing Germany.

Key term

Key term

Make-believe constitution
A constitution that was not genuine and merely hid a dictatorship by one party: the SED.

Key dates

People's Congress approved the GDR constitution: 30 May 1949

GDR set up: 12 October 1949

Key question
What impact did the division of Germany have on Berlin?

not seem to be so very different from West Germany's. In reality, however, it was as British historian Peter Merkl observed, a **make-believe constitution** camouflaging a one-party dictatorship. In May a new People's Congress was elected. The voters, as in the other Soviet-dominated countries in Eastern Europe, had been presented with just one list of candidates, all of whom represented the views of the SED.

At the end of May the congress met and approved the draft constitution, but Moscow, where the real power lay, kept the SED in suspense. The Soviets believed that there was still a slim chance of stopping the setting up of the FRG. However, once the West German elections, in which the KPD won only 5.7 per cent of the voters, had taken place in August, Stalin realised that there was no longer any alternative to forming the German Democratic Republic (GDR), even though for him it was an exercise in damage limitation, which would ensure that the Soviet zone did not become sucked into a united Western-orientated Germany. On 12 October the government of the new state was formed and the Soviet military occupation of the zone came to an end, although a Soviet Control Commission was set up, which, like the Allied High Commission in the West, retained considerable reserve powers.

Berlin

The division of Germany ensured that Berlin remained a divided city within a divided state within a divided continent. At the end of November 1948 the Germans in West Berlin, in response to threats and intimidation from the SED, set up their own city government with an elected assembly, which had an overwhelming anti-Communist majority. Britain, France and the USA permitted West Berlin to send representatives to sit in the West German parliament in Bonn but, as the city was still legally under four power control, they had no voting rights.

There was as yet no physical barrier between East and West Berlin. Nevertheless, the Soviet sector of Berlin became the capital of the new GDR. The frontier was still open in the city. The Berlin Wall was not built until August 1961 (see page 119).

8 | Key Debate

Was the division of Europe and Germany inevitable in 1948–9?

In the autumn of 1947 the USA had hoped that it could, through economic assistance alone, set up a strong but friendly Western Europe that would be able to withstand pressure from the Soviet bloc. US officials believed that a strong economically and politically integrated Western Europe could also act as a magnet that would pull the Soviet satellites out of Moscow's orbit. By the spring of 1948, however, it was clear that European economic integration was not happening. Military and economic weakness and the reluctance of Britain and France to go too far down the road of integration meant that the Western Europeans desperately needed assurances of US military support. The US presence was also the key to persuading France and the Benelux states that they had nothing to fear from a revived West Germany.

The more the USA was drawn into establishing in Western Europe what the US historian Geir Lundestad has called an **empire by invitation**, the more it provoked Soviet reaction and the consolidation of the Soviet bloc, without Yugoslavia. The Prague *coup* (see page 67) appeared to confirm all the worst fears about the USSR, and was an important factor leading to the decision to create West Germany and negotiate the North Atlantic Treaty. Stalin's unsuccessful attempt to force the Western allies to drop their plans for West Germany by blockading West Berlin merely accelerated the division of Germany and left him with no option but to form an East German state.

With hindsight the division of Germany and Europe seemed inevitable. Yet for Stalin the creation of a potentially independent West German state was a serious blow. East Germany has been described by the German revisionist historian Willy Loth as his 'unwanted child'. Until his death, Stalin saw the GDR as only a temporary structure that he would be happy to dismantle, if he could somehow create a neutral Germany independent of a US-dominated Western Europe. By moving so quickly to set up a separate West Germany and a North Atlantic security system, were Britain, France and the USA responsible for the partition of Europe into two blocs? The eminent US diplomat George Kennan warned in September 1948 that this policy would lead to 'an irrevocable congealment of the division of Europe into two military zones: a Soviet zone and a US zone. Instead of the ability to divest ourselves gradually of the basic responsibility for the security of Western Europe, we will get a legal perpetuation of that responsibility'. In Britain, too, there were critical voices. In July 1948 General Robertson, the British Military Governor in Germany, in a memorandum to Bevin suggested that:

> it would be impossible for the Western Allies to concede total evacuation because once British and US troops left Germany, the Soviets would have the country at their mercy. There is no reason, however, why the armed forces of the Allies should not withdraw into given frontier areas, leaving Berlin and the main part of Germany to a single central government. …

From the reaction to this advice in London, Paris and Washington, it was obvious that most Western Europeans and their governments preferred a divided Germany and a West Europe protected by a US military presence to the uncertainties and risks to which a neutral unified Germany would have exposed them. It was by no means clear that Stalin would in reality have tolerated a genuine independent and neutral Germany.

Empire by invitation
The Western Europeans were in effect asking to be put under US protection and so become a part of a US 'empire' or a US-dominated region.

Key term

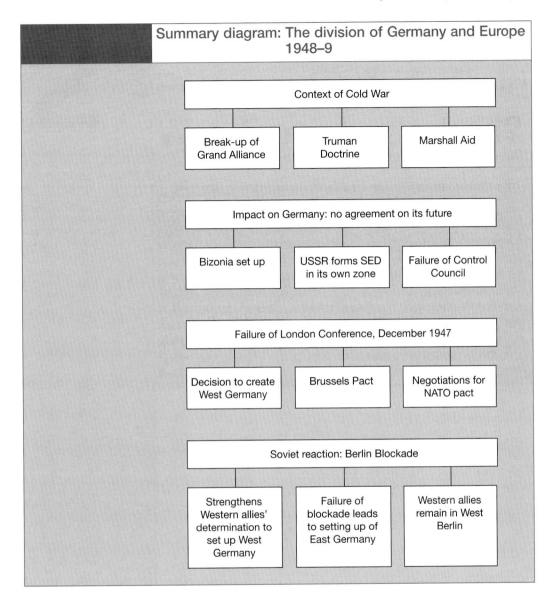

Summary diagram: The division of Germany and Europe 1948–9

Study Guide: AS Question

In the style of OCR

How far do you agree that by 1949 the USA was winning the Cold War in Europe?   (50 marks)

> ### Exam tips
>
> *The cross-references are intended to take you straight to the material that will help you to answer the question.*
>
> This question requires you to analyse and evaluate the extent to which the USA was defeating the USSR by 1949. You are not required to write an explanation, but to make a judgement based on evidence that assesses the situation in 1949. Your evaluation should be balanced. Arguments in support of the statement might include:
>
> - The USA had outmanoeuvred the USSR by defeating the Berlin Blockade (page 69).
> - The USA had moved its military potential to Europe by locating B-29 bombers in the UK (page 70).
> - The USA's Marshall Plan had prevented Greece and Turkey from falling to communism (pages 48–50).
> - The USA had demonstrated its superior atomic power (pages 39–40).
> - NATO, largely funded by the USA, was established in 1949 (pages 72–3).
> - The West German state was established and excluded the USSR from the Ruhr (pages 73–5).
>
> On the other hand, the counter-argument is:
>
> - The USSR had extensive secret agents operating in the West that countered US intelligence (pages 51–4).
> - The USSR controlled most of Eastern Europe and denied its satellites democratic rights (pages 66–7).
> - The USSR had a large and effective army and many battalions stationed in Europe.
> - The USSR tested its atomic bomb in 1949.
> - In 1949 China became a communist ally of USSR.

Study Guide: A2 Questions

In the style of AQA

'It was the Western Allies, rather than the Soviets, who were responsible for the division of Germany in 1948–9.' Assess the validity of this view. (45 marks)

> ### Exam tips
>
> *The cross-references are intended to take you straight to the material that will help you to answer the question.*
>
> You must explain and give your opinion about why the partition of Germany happened, drawing on the evidence from the last two chapters. You will need to know the following material, although you should not, of course, simply present it as a narrative of what happened:
>
> - Refer to Allied disagreements over reparation payments, the threatening ambiguity of the USSR's German policy as instanced by the creation of the SED, the formation of Bizonia and then the impact of the Marshall Plan, which all contributed to the failure of the London Foreign Ministers' Conference in December 1947 (page 64).
> - The momentum towards division was accelerated by the shock of the Prague *coup*, which seemed to show that Western Europe was threatened by Soviet aggression (page 67).
> - This led to the signature of the Brussels and North Atlantic Treaties but, even more importantly, to plans for going ahead with constructing a new West German state (page 65).
> - The Berlin Blockade and its successful defeat by the Western allies merely confirmed in Western eyes the correctness of their policy, while forcing the Soviets to create the GDR as a counterweight to the FRG (pages 69–75).
>
> As long as you are sure of your evidence in this type of question, do not be at all afraid to express your own opinions clearly. You may well agree with George Kennan and General Robertson (page 76) that there were alternatives to the partition of Germany. On the other hand, you may wish to stress that the vulnerability of Western Europe to Soviet pressure and the ever-present fear in France of a revived Germany made the partition of Germany and the creation of a Western European–American military bloc the only viable policy at the time. Choose an argument and try to stick to it throughout your answer. Your conclusion should evolve naturally from what you have said.

In the style of Edexcel

Study Sources 1–3 below.

Source 1

From: Martin McCauley, Russia, America and the Cold War, 1949–1991, *published in 1998.*

Russia and America competed with one another as systems. The systems can be perceived as Communism and capitalism, freedom and tyranny, the command economy versus the market economy, individualism and collectivism. Both dominant ideologies were utopian*. Marxists inhabited the kingdom of certainty. The Soviet Union would one day be the leading world power and America, which appeared so powerful and threatening, would become socialist. America also had a utopian ideology, born of the conviction that America had the right and duty to enlighten the world. To become rich, happy and free other nations had just to copy the United States. It was almost inevitable that Russia and America, given their utopianism, would construct empires. The number of countries which were in their respective zones of imperial influence would be used as a bench mark to determine which was gaining the upper hand. By the 1970s, superpower rivalry, beginning in Europe in 1945, had encompassed the globe.
[*utopian; based on a vision of an ideal society]

Source 2

From: Harriet Ward, World Powers in the Twentieth Century, *published in 1985. This author is an historian who argues that the success of the Berlin airlift led to Stalin's lifting of the blockade.*

The Russians blockaded West Berlin, presumably hoping to starve the West Berliners into amalgamation with the Soviet zone. The West's reply to the Berlin Blockade was the airlift: an amazing Anglo-American feat by which, for 10 months, all the essentials of life were flown in to the 2.5 million West Berliners. In May 1949 the USSR gave in and lifted the Blockade. Not surprisingly, the Berlin Blockade hardened Western attitudes. America's promised backing of the Brussels Pact was enlarged into a full-scale military alliance of 12 nations, centred on the colossal strength of the United States.

Source 3

From David Williamson, Europe and the Cold War, 1945–91 second edition, *published in 2006.*

The more the USA was drawn into establishing in Western Europe what the US historian Geir Lundestad has called an empire by invitations, the more it provoked Soviet reaction and the consolidation of the Soviet bloc, without Yugoslavia. The Prague *coup* appeared to confirm all the worst fears about the USSR, and was an important factor leading to the decision to create West Germany and negotiate the North Atlantic Treaty.

Stalin's unsuccessful attempt to force the Western allies to drop their plans for West Germany by blockading West Berlin merely accelerated the division of Germany and left him with no option but to form an East German state.

… Until his death, Stalin saw the GDR as only a temporary structure that he would be happy to dismantle, if he could somehow create a neutral Germany independent of a US-dominated Western Europe. By moving so quickly to set up a separate West Germany and a North Atlantic security system, were Britain, France and the USA responsible for the partition of Europe into two blocs?

How far do you agree with the view that the actions of the Western Allies were primarily responsible for the division of Europe into two power blocs by 1950?

Explain your answer, using the evidence of Sources 1, 2 and 3 and your own knowledge of the issues related to this controversy.

(40 marks)

Exam tips

The cross-references are intended to take you straight to the material that will help you to answer the question.

In asking you to assess the significance of the actions of the Western Allies, the question encompasses a number of the controversies you have already encountered in your reading of Chapters 1–4. Clearly, you also need to consider the way the actions and attitudes of the USSR have been viewed. When can the actions of the USSR and the West be seen as defensive reactions to perceived threats? When do they appear to be more actively responsible for creating division?

The sources raise the issues of: the competition of communist and capitalist systems (pages 45 and 47); the push to construct rival empires and the US 'empire by invitation' (pages 48–51, 51–4, 57, 65–6); Stalin's wish for a neutral Germany (page 45); fears of a US-dominated Western Europe (pages 56 and 64); the effect of the Prague *coup* (pages 65 and 67) and the Berlin Blockade (pages 69–71) in increasing tension and hardening Western attitudes; Western initiative in setting up West Germany and NATO (pages 72–5).

Which of these points can be found in which of the sources? How can the points be grouped? What links can be made between them: for example, are there references to a US 'empire' in more than one source? What are the points of corroboration and what elements of difference are there in these references?

You will need to make the issues in the sources directly relevant to the question. Some are clearly about actions. Where does material about fears fit? The material on the fears and attitudes of both sides is important in explaining why the powers acted as they did to each other's actions. This enables you to assess how far the responsibility for division lies more with one side than the other, but be careful not to deal with this material about fears in isolation from the question.

How will you deploy your own knowledge to develop issues raised in the sources? For example, the sources make no direct reference to the Marshall Plan; there is scope for you to integrate your own knowledge here and to explore how far this was seen as US economic imperialism.

What other relevant issues could you add from your own knowledge? The impact of the atom bomb (pages 39 and 70) on superpower relations could be included as an additional factor.

5 The Consolidation of the Rival Blocs

POINTS TO CONSIDER
The period 1950–5 witnessed the consolidation of the division of Europe into a Soviet bloc and a Western bloc. This chapter considers the developments that led to this through the following sections:

• Western integration 1950–2
• Stalin's failure to stop West German rearmament
• Eastern integration
• Western attempts to destabilise the Soviet bloc
• Leadership changes in the USA and USSR
• The East German revolt, June 1953
• The Eastern European settlement 1953–5
• The Warsaw Pact Treaty
• The Geneva Conference, July 1955

Key dates

1949	October	People's Republic of China proclaimed
1950	June 25	Outbreak of Korean War
	October 24	French Assembly approved Pleven Plan
1951	April 18	European Coal and Steel Community (Schuman Plan) Treaty signed
1952	March 10	Stalin's note, proposing a neutral united Germany
	May 27	European Defence Community (EDC) Treaty signed in Paris
1953	March 5	Stalin died
	June 16–17	Strikes and riots in the GDR
	July	Korean War ended
1954	August 31	EDC rejected by the French Assembly
1955	May 5	The FRG became a sovereign state and joined NATO
	May 14	Warsaw Pact signed
	September 20	USSR recognised sovereignty of GDR

1 | Western Integration 1950–2

Despite the foundation of NATO in April 1949, there was a strong feeling in the Western alliance in the winter of 1949–50 that it was losing ground to the Soviet Union. In September the USSR had successfully exploded its first atom bomb, while a month later China fell to the Communists. Stalin also rapidly began to expand the Red Army. Meanwhile, Western European integration was developing only slowly. NATO was still in its infancy and lingering fears of German domination among the Western European states stopped the USA from building up the new Federal Republic's economic and military strength to a point where it could play a major role in the defence of Western Europe. Until the FRG was fully integrated into a Western European and economic and military system there was a real danger that Stalin might be able to win the Germans over by offering them unity and markets stretching from the river Oder, which formed the border between the GDR and Poland (see the map on page 42), to the Pacific Ocean.

At the same time US pressure to rearm West Germany and Truman's decision to develop the hydrogen bomb triggered in Western Europe a wave of anti-Americanism and the emergence of a powerful peace movement, which the USSR was able to exploit. In January 1950 Truman had authorised research on the hydrogen bomb (see page 11). When it was tested on 1 March 1954, its explosive power was the equivalent to more than the total number of bombs dropped by both sides in the Second World War.

The Schuman Plan

It was against this background that the Americans tried hard to find a formula that would overcome Western European fears of the growing economic power of the FRG and so enable the North Atlantic alliance to benefit from its reserves of industrial strength. The French came to realise that the only effective way of controlling the FRG was to integrate it firmly into a Western European economic and political union. But to make this work, Britain would also have to join, to balance the developing power of West Germany. Yet this solution was a non-starter because Britain refused to commit itself to further integration and, instead, insisted on cultivating its special relationship with the USA and the **Commonwealth**. The alternative was to use NATO as a means of rearming West Germany and of aligning it firmly with the Western powers within an Atlantic rather than a Western European framework.

The French were unconvinced. To them NATO was primarily a military alliance and they feared that within it West Germany would be able to develop its vast strength unchecked. They argued that the Americans and the British were subordinating the German problem to the Cold War, and that when it was over, France would once again be confronted with a strong Germany.

Key question
Why did the Cold War make Western integration so necessary?

Key date
The Communist forces in China under Mao Zedong finally defeated the Nationalists and declared China to be a People's Republic: October 1949

Key question
What did the French hope to achieve with the Schuman Plan and how did it help to end the bad feeling between France and Germany?

Key term
Commonwealth
Made up of the states that originally formed part of the British Empire.

To avoid this fate Schuman, the French Foreign Minister, announced in May 1950 a plan, devised by Jean Monnet, who was in charge of the French economic modernisation programme, to create the European Coal and Steel Community (ECSC). The Schuman Plan, as it was called, would enable the Western allies to exploit Germany's coal and steel resources for their own rearmament programmes without running the risk of simultaneously building up a strong and independent West Germany. As far as the French were concerned, it was a substitute for German rearmament. It was received enthusiastically by Adenauer, the West German Chancellor, as he realised that only through integration could West Germany forge a partnership with the Western democracies and gain security from the USSR. Italy and the Benelux states also welcomed it, but Britain, not wishing to lose control of its own coal and steel industries, which the Labour government had only just nationalised, did not.

The French called a conference of the six powers in Paris in late summer 1950 to begin work on the nuts and the bolts of the scheme. Initially, they intended to set firm limits on the amount of steel produced by the Germans, break up the great steel companies and end the ownership of the Ruhr coal mines by German industrialists, but the enormous demand for coal and steel caused by the outbreak of the Korean War strengthened Germany's negotiating position. In December, the Americans had to intervene to force a compromise on both sides, which then enabled the Schuman Plan Treaty to be signed on 18 April 1951.

Key date
The Korean War broke out: 25 June 1950

Key figures in Western European integration
Robert Schuman, 1886–1963, was elected to the French parliament in 1919, was Prime Minister 1947–8, and then Foreign Minister. In 1958 he became President of the European Assembly. **Jean Monnet**, 1888–1979, initially worked as a civil servant in the French Ministry of Commerce. In the two world wars he became an expert on international economic collaboration. In 1945 he was appointed Planning Commissioner for France. In 1952–5 he was President of the ECSC. He then became the President for the Action Committee for the United States of Europe.

Both were key figures in European integration and wanted to see a 'united states of Europe'.

Key question
How did the ECSC lay the foundations for European integration?

European Coal and Steel Community (ECSC)

The ECSC replaced the International Ruhr Authority (see page 69) in July 1952 with a new supranational organisation, controlled by the six member states. It regulated their coal and steel industries, guaranteeing that the economic needs of each member for these vital raw materials would be met. The ECSC laid the foundations for Western European economic, and ultimately political, integration; and, together with the military security that NATO provided, it immeasurably strengthened the Western bloc. Michael Hogan argues that 'it amounted to the treaty of peace that had never been signed' between Germany and France, as it went far towards removing the fears and animosities that had bedevilled European politics since 1870.

The Korean War and German rearmament

The military planning staff in Washington had advised Truman as early as 1947 to build up a West German army. The case for it became even stronger when the East Germans formed a strong **paramilitary police force** in 1949. Behind the scenes Adenauer was already floating the idea that the FRG should contribute troops to 'an international legion', but politically West German rearmament remained a controversial issue. The prospect of it still alarmed the West European states, and the French argued that it would antagonise the USSR and trigger a Third World War.

The Korean War changed the situation dramatically. The invasion of South Korea by North Korean troops on 25 June 1950 seemed to mark the start of a new global conflict in which the Soviets would finally overrun Western Europe. This impression was underlined when Ulbricht, the East German leader (see page 91), not only supported North Korean aggression but recommended similar action as a way of unifying Germany. In this context West German rearmament seemed certain.

The war in Korea

In 1945 the Western allies and the USSR agreed that when Japan was finally defeated, Korea, which had been under Japanese control since 1910, should be given back its independence. At the end of the war with Japan in August 1945, Soviet troops had occupied northern Korea and US troops the south. Korea was consequently divided into two zones of occupation along the 38th parallel. As in Germany the two powers could not agree on the future of the state. The USSR sealed off the frontier in 1945, but hoped to arrive at some agreement with the USA that would guarantee their interests in the Korean peninsular. From 1945 to 1948 attempts by the United Nations to unify Korea failed. After an election supervised by the UN in South Korea, Syngman Rhee became President and his government was recognised as the legal government of a united Korea by all states except the USSR. In response the North Koreans formed the Korean People's Republic.

Relations between the two states rapidly became very bad as both claimed to be the true representative of the Korean people. After persistent appeals to the USSR, Stalin finally gave Kim Il Sung, the North Korean leader, the go-ahead to attack the south. North Korean forces crossed the frontier on 25 June 1950. After initial success they were pushed back to the Manchurian border by United Nation troops under US leadership. The war was prolonged by large-scale Chinese intervention in November, which dramatically halted the US advance. Although President Truman rejected the advice of his Commander-in-Chief, General MacArthur, to use nuclear weapons against the Chinese, their counter-attack was eventually halted some 70 miles into South Korea in 1951, and the war settled down into a stalemate until a ceasefire was signed in July 1953. Stalin gave limited support to the Chinese.

Soviet fighter planes, which were painted in Chinese colours and flown by Soviet pilots in Chinese uniform, defended the Yalu river crossings and gave some limited air support to the Chinese army.

The proposed European Defence Community

Key question
Why did the French propose the Pleven Plan?

Key date
French Assembly approved Pleven Plan: 24 October 1950

The French were particularly anxious that Adenauer should not exploit NATO's need for West German troops to modify the Schuman Plan, and so allow the FRG's coal and steel industries to escape the restraints of supranational control. Consequently, on Monnet's suggestion, the French Prime Minister, **René Pleven**, announced on 24 October the so-called Pleven Plan, a proposal for a European Defence Community (EDC). Essentially its purpose was to set up a European army under supranational control, which would be linked to the ECSC. To ensure that the FRG was kept on a tight rein its troops would join not in divisions (units of about 10,000 troops), but instead in battalions (much smaller units composed of only about 800 troops).

The Spofford Compromise

Key question
Why was the Spofford Compromise necessary?

Key figure
René Pleven
1901–93; French Prime Minister 1951–2. In the 1950s he headed several governments and was also Minister of Justice. He served in the Free French under General de Gaulle during the war.

Militarily the first version of the Pleven Plan was unworkable. It was essentially a French plan aimed more at controlling German rearmament than at military effectiveness. The British refused to join and only Belgium and Luxemburg showed any real interest, while the Americans felt that it was a military nonsense. However, after prolonged discussions in Washington, a workable compromise was hammered out that would ultimately enable German troops to be recruited. Charles Spofford, the deputy US representative on NATO's Atlantic Council, suggested that, while the political problems caused by the EDC proposal were being sorted out, certain practical steps to strengthen defences in Western Europe, 'upon which there already exist large measure of agreement', should be taken immediately. This was accepted by both France and Britain and the other NATO members, and from this emerged the Spofford Compromise. This proposed that, parallel with the creation of a European army, NATO itself would create an integrated force in Europe. In it would serve medium-sized German units, which would be subject to tight supervision by the Western allies.

Strains within NATO, December 1950–June 1951

At first it seemed as though the Spofford Compromise had broken the deadlock over German rearmament. Preliminary negotiations about setting up the EDC began in Paris in February 1951, and at the same time Adenauer began to discuss plans with the Western allies for creating 12 West German **divisions** for NATO. The Western powers also began to normalise relations with the FRG. They officially terminated the state of war with Germany and opened negotiations to replace the Occupation Statute (see page 73) with a more appropriate treaty which recognised the FRG's new status.

Throughout the first half of 1951 the West German rearmament question and US policy in Korea put an immense strain on the unity of the alliance. France and many other of the smaller western European states dreaded German rearmament, while America's allies in NATO were worried that the USA would use nuclear weapons in Korea and so trigger a third world war.

West German rearmament

In Western Germany the Social Democrat Party bitterly attacked Adenauer's intention to join the EDC on the grounds that this would permanently divide Germany. He therefore attempted to drive a hard bargain with the Western allies in order to convince his electorate that rearmament would lead to the FRG being given equality of treatment by its former occupiers. This, of course, frightened French public opinion, which would not allow their government to make any more concessions to the Germans.

Disagreements about Korea and China

The escalating conflict in Korea put further pressure on the Alliance. When Chinese troops came to the assistance of the North Koreans in November 1950, Western Europeans were alarmed by rumours that the USA would retaliate by dropping nuclear bombs on China, and feared that this would lead to an all-out war and the withdrawal of US troops from Europe. The British Prime Minister, **Clement Attlee**, with the support of the French government, flew across to Washington to try to persuade the USA to open negotiations with China. Truman refused on the grounds that he could not **appease** Communism in Asia while containing it in Europe, but he did reassure him that the atom bomb would not be used.

The impact of rearmament on Western Europe

Once China had sent troops into Korea, it was clear that the war would last for a long time. This strengthened the hand of the Republican Party in the US Congress, which believed that Washington should take a much tougher line towards both the USSR and China, and forced Truman to make rearmament his government's overriding priority. Marshall Aid was first diverted to Western European industries that were vital for rearmament and then in 1951 stopped altogether in favour of a military assistance programme. Inevitably this led to massive pressure on

Key question
How did the rearmament programmes of 1950–1 threaten to destabilise the Western alliance? Why did this not happen?

Key figure

Clement Attlee
1883–1967; leader of the Labour Party and British Prime Minister 1945–51.

Key term

Appease
To conciliate a potential aggressor by making concessions. In the 1950s appeasement was a 'dirty word' associated with Britain's and France's appeasement of Nazi Germany in the 1930s.

the Western European states to rearm more rapidly, and the sheer expense of rearmament threatened to destabilise the North Atlantic Alliance at a time of acute danger.

In Western Europe the NATO states increased their expenditure on rearmament from $4.4 billion in 1949 to $8 billion in 1951. This at first triggered a boom in industrial production, but because expensive raw materials such as coal, copper and rubber had to be imported in considerable quantities, it also caused inflation and serious balance of payments problems. As a result of inflation between July 1950 and June 1951 the cost of living increased by about 20 per cent in France and by about 10 per cent in Italy, the FRG and Britain.

There was also increasing evidence that the shift in investment from civilian to defence production and higher taxes was undermining political stability. In Britain a serious split developed in April in the Labour Cabinet over the cost of rearmament, while in the French and Italian elections of May and June 1951 both the Communists and the right-wing nationalist parties made a strong showing. In West Germany there were ominous signs that the extreme right appeared to be making a comeback in the state elections in Lower Saxony.

It was no wonder then that **Robert Marjolin**, the Secretary-General of the Organisation for European Economic Co-operation (OEEC), was convinced that Western Europe was facing a great economic crisis, which could only be solved by a 'second Marshall Plan'. While it was unrealistic to expect any help on this scale from Washington, in July 1951 the OEEC and NATO did co-operate in a successful attempt to ensure that rearmament did not stifle the economic recovery of Western Europe. In August the OEEC called for a dramatic 25 per cent expansion of Western Europe's industrial production over the coming five years. It proposed financing both rearmament and domestic prosperity through increased production. In other words both **guns and butter** were to be produced! Thanks to the combination of the rearmament boom triggered by the Korean War and the steadily growing world demand for industrial goods and vehicles this proved a realistic plan. For the next 20 years Western Europe enjoyed a period of unparalleled prosperity, which in turn encouraged further economic and political integration and consolidated the Western bloc.

The signature of the EDC and the General Treaty

Under US pressure detailed negotiations on the EDC started in Paris in October 1951. Simultaneously talks began in Bonn between the High Commissioners and Adenauer on replacing the Occupation Statute. Both sets of negotiations proved complicated and dragged on until May 1952. In Bonn the sticking point was how much independence the Western allies were ready to give the FRG, and in Paris the key issue was still French determination to prevent Germany from becoming a major military power again. Thus, France vetoed German membership of NATO and

Key figure

Robert Marjolin
1911–86; a brilliant economist who was the first Secretary of the OECC, 1948–55. He later played a key role in the European Commission.

Key term

Guns and butter
A country's economy can finance both rearmament and a rising standard of living for its inhabitants.

Key question
Why did it take so long for the EDC treaty to be signed?

Key date

EDC Treaty signed: 27 May 1952

continued jealously to restrict the size of German units that could be integrated into the EDC. The General Treaty was signed on 26 May, and the EDC Treaty a day later in Paris as a result of US pressure on the French government. After that there began the long struggle to have the treaty **ratified** by the national parliaments of France and West Germany.

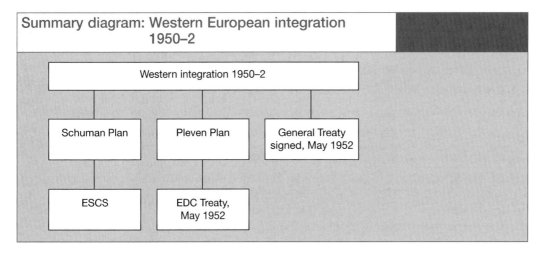

Summary diagram: Western European integration 1950–2

Western integration 1950–2

Schuman Plan

Pleven Plan

General Treaty signed, May 1952

ESCS

EDC Treaty, May 1952

2 | Stalin's Failure to Stop West German Rearmament

Stalin attempted to counter the threat of NATO and German rearmament in two ways.

- First, he tried to exploit fears in West Europe of a new world war by launching the Communist-led World Peace Movement, which campaigned for disarmament and world peace.
- More ambitiously he also attempted to stop West Germany's military and economic integration into Western Europe.

From the autumn of 1950 until the spring of 1952 Stalin put forward, either at international level or through the GDR, a series of initiatives aimed at achieving a united but neutral Germany. In March 1952, in a note to the Western allies, he made a far-reaching proposal for free elections, supervised by a commission of the four former occupying powers, which would lead to the setting up of an independent Germany. The new reunified Germany would not be allowed to make alliances against former enemies, and so could hardly join the EDC; but, on the other hand, it would not be burdened with demands for reparations, denazification and the **socialisation of the economy**. It would also be allowed to have its own limited armed forces.

The SED celebrating its second party conference in July 1952. Note the pictures of Marx, Engels, Lenin and Stalin.

Profile: Walter Ulbricht 1893–1973

1893	– Born in Saxony, Germany
1914–18	– Fought in the First World War
1919	– Joined the German Communist Party
1928–33	– Was a member of the *Reichstag* (parliament)
1933–45	– In exile in Moscow, he was secretary of the German Communist Party politburo
1943	– Co-founder of the National Committee for a Free Germany
1946–71	– First Secretary of the SED
1960–73	– Chairman of the GDR's State Council
1973	– Died

When the GDR was founded, Ulbricht exercised the real power on the basis of his role in the SED. Otto Grotewohl, the **Minister President** of the GDR, was effectively a figurehead. Ulbricht was initially determined to turn East Germany into a Communist state. He was often dismissed by the West Germans and Western allies as a Communist stooge, but in reality he was quite capable of standing up to the USSR, and some historians believe that he deliberately provoked a revolt in East Germany in June 1953 in order to bring about Soviet intervention. Similarly, he put pressure on Khrushchev to build the Berlin Wall in 1961 (page 119).

Key term

Minister President
Prime Minister.

Was Stalin really serious with this offer? Many West Germans believed that Adenauer should have responded more positively to Stalin's initiative. They were convinced that it was a 'missed opportunity', an opinion that has been echoed by modern historians, of whom Steininger and Loth are the most persuasive. Adenauer, however, like the Americans and the British, wanted to see the FRG firmly integrated into the West and not replaced by a unified neutral Germany, which would be vulnerable to Soviet pressure.

Thus, Stalin's initiative was never fully explored by the Western powers. In July 1952 Ulbricht was given the go-ahead for an accelerated socialisation programme in East Germany, which suggested that Stalin had now finally given up the idea of sacrificing the GDR to stop the rearmament of the FRG.

3 | Eastern Integration

On the surface, the Soviet bloc appeared stable, yet its unity was fragile. Unlike the West it was essentially held together by coercion, and had no international organisations comparable to NATO, the OEEC and the ECSC:

Key question
How did Eastern 'integration' differ from Western integration?

- The Cominform (see page 50) was set up to create ideological unity in Eastern Europe, but by 1949 it was rapidly lapsing into inactivity.
- Similarly the Council for Mutual Economic Assistance (Comecon), which was created to counter the Marshall Plan, was in reality, to quote one historian, R.L. Hutchings, just a 'paper organisation until the late 1950s'.

The only effective ties strengthening the bloc were the network of bilateral treaties 'of friendship, co-operation and mutual assistance' signed between the USSR and the individual satellite states and also between these states themselves. Each of these treaties contained the following agreements:

- a mutual defence agreement
- a ban on joining a hostile alliance such as NATO
- recognition of equality, sovereignty and non-interference in each other's internal affairs (although in practice this did not deter the USSR from intervening in the domestic policies of its satellites).

There was also a series of interstate agreements covering economic, scientific and technical co-operation.

Stalin and Eastern Europe

Stalin achieved obedience to the Soviet line by frequently summoning the leaders of the Eastern bloc states to Moscow, and also through the direct participation of Soviet ambassadors and advisers in the internal affairs of the satellites. In the background, of course, there was always the threat of the Red Army. The

Key question
How did Stalin control Eastern Europe?

armed forces of the satellite states, unlike the NATO armies, formed a completely integrated system centred in Moscow. Each army was issued with Soviet equipment, training manuals and armaments. Even the style of uniform was identical. The **Stalin cult** was also a unifying factor in the Eastern bloc. He was celebrated everywhere as the builder of Socialism in the USSR and the liberator of Eastern Europe. To survive in this period local politicians had, in the words of R.L. Hutchings, to be 'more like Stalin than Stalin himself', and the societies and economies of the satellite states had to be based on the Soviet model. Farms were collectivised, heavy industry was to be developed in a series of Five Year Plans and central planning for the economy was introduced.

Key term

Stalin cult
The propaganda campaign vaunting Stalin as the great ruler of the USSR.

Summary diagram: Eastern integration 1949–53

Treaties and international organisations:

- Cominform 1947
- Comecon 1949
- Bilateral treaties of friendship
- Treaties on scientific and technical co-operation

Direct intervention by USSR into the satellite states:

- Eastern bloc leaders regularly summoned to Moscow
- Direct intervention by Soviet ambassadors
- Stalin cult
- Armed forces of the Eastern bloc had the same equipment as the USSR

Key question
How did the West try to destabilise the Soviet bloc in the period 1949–52?

4 | Western Attempts to Destabilise the Soviet Bloc

Tito's break with the Kremlin in 1948 (see pages 66–8) indicated to the USA and the Western powers that the unity of the Soviet bloc was more fragile than it appeared to be. The Tito–Stalin split encouraged the USA to explore various ways of weakening the USSR's position in Eastern Europe:

Key figure

Enver Hoxha
1908–85; Prime Minister of Albania 1944–54 and First Secretary of the Albanian Communist Party's Central Committee until his death, which made him the effective ruler of Albania. He hated Tito and was later highly critical of the USSR.

- So as not to discredit Tito in the eyes of his fellow Communists, Truman secretly granted Yugoslavia economic and military assistance.
- Between 1949 and 1952 there was a series of unsuccessful operations planned by the Americans and British involving landing agents and paramilitary forces in Albania to overthrow the Communist government of **Enver Hoxha**.
- Attempts were made to undermine Soviet power in the other satellite states by complaining in the United Nations about human rights abuses.
- The West restricted trade with the satellite states, so that they would be forced to look to the USSR for goods, which it could only supply at considerable cost to itself.

- Eastern European refugees were helped financially, so as to encourage others to flee from the Soviet bloc.
- Radio Free Europe, which broadcast anti-Soviet propaganda to the states behind the Iron Curtain, was set up and paid for by US money.

All these measures were aimed at weakening Soviet power in Eastern Europe over the long term. The USA and its allies were not, however, ready to risk war with the USSR, especially as it was now a nuclear power.

5 | Leadership Changes in the USA and USSR

The election of Eisenhower

In November 1952, Dwight D. Eisenhower, standing as a Republican, won the US presidential election. During the election campaign there had been much talk about 'rolling back the frontiers of Communism', but, like his predecessor, he was not ready to risk war, and privately he expressed considerable doubts 'about how much we should poke at the animal through the bars of the cage'. Western military integration and support for Adenauer remained the cornerstone of US policy.

> **Key question**
> What impact did the new leaders in the USA and USSR have on the Cold War?

Profile: Dwight D. Eisenhower 1890–1969

1890	– Born in Texas
1942	– Commanded Allied forces in North Africa
1944	– Supreme Commander of the troops invading France
1950–1	– Commander of NATO
1952	– Elected President of the USA
1953	– Ended Korean War
1956	– Opposed Suez operation; re-elected President
1961	– Retired
1969	– Died

In his presidential campaign in 1952 Eisenhower had promised to cut military spending, while standing up to the Russians. He was worried that massive defence expenditure created an '**industrial and military complex**' which had a vested interest in the arms race. He ended the Korean War in 1953 (see page 87) and managed to reduce annual government spending on arms by nearly $10 billion by 1956. It increased again between 1957 and 1959, but declined during his final year as president. Eisenhower was interested in avoiding confrontation where possible. Under him, however, the USA did come to rely increasingly on nuclear weapons as a way of cutting costs and minimising the reliance on expensive conventional weapons.

> **Key term**
>
> **Industrial and military complex**
> The powerful combination of the armed forces and the defence industries.

Death of Stalin:
5 March 1953

Changes in the Soviet leadership

In March 1953 Stalin's death also led to changes in the Soviet leadership. His one-man dictatorship was replaced by a collective leadership composed of Malenkov, Khrushchev, Molotov, Bulganin and, for a short time, Beria. At home this group was determined to improve living standards and cautiously to dismantle the apparatus of terror created by Stalin. To carry out these reforms they needed a more relaxed international climate. Shortly after Stalin's death Malenkov declared in the Supreme Soviet:

> At the present time there is no disputed or unresolved question that cannot be settled by mutual agreement of the interested countries. This applies to our relations with all states, including the United States of America.

The Soviet leadership 1953–6
For three years after Stalin's death powers rested with a group of leading Communists, who exercised a collective leadership, that is to say they jointly controlled the USSR:

- Nikita Khrushchev, 1894–1971; First Secretary of the Russian Communist Party 1953–64 and Premier 1958–64
- Georgi Malenkov, 1902–88; Deputy Prime Minister of the USSR 1953–5
- Vyachlav Molotov, 1890–1986; Minister for Foreign Affairs 1939–48, 1953–6
- Lavrenty Beria, 1899–1953; Head of the Soviet Secret Police 1938–53
- Nikolay Bulganin, 1896–1975; Soviet Minister of Defence 1953–5 and Chairman of the Council of Ministers 1955–7.

The West's reactions to the new Soviet policy

Given this desire for *détente* by the Soviet leadership, it looked briefly as though the German question might be reopened. The obvious dangers in this for NATO were that it would:

- slow down the progress of Western military integration
- give the French Assembly an excuse not to ratify the EDC treaty
- weaken the position of Adenauer.

Eisenhower therefore responded cautiously and on 16 April 1953 announced that any improvement in Soviet–US relations would depend on free elections in Eastern Europe.

In May, Churchill, who had become Prime Minister again after the Conservatives had won the British general election in October 1951, suggested a four power conference. This proposal was unpopular with both Adenauer and Eisenhower who feared that it might reopen the German question, but such was the desire for peace throughout Western Europe, particularly in the FRG, that both statesmen reluctantly had to agree to discuss a possible agenda for talks at a preliminary Western conference, although this did not meet until December in Bermuda.

6 | The East German Revolt, June 1953

The causes of the revolt

In the spring of 1953 Beria urged his colleagues in the Soviet Council of Ministers to 'sell' the GDR for the payment of $10 billion to West Germany since it was proving an expensive and potentially unstable state to keep going. Ulbricht's programme of forced collectivisation of farms and of socialisation was causing a mass exodus of East Germans fleeing westwards through the open frontier in Berlin. Although Beria failed to convince his colleagues, who still clung to the idea of working slowly and cautiously towards a unified socialist Germany, Ulbricht (see page 91) was ordered to pursue a more conciliatory approach in East Germany and to abandon his programme for rapid socialisation. These concessions, however, were made too late and also failed to scale down the high production targets that had been set for the workers by Ulbricht.

Key question
Why did the revolt break out?

The uprising

A series of strikes and riots broke out throughout East Germany on 16 June. At the request of the East German government, Soviet troops backed by tanks intervened the following day to suppress them. Sporadic demonstrations and riots then continued throughout the summer.

The workers demanded increased pay, more political freedom and the re-establishment of the SPD, which had been amalgamated with the KPD in 1946 (see page 43). By the following day waves of spontaneous and uncoordinated strikes and demonstrations had erupted across the whole of the GDR. Crowds collected outside prisons, state and party offices and called for the resignation of the government, but only in two cities, Görlitz and Bitterfeld, were there determined efforts to form **democratic local governments**. Elsewhere there were no plans to control radio stations or the railways or to seize arms. In East Berlin alone there were 100,000 people on the streets. The government, distrusting the loyalty of its own police forces, appealed to the Soviets to intervene. By 18 June a combination of Soviet military intervention and the withdrawal of production targets restored order, although sporadic strikes, protests and demonstrations continued for a few more days.

Key question
How was the East German uprising crushed?

The East German uprising: 16 June 1953

Key date

Democratic local governments
Town and regional councils that were elected democratically.

Key term

The consequences

The uprising took both the Soviets and the Western powers by surprise, and has been called by one historian, Christian Ostermann, 'one of the most significant focal points in the history of the Cold War'. The US government at first welcomed the crisis, as it upset the whole Soviet peace offensive and made the calling of a four power conference much less likely. For this very reason

Key question
What were the consequences of the East German uprising?

East German workers hurl stones at Soviet tanks on 17 June 1953.

Churchill tried to play down Soviet intervention and stressed, correctly in fact, that Soviet troops had acted with considerable restraint. The Americans, on the other hand, hoped that the sight of Soviet troops on the streets of East Berlin would fuel West German fears of the USSR and persuade the voters to re-elect Adenauer in the September election. Yet there was a considerable danger that if the USA was seen to do nothing to help the East Germans there could, as one US official said, 'be a terrible let down in East and West Germany, which will seriously affect the American position and even more seriously affect Adenauer's position'.

Eisenhower's advisers therefore came up with a two-pronged strategy. The USA would respond to pressure from public opinion in West Germany for international intervention to help the East Germans by calling for a four power foreign ministers' conference on the future of Germany, but at the same time, through provocative broadcasts from its radio stations in West Berlin, it would do all it could to prolong the unrest in East Germany.

This policy certainly strengthened support for Adenauer in the FRG, who duly won the election in September with a greatly increased vote; but it also made it much more difficult for the Soviets to make any real concessions on the status of the GDR. The revolt led not only to Beria's arrest and execution on the orders of his political rivals, but also to a re-think of Soviet policy towards the GDR. The unpopularity of the Socialist Unity Party (SED) in East Germany and the hatred for the Communists in the FRG forced the Soviets to come to the conclusion that the prospect of a friendly united neutral Germany was unrealistic and that therefore they had little option but to concentrate on consolidating the GDR.

7 | The Western European Settlement 1953–5

The collapse of the EDC

On 15 May 1953 the European Defence Community (EDC) and the General Treaty were at last ratified by the West German parliament, but only after prolonged opposition from the Social Democrats. Soviet intervention in East Germany on 17 June was then seen by most West Germans as a confirmation that Adenauer's policy of joining the EDC was correct. In France, however, the situation was very different. France began to have second thoughts about the EDC almost as soon as it had signed it, and the government adopted the tactics of dragging out the ratification process as long as possible.

Stalin's death, the end of the Korean War in July 1953 and the Soviet peace offensive all appeared to have made the EDC less necessary. Finally, after failing to gain major changes in the treaty the French Chamber rejected it on 30 August 1954. Two years earlier such a defeat would have led to Adenauer's resignation and probably to renewed Franco-German rivalry, which would have fatally undermined the unity of Western Europe. By 1954, however, Adenauer's position was immeasurably stronger. He had won the 1953 election, the economy of the FRG was booming and he enjoyed the support of the new US Secretary of State, John Foster Dulles. France, on the other hand, was weakened by its **defeat in Indo-China**, where it had been waging a bitter colonial war since 1945, and was therefore vulnerable to Anglo-American pressure.

The FRG joins NATO

The immediate priority of Britain and the USA was to secure the FRG's entry into NATO. France's fears of a rearmed Germany were overcome by Adenauer's agreement to limit the Federal army to the size envisaged in the EDC treaty, his voluntary renouncement of nuclear weapons and Britain's commitment permanently to keep four divisions of troops supported by air power in West Germany. In October 1954 a fresh settlement was hammered out that recognised the sovereignty of the FRG and its membership of NATO. The Western allies again committed themselves to work towards a united federal Germany integrated into a democratic Western Europe. Until this happened their troops would remain in the FRG and Berlin would still be under four power control. On 5 May 1955 the treaty came into force and four days later the FRG joined NATO.

Key question
Why did the French finally reject the EDC?

Key dates
Korean War ended: July 1953

EDC rejected by the French Assembly: 31 August 1954

Key term
Defeat in Indo-China
From 1945 to 1954 France attempted to hold on to its colony, Indo-China, and fought a bitter war against the Communists led by Ho Chi Minh. In March 1954 French troops surrendered at Dien Bien Phu.

Key question
Why did Britain and the USA want the FRG to join NATO?

Key date
FRG became a sovereign state and joined NATO: 5 May 1955

Profile: John Foster Dulles 1888–1959

1888	– Born in Washington DC
1919	– Served at the Versailles Conference
1945	– Senior US adviser to the San Francisco conference of the United Nations
1951	– Negotiated US–Japanese peace treaty
1952–9	– US Secretary of State
1959	– Died of cancer

Dulles was convinced that the USA should challenge the USSR aggressively. He wrote in 1950 that 'dictatorships usually present a formidable exterior', but inside 'they are full of rottenness'. In the 1952 presidential elections he promised that the US would roll back Soviet power in Eastern Europe, but once he became Secretary of State the reality was very different. Neither in East Germany (1953) nor in Hungary (1956) did the USA intervene. In practice, Dulles and Eisenhower believed that all that could be done was simply to preserve the status quo and protect Western Europe. John Gaddis has pointed out that 'the United States therefore refrained from exploiting Soviet weaknesses. Far from shifting the status quo, as he had promised to do, while seeking office, Eisenhower used nuclear weapons to shore it up and stabilise it'.

Chancellor Adenauer addressing the first volunteers for the new West German army in January 1956.

Vienna Settlement of 1815
Re-drew the map of Europe after Napoleon had finally been defeated.

These treaties effectively completed the postwar settlement of Western Europe. A German historian, Hans-Peter Schwarz, has compared them to the **Vienna Settlement of 1815**, which created a generation of peace after the Napoleonic wars. Yet they also deepened the division of Europe. While theoretically the door was kept open for German unification, in reality the integration of the FRG into NATO made unity in the foreseeable future unlikely.

The very success of Western integration intensified what the German historian Christoph Klessmann has called 'the reactive mechanism' of the Cold War: the more the FRG was integrated into the West, the more tightly bound was the GDR into the Soviet bloc.

8 | The Warsaw Pact Treaty

The Soviets reacted, to quote John Gaddis, 'surprisingly mildly' to West Germany's membership of NATO and did not let it interfere with their plans for the coming Geneva Conference. Nevertheless, on 14 May 1955 the USSR and the Eastern European states signed the Warsaw Pact, which the GDR eventually joined in January 1956. The pact committed its members to consult on issues of mutual interest and to give all necessary assistance in the event of an attack on any one of them in Europe. Essentially it was a treaty made for its political rather than military impact on the international situation, as it lacked organisation and for its first few years was, as Hutchings puts it, 'little more than a shell'. It still kept open the option of a neutral Germany by declaring that if a 'general European Treaty of **Collective Security**' was signed, the Warsaw Pact would lapse.

Key question
To what extent was the Warsaw Pact the consequence of West Germany's membership of NATO?

Signing of the Warsaw Pact: 14 May 1955

Key date

9 | The Geneva Conference, July 1955

By the summer of 1955 the Cold War had reached a stage of equilibrium. Increasingly, the nuclear weapons possessed by the two superpowers, the USA and USSR, appeared to rule out war and make peaceful coexistence the only practical option. In May the Soviets agreed to evacuate **Austria** provided it remained neutral, and in July 1955 the leaders of Britain, France, the USA and USSR met for the first time since Potsdam at Geneva. Here, however, the limits to the new spirit of coexistence, or *détente*, were quickly reached. No agreement was achieved on the future of Germany or on disarmament, but at least conversations were conducted in an atmosphere of friendship and the division of Europe was treated as a diplomatic fact of life.

In September, Adenauer visited Moscow to negotiate the return of the last German prisoners of war and to establish normal diplomatic relations with the USSR. Far from leading to a breakthrough in the German question the division between the two Germanies widened still further. To reassure East Germany of continued Soviet support Nikita Khrushchev acknowledged the GDR as an independent state in its own right. Adenauer, worried that an exchange of ambassadors with the USSR might be interpreted to mean that his government recognised the legal existence of the GDR, immediately announced the Hallstein doctrine.

This stated that the FRG would consider the recognition of the GDR by any state, other than the USSR, as an unfriendly act which would lead to an immediate break in diplomatic relations. The Hallstein doctrine showed clearly the limits to the 'Geneva spirit'.

Key question
What significance, if any, did the Geneva Conference have?

Collective security
Security gained through joining an alliance where the security of each state is guaranteed by the alliance.

Austria
In 1945 Austria, like Germany, had been divided into four zones. At Geneva, the USSR agreed to independence provided it remained neutral and did not join NATO.

Key terms

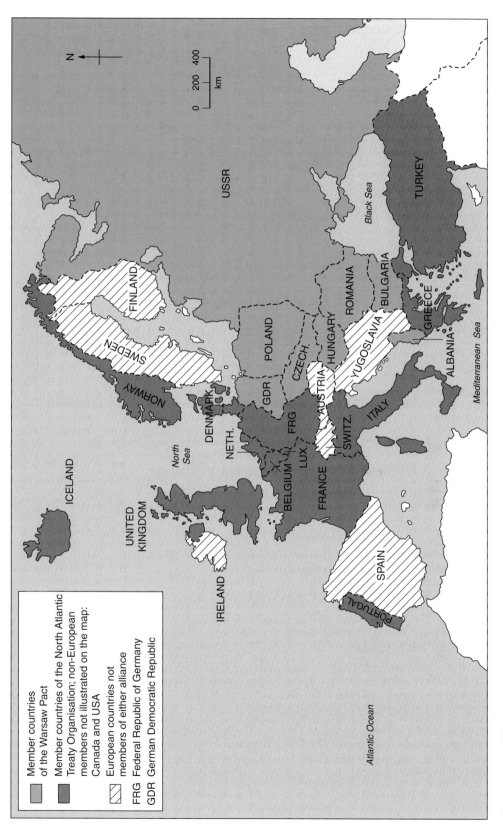

Figure 5.1: NATO and the Warsaw Pact 1956.

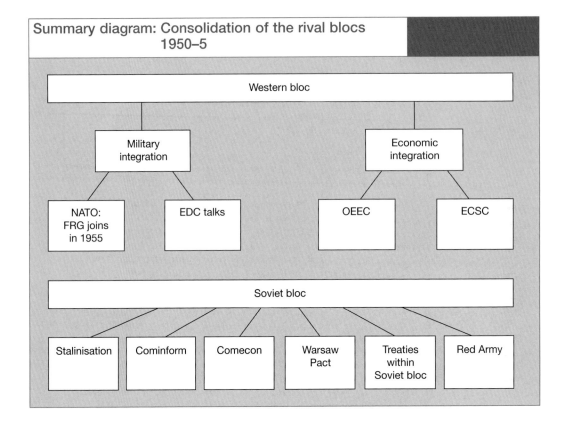

Summary diagram: Consolidation of the rival blocs 1950–5

10 | Key Debate

Many historians have contributed to the analysis of the Cold War during the crucial years of 1950–5. The key questions that scholars try to answer are:

- Was it the policies of the USSR or the USA and the Western allies that were responsible for the intensification of the Cold War and the hardening of the division of Europe and Germany?
- Or was the Cold War an inevitable clash between two opposed powers?

Traditionalist historians

Traditionalist historians, who were writing before the archives in either the USSR or the Western states were open, such as David Rees and Herbert Feiss, view the Cold War as being driven essentially by the USSR and argue that the West merely responded to Soviet threats. In the USSR, Soviet historians and Eastern Europe could only follow the party line and essentially interpret the Cold War as an inevitable struggle in which the USSR was defending socialism from Western 'capitalists' and 'fascists'.

Revisionist historians

Both Willy Loth and Rolf Steininger, revisionist historians who have been able to study the sources in the archives, argue that Stalin, after the failure of the Berlin blockade, was very anxious to halt the integration of Germany into the Western bloc. They stress particularly that the Stalin note of March 1952 really did offer the chance of creating an independent united, but neutral, Germany. They also stress that it was the East German riots in June that prevented a settlement in 1953.

John Gaddis

On balance, the post-revisionist John Gaddis comes down on the side of arguing that, while Stalin may very briefly have flirted with the idea of tolerating an independent united Germany, he was determined to keep the USSR's grip on a socialist East Germany, which was firmly integrated into the Soviet bloc. Gaddis, however, does argue that briefly Beria really did champion the idea of 'selling' the GDR to the West Germans, but that it was the West that rejected this proposal.

Geir Lundestaad

Geir Lundestaad, a post-revisionist historian, took issue with the revisionist historians such as William Appleman Williams and Gabriel Kolko, who, writing in the 1960s and 1970s under the influence of the Vietnam War, saw the USA as the 'aggressor'. After studying the sources in the Western European archives he argued that the Americans, far from imposing their power on Western Europe, in fact created an empire by invitation. Lundestaad argues that it was the Western Europeans who 'invited' the USA to construct what amounted to an empire in Western Europe in order to defend it against Communism. He stresses how anxious the Western Europeans were, for instance, to support NATO and to rely on US military superiority.

Study Guide: AS Question

In the style of OCR

To what extent had Stalin's European policy, 1945–53, failed by
the time of his death?   (50 marks)

Exam tips

*The cross-references are intended to take you straight to the material
that will help you to answer the question.*

Consider initially what the question actually means and what
information you need to draw on to answer it. Examiners often use
the words 'to what extent'; they indicate that you must make some
sort of judgement or evaluation. Thus, before you can assess
whether or not Stalin's European policy was a failure, you must be
sure what his European policy was. Look back over your notes of the
last five chapters and work out how you will plan your essay. Each
paragraph should deal with an important argument that explores and
answers a particular aspect of the question. In the introduction
summarise the main thrust of your arguments and clarify any
obscure points in the question:

- Could it be that in some areas, such as the role played by the
  Communist parties in Western Europe, Stalin's policy had failed
  by 1953 (pages 54–5)?
- Similarly, his attempts to create a pro-Soviet Germany, or at the
  very least to stop the integration of Western Germany into a
  US-dominated Western bloc, had also very obviously failed by
  his death (pages 90–2).
- On the other hand, he had created a ring of satellite states in
  Eastern Europe and made the USSR the greatest military power
  in Europe (pages 84 and 92–3).

As with most historical problems, it is likely that you will conclude
that there is no clear-cut answer: Stalin's European policy was a
failure in some areas and a success in others. As you write out your
essay do not lapse into narrative. Always remember that you must
argue relevantly.

Study Guide: A2 Question

In the style of AQA

'By July 1955, it seemed as if the Cold War might end.' Assess the validity of this view. (45 marks)

Exam tips

The cross-references are intended to take you straight to the material that will help you to answer the question.

Your task is to provide a reasoned judgement as to whether the end of the Cold War could have come about in 1955 or whether attitudes were too entrenched to permit this. In arguing these issues you are likely to want to cite material from earlier chapters in this book as well as looking fairly closely at this chapter. First, you will need to identify the situation in July 1955 when the Geneva Conference took place (page 100) and consider the implications of Stalin's death in 1953 for developments in the period 1953–5. Try to offer some comment on the state of the Cold War in 1955. You will then need to balance your picture of these years against the longer-term factors influencing the Cold War. You should evaluate the extent to which an end to the Cold War was possible by:

- discussing how serious an international struggle the Cold War really was
- analysing the aims of both the USA and the USSR in the main areas of tension in the Cold War, e.g. Germany and Eastern Europe.

Try to argue throughout your answer and provide a well-supported conclusion showing your own judgement.

6

The Khrushchev Era and the 'Second Cold War' 1956–63

POINTS TO CONSIDER

This chapter covers the eventful period when the Soviet leader, Nikita Khrushchev, was trying to consolidate the USSR's grip on Eastern Europe, while also attempting to 'destalinise', or liberalise, conditions within it. It focuses on the following interlinked events and their impact on East–West relations:

- The year of crises: 1956 (Poland, Hungary and the Suez Crisis)
- The legacy of the crises
- The Berlin Crisis 1958–61
- The Cuban Missile Crisis 1962

The chapter then finishes by assessing the question of whether the period 1956–63 can be described as the 'Second Cold War'.

Key dates

1956	February 25	Khrushchev attacked Stalin at 20th Party Congress
	June	Riots in Poland
	23 October–4 November	Hungarian uprising defeated
1957	March 25	Treaty of Rome signed
1958	November 27	Khrushchev's Berlin ultimatum
1959	January	Castro set up a revolutionary government in Cuba
1960	May 1	US U2 spy plane shot down over USSR
	May 16–17	Paris Summit broke down
1961	August 13	Frontier between East and West Berlin closed
1962	September 13	USA warned USSR on installation of missiles in Cuba
	October–November	Cuban Missile Crisis

1 | The Year of Crises 1956

Destalinisation

Destalinisation had a big impact on the relations between the USSR and its satellite states. It appeared to promise a return to the policy of 'different roads to socialism', which Stalin briefly tolerated between 1945 and 1947 (see page 51). The pace of destalinisation accelerated after the fall of Beria (see page 97). His secret police network, which had spies throughout Eastern Europe, was dissolved and politicians such as Gomulka in Poland and Kadar in Hungary were released from prison and returned to public life. This raised expectations in the satellite states that they would be given more independence from Moscow.

Khrushchev's speech at the 20th Party Conference, February 1956

A further wave of destalinisation followed after Khrushchev's famous speech at the 20th Party Conference, February 1956, denouncing Stalin and recognising the rights of the satellite states to find their 'national ways to socialism'. Although the speech was supposed to be secret, the US security service, the CIA, acquired a copy and ensured that it was broadcast to Eastern Europe. By raising hopes of political change this contributed to the unrest in Poland and Hungary later in the year.

Expectations of reform were further increased by the improvement in relations between the USSR and Yugoslavia, which was 're-admitted' to the Socialist bloc after Khrushchev and Bulganin had visited Belgrade in May 1955. The blame for the break in 1948 was attributed fairly and squarely to Stalin (see pages 66–8). Khrushchev was, of course, primarily interested in bringing back Yugoslavia into the Soviet sphere of influence, while Tito, the Yugoslav leader, ambitiously believed that, as a result of his experience in defying Stalin, he was a role model for the new generation of Soviet leaders and would now become a leading figure in the Soviet bloc. In June 1956, after talks in Moscow, Khrushchev and Tito issued a communiqué in which they agreed that:

> the path of socialist development differs in various countries and conditions, that the multiplicity of forms of socialist development tends to strengthen socialism and that any tendency of imposing one's opinions on the ways and forms of socialist development is alien to both.

This was an optimistic doctrine assuming that the satellite states wished to remain within the Soviet bloc. What would happen, however, if one or more of these states decided to take a controversial road to socialism, with which the USSR did not agree? Would it intervene militarily or run the risk of seeing the Soviet bloc disintegrate?

Key question
Why did destalinisation cause serious crises within the Soviet bloc?

Destalinisation
The attempts to liberalise the USSR after the death of Stalin in 1953.

Key term

Key question
What was the significance of Khrushchev's speech at the 20th Party Conference?

Khrushchev attacks Stalin's record at the 20th Party Congress: 25 February 1956

Key date

Profile: Nikita Khrushchev 1894–1971

1894		– Born in Kursk
1918		– Joined the Bolshevik Party
1935		– First Secretary of the Moscow City Committee
1938		– Head of the Ukranian Communist Party
1939		– Joined the Politburo
1941–5		– Served as Political Commissar on various fronts including Stalingrad
1950		– In charge of Soviet agriculture
1953		– Elected First Secretary of the Party (Party leader)
1956	February	– Denounced Stalin in a secret speech
	November	– Sent troops into Hungary
1958		– Became Soviet Prime Minister
	November	– Sent Berlin Ultimatum to the Western powers
1960		– Recalled Soviet specialists from China
1961	August	– Sanctioned the building of the Berlin Wall
1962		– Erected Soviet rocket firing pads in Cuba
1964		– Ousted from office
1971		– Died

By the time the 20th Party Congress met in February 1956 Khrushchev was already the most powerful figure in the USSR. He was convinced that Communism would eventually win the economic and ideological competition with capitalism. Although this competition was to be peaceful, he did not hesitate to play on the West's fear of nuclear war to achieve his ends. His opportunism and '**nuclear sabre rattling**' made the world a much more dangerous place than it had been in Stalin's time. Khrushchev was a paradoxical figure. As the British historian Geoffrey Roberts has observed, 'he emphasised peaceful economic competition between socialism and capitalism, but he projected an equally, if not more competitive policy in the political, ideological and military spheres'.

Key term

Nuclear sabre rattling
Threatening or hinting at the possibility of nuclear war in order to intimidate the Western powers.

Key question
Why did Khrushchev decide against using Soviet troops to restore order in Poland?

Key date

Riots in Poland:
June 1956

The Polish Crisis, June–October 1956

The limits to this doctrine of allowing the Eastern European states to develop socialism in their own way were tested first of all in Poland in the autumn of 1956. At the end of June riots broke out in Poznan when the local factory workers protested about the imposition of increased work targets. They were put down with heavy casualties, but to overcome the bitterness this caused, the Polish Communist Party turned again to its popular former leader, Gomulka, who had just been released from prison (see page 66). The Soviet government, fearing that he would seek to restore Polish independence, sent a high-powered delegation to Warsaw on 19–20 October, and ordered the Red Army units

Profile: Wladyslaw Gomulka 1905–1982

1905   – Born in Krosno
1943–8   – Head of the Polish Workers' Party
1948   – Dismissed under pressure from Stalin and accused of 'Titoist tendencies'
1951–5   – Imprisoned
1956–70 – First Secretary of the Polish Communist Party
1970   – Replaced as First Secretary by Edward Gierek after failing to suppress strikes in the Gdynia shipyards
1982   – Died

Gomulka was hated by the Stalinists in Poland, but initially in 1956 he was a hero to the Polish people, and in October was the only person who could restore order. As First Secretary of the Polish Communist Party he made considerable reforms:

- he ended collectivisation of agriculture
- he attempted to reform the running of the economy by decentralising decision making (that is, he allowed local managers some say in making the decisions about their factories)
- he developed trade with the West
- he provided some limited freedom of speech.

However, he still preserved the one-party Communist state and did not allow the workers' councils any real power or influence. For a time, as British historian John Young observed, 'he basically satisfied the Soviets while supposedly respecting Polish sovereignty'. Yet he increasingly became more authoritarian. In March 1968, for instance, he ruthlessly broke up student protest demonstrations in Warsaw and elsewhere. In December 1970 his attempts to impose price increases on the Polish people caused a wave of strikes and riots in the Polish sea ports. Gomulka attempted unsuccessfully to repress these by shooting the protesters. In December 1970 he was replaced by Edward Gierek, who withdrew the price increases and attempted to pursue a more co-operative policy with the workers.

stationed in Poland to advance on the city in an attempt to stop his election. Gomulka refused to be cowed and his election went ahead. On 24 October Khrushchev told a Central Committee meeting in Moscow that:

> the discussions between the delegations ranged from being very warm to rude. Gomulka several times emphasised that they would not permit their independence to be taken away and would not allow anyone to interfere in Poland's internal affairs. He said that if he were leader of the country he would restore order promptly.

Faced with the prospect of having to fight the Poles at a time when the situation in Hungary was rapidly deteriorating (see below), Khrushchev wisely withdrew the troops and chose to believe Gomulka's assurances that Poland would remain a loyal member of the Warsaw Pact. As the Soviet leader was to observe, 'finding a reason for an armed conflict now would be very easy, but finding a way to put an end to such a conflict would be very hard'.

The Hungarian uprising

Key question
Why did the USSR face a challenge to its authority in Hungary?

Just as the worst of the Polish crisis was over, the USSR was faced in Hungary with the most serious challenge to its power since the Second World War. As part of his destalinisation campaign Khrushchev had, with Tito's backing, put pressure on the Hungarian Communist Party in July to replace its old-style Stalinist leader, Mátyás Rákosi, with the more liberal Ernö Gerö. Tito had considerable ambitions in Hungary, as he hoped that an independent Communist regime would emerge in Budapest that would look to Belgrade rather than Moscow and so strengthen his overall influence within the Soviet bloc.

In the early autumn the pressures for further change, which Tito encouraged, continued to grow. A turning point was reached on 23 October when a large demonstration in Budapest, called in support of the Polish reformers, escalated out of control. Even before he had received a formal request for help from Gerö, Khrushchev decided to send in 30,000 troops backed with tanks and artillery. A new government under Imre Nagy, who was an independent minded and reforming Communist, supported by Tito, was formed.

Key terms

Legal and mutually agreed framework
A legal agreement freely negotiated that would allow the USSR to maintain bases in Hungary.

Nationalise
To take over ownership of privately owned industries, banks, etc., by the state.

Khrushchev at first tried to reconcile his pledges to concede greater independence to the satellite states with Soviet security needs. He issued on 30 October the 'Declaration on the Principles of Development and a Further Strengthening of Friendship and Co-operation between the USSR and other Socialist Countries', which attempted to provide a **legal and mutually agreed framework** for Soviet military bases in Eastern Europe. He also began to pull out the troops from Hungary, but then Nagy threatened the whole foundations of the USSR's power in Eastern Europe by announcing that he intended to withdraw Hungary from the Warsaw Pact. He was also planning to share power with non-Communist groups.

The Suez Crisis

Key question
In what ways did the Suez Crisis influence Soviet action in Hungary?

Soviet policy during the Hungarian uprising cannot be fully understood without also looking at the Suez Crisis. The USSR had been so successful in cultivating good relations with Colonel Nasser, the Egyptian leader, that the Americans decided to bring him to heel by cancelling their loan for building the Aswan dam in July 1956. This merely prompted Nasser to turn to the USSR for finance and to **nationalise** the Suez Canal, which was owned by an Anglo-French company, so that he could get further revenue from tolls that the ships had to pay when using the canal.

On 16 October the British, French and Israelis worked out a joint plan for invading Egypt. The Israelis were to invade Egypt through the Sinai and advance towards the canal. The British and French would intervene and send troops to 'protect the canal'.

Israel attacked on 29 October. The British and French immediately sent an ultimatum demanding the withdrawal of both the Israelis and Egyptians from the canal. When the Egyptians refused, British planes began to bomb Egyptian airfields on 31 October, at the very time that the Hungarian crisis was reaching its peak, and on 5 November Anglo-French forces landed in the canal zone. Khrushchev was convinced that Nasser would be quickly removed and that Soviet influence in the Middle East would suffer a disastrous blow. If this was combined with further setbacks in Hungary, Soviet power and prestige might never recover. Consequently that same day he told the Central Committee of the USSR:

> We should re-examine our assessment and should not withdraw our troops from Hungary and Budapest. We should take the initiative in restoring order in Hungary. If we depart from Hungary, it will give a great boost to the Americans, English and French – the **imperialists**. They will perceive it as a weakness on our part and will go on the offensive. We would then be exposing the weakness of our positions. Our party will not accept it if we do this. To Egypt they will then add Hungary. We have no other choice. ...

On 4 November Soviet troops advanced into Hungary and, after a few days of fierce fighting, a new government loyal to the USSR under János Kádér was installed. Khrushchev had nothing to fear from Western intervention. Eisenhower, suspecting that the USSR

Key date

The Hungarian uprising defeated: 23 October–4 November

Key term

Imperialists
Britain and France, who both still had extensive colonial empires. The Soviets also regularly called the Americans imperialists.

Russian officers in Budapest, November 1956, advance threateningly towards a Western photographer. Why were they so hostile towards Western journalists?

might be willing to risk war rather than lose Hungary, made it absolutely clear to the Soviet leaders that there was no question of US intervention to save Nagy.

However, much to Khrushchev's surprise, Nasser was saved by the Americans, who viewed the Suez War as an attempt by Britain and France to prop up their disintegrating empires in the Middle East and Africa. The British had assumed they would get US support, but Eisenhower, in the middle of an election campaign, refused to give this. Not only did the Americans condemn the attack in the United Nations, but they also refused a loan to Britain. Through massive diplomatic and financial pressure on London and Paris, Eisenhower managed to halt the fighting on 6 November just at the point where the British and French troops were near to capturing the whole length of the Suez Canal.

Khrushchev cleverly exploited this split in the Western alliance and on 5 November threatened nuclear missile attacks on Britain, France and Israel if they did not stop the war. Although it was known at the time by **Western intelligence** that the USSR did not yet possess the rockets to propel such missiles, the ceasefire on the following day made it look as if it was the Soviet ultimatum rather than US financial pressure that had saved Egypt. Khruschev himself was thus able to take the credit in the Middle East and the Communist world for having defeated the British and French 'imperialists'.

Key term

Western intelligence
Information gained by Western spies in Eastern Europe.

Summary diagram: The year of crises 1956

Polish and Hungarian Crises

General causes

- Destalinisation
- Impact of Khrushchev's speech at 20th Party Conference
- Tito's influence – different routes to Socialism

Poland	Hungary
• Riots of June 1956 • Soviet objection to appointment of Gomulka • Advance of Red Army averted by Gomulka's promise to resolve order	• Stalinist leader replaced by Gerö • Tito encourages a more independent line • Riots on 28th October triggered Soviet military intervention • Nagy appointed as compromise leader • Announcement that Hungary intended to withdraw from Warsaw Pact prompts Soviet military intervention • Khrushchev convinced that his ally in the Middle East, Colonel Nasser would be toppled by Anglo-French action

Impact of Suez Crisis on Cold War

- Fear of Nasser's defeat strengthens Khrushchev's resolve to crush Hungarian revolt
- Khrushchev attempts to exploit Anglo-French/US split by threatening to fire nuclear missiles at London and Paris
- USSR's position in Middle East strengthened
- Khrushchev encouraged to develop policy of nuclear diplomacy

2 | The Legacy of the Crises

Legacy for the USSR

The Polish and Hungarian crises had shown how difficult it was for the Soviet government to encourage the satellite states to reform without creating a demand for their transformation into genuine democratic regimes. They also highlighted the problems the Soviet bloc had in the post-Stalinist era in agreeing on common policies, as there was no framework for regular consultations.

Moscow Conference of international Communist leaders, October 1957

Khrushchev attempted to remedy this at the conference attended by the international Communist leaders at Moscow in October 1957. Although opposed by the Poles and the Yugoslavs, this conference passed a motion recognising the USSR as 'the first and mightiest' of the socialist countries, while still acknowledging the legitimacy of the principle of 'different roads to socialism'. It also made very clear that a Communist leader under pressure could appeal to the Soviet bloc for 'mutual aid', which in effect meant military assistance to counter any major disturbances. An element of diversity was still tolerated and considerable economic help was given to the satellite states by the USSR, but it was understood that they must in all essentials stick to the Soviet political and economic model. Almost inevitably this doctrine led to a fresh break with Tito, who now joined with India and Egypt to form the **non-aligned movement** of neutral states.

Khrushchev's position strengthened

One of the important legacies of the Hungarian and Suez crises was that Khrushchev's position was greatly strengthened in the USSR. Dulles, the US Secretary of State, had perceptively warned that he was 'the most dangerous person to lead the Soviet Union since the **October Revolution**'. Dulles felt that, whereas Stalin attempted to calculate carefully the consequences of his actions, Khrushchev was prepared to take dangerous risks to achieve his ends.

After his propaganda success in the Suez Crisis, Khrushchev was convinced that the mere threat of nuclear weapons would enable him to force the West to make concessions in Berlin and elsewhere. His policy of '**nuclear diplomacy**' gained more credibility when the USSR launched the world's first intercontinental ballistic missile (ICBM) (see page 11) in August 1957, and followed it up by sending a satellite, the **Sputnik**, into orbit in October. Although the overall military balance still favoured the West, Khrushchev deliberately exaggerated the extent of the Soviet successes in order, as he wrote in his memoirs, 'to exert pressure on American militarists – and also influence the minds of more reasonable politicians – so that the United States would start treating us better'.

Key question
What were the consequences of the 1956 crises for the Soviet bloc?

Non-aligned movement
Not allied with either the USSR or the West.

October Revolution
The second Russian Revolution in October 1917, in which the Bolsheviks seized power.

Nuclear diplomacy
Diplomacy backed up by the threat of nuclear weapons.

Sputnik
This satellite weighed 84 kg and was able to orbit the earth. In Russian the word means 'fellow traveller', or supporter of the USSR.

Key terms

Key question
Why did Dulles think that Khrushchev was such a dangerous Soviet leader?

Key question
What were the consequences of the 1956 crises for the Western bloc?

Legacy for NATO

The immediate damage done to NATO by the Suez Crisis was quickly repaired, as was the Anglo-American special relationship; yet in continental Western Europe as a whole, a certain distrust of US policies lingered. Once the Soviets were in a position to threaten the US East Coast cities with their new ICBM missiles, the European leaders wondered whether the Americans would still defend Western Europe from a possible Soviet attack. Rather than see New York and Washington destroyed would they not do a deal with the Soviets and surrender Western Europe or at least West Germany?

These fears were strengthened by several current developments. The Americans and British were reducing their **conventional forces** in Europe and equipping those that remained with **tactical nuclear weapons**. In October 1957 Adam Rapacki, the Polish Foreign Minister, also put forward plans for a **nuclear-free zone** in Central Europe, which Adenauer, the Chancellor of the FRG, believed was a 'Russian trap' leading to the reunification of a neutralised Germany. Adenauer feared that a neutral united Germany could easily be overrun by the USSR. Not surprisingly, therefore, Adenauer became more responsive to French plans in early 1958 for developing a Franco-German-Italian nuclear bomb that would be independent of the British and Americans.

Doubts about the USA's loyalty to its European allies also influenced Adenauer's thinking about the future of the new European Economic Community (EEC), and his attitude to General de Gaulle, who returned to power in France in May 1958. The two statesmen had very different plans for its future. Adenauer wanted it to develop into a closely integrated community linked to the USA, while de Gaulle hoped that it would become an association of independent states, completely free from US influence, and under French leadership. If, however, the Americans decided to pull out of Europe or sacrifice West Berlin to the USSR, de Gaulle's vision of Europe was the only alternative Adenauer could fall back on.

Key terms

Conventional forces
Military forces that do not rely on nuclear weapons.

Tactical nuclear weapons
Small-scale nuclear weapons that can be used in the battlefield.

Nuclear-free zone
An area, such as Central Europe, in which nuclear weapons would be neither used nor based.

Key date

The Treaty of Rome signed: 25 March 1957

The EEC and EFTA
The European Economic Community (EEC) was set up by the Treaty of Rome, which was signed with general US approval by the FRG, France, Italy and the Benelux states in March 1957. Its aim was to create a common market or customs union within 12 years, while also gradually forming a more integrated political structure. British plans for setting up a much larger free trade zone were turned down by the leaders of the six powers on the grounds that it would not provide an effective basis for European economic and political co-operation. This led to Britain forming the European Free Trade Association (EFTA) with Denmark, Norway, Sweden, Switzerland, Austria and Portugal. Thus, a major economic split in Western Europe developed just at the time that it was about to face renewed pressure from the Soviet bloc.

3 | The Berlin Crisis 1958–61

The first stages

In the autumn of 1956 the GDR had acted, in contrast to Poland and Hungary, as a loyal ally of the USSR. Yet the GDR, despite Soviet recognition in September 1955 (see page 100), remained a fragile and artificial state totally dependent on Moscow and on the presence of 20 divisions of Russian troops stationed within its frontiers. It was confronted by a prosperous West Germany, the miraculous economic recovery of which inevitably attracted many of its youngest and most ambitious citizens.

Through the open frontier in Berlin it was still possible to flee from the drab life of socialist planning and rationing to the bright lights of the FRG, and both Adenauer and the USA did everything to encourage this. Between 1945 and 1961 about one-sixth of the whole East German population had fled westwards. One way of stopping this exodus was dramatically to improve the standard of living in the GDR, but to achieve this, it was essential to stop skilled workers and professionals quitting in large numbers to the FRG. This meant that something had to be done about the status of West Berlin.

Khrushchev's aims

By the autumn of 1958 Khrushchev was increasingly confident that the USSR could force the USA into making concessions over West Berlin, and indeed perhaps over the whole German question. By grossly exaggerating the extent of Soviet nuclear power and by putting pressure on West Berlin he was sure that he could squeeze concessions from the Western allies without the risk of war. He graphically observed: 'Berlin is the testicles of the West ... every time I want to make the West scream I squeeze on Berlin'. Also, as China pointed out, if the GDR could not be turned into a viable state able to hold its own with the FRG, the whole prestige of international Communism was at stake.

Apart from strengthening the GDR what other aims had Khrushchev in mind? He also hoped to:

- stop or at least delay the decision by NATO to equip the FRG with nuclear weapons
- show his critics within the USSR and the Chinese that he was not 'soft on the imperialists'
- divide the Western powers
- force them to accept the USSR as a political and military equal and to come to the conference table to draw up a German peace treaty, which would recognise the division of Germany and the GDR's postwar frontiers with Poland.

In the words of a US historian, Hope Harrison, 'Khrushchev always saw and used West Berlin ... as a lever to compel the West to recognise the post-war status quo and the existence of East Germany'.

Key question
What was Khrushchev intending to achieve by triggering a crisis over Berlin?

Key date

Khrushchev's Berlin
ultimatum:
27 November 1958

The Berlin ultimatum, November 1958

The long and dangerous crisis began on 10 November when
Khrushchev called for a peace treaty with the two German states:

> The time has obviously arrived for the signatories of the Potsdam
> Agreement to renounce the remnants of the occupation regime in
> Berlin, and thereby make it possible to create a normal situation in
> the capital of the German Democratic Republic. The Soviet Union,
> for its part, would hand over to the sovereign German Democratic
> Republic the functions in Berlin that are still exercised by Soviet
> agencies. This, I think, would be the correct thing to do.

On 27 November he followed this up with a six-month ultimatum
demanding the demilitarisation of West Berlin, the withdrawal of
Western troops, and its change of status into a free city. If the
Western allies refused to sign a peace treaty with the two German
states, Khrushchev threatened to conclude a peace agreement just
with the GDR and to recognise its sovereignty over East Berlin.
This would then enable it to control access to West Berlin and
interfere at will with traffic using the **land corridors** from the
FRG. The Western allies would thus be compelled to deal with
East German rather than Russian officials and so in effect
recognise the sovereignty of the GDR, which would shatter the
Hallstein Doctrine (see page 100). He was, however, as we shall
see, to have second thoughts about putting quite so much power
into the hands of Walter Ulbricht, the leader of the GDR.

Key term

Land corridors
Roads, railways and
canals, which the
Soviets had agreed
in 1945 could be
used to supply West
Berlin.

Khrushchev making a speech in an aggressive mood.

The Western reaction 1959–60

Although the Western allies rejected the ultimatum, Khrushchev was successful in forcing them to the conference table to discuss the 'German question'. In February 1959 they agreed that a Foreign Ministers' conference should meet in Geneva in the summer. Khrushchev was also delighted to see splits beginning to appear in the Western alliance. In the preceding months Adenauer viewed with increasing concern statements from London and Washington signalling the desire for compromise and concession, and inevitably drew closer to de Gaulle, who urged a much tougher line against the Soviets. He was particularly alarmed by the decision of British Prime Minister Harold Macmillan to visit Moscow in February and by Eisenhower's invitation to Khrushchev to visit the USA in the coming autumn.

Key question
What was the Western reaction to the Berlin ultimatum?

The Geneva Conference, May–August 1959

At the Geneva Conference both sides put forward proposals for German unity, but no agreement was secured. The Western powers came up with their usual demand for free elections, while the USSR suggested that the two Germanies should form a **confederation**, which would only very slowly evolve into a united state. However, as the Soviets did succeed in persuading the West to discuss the Berlin problem as a separate issue, Khrushchev believed that his threats were paying off, and he continued the pressure, renewing the ultimatum in June.

Confederation
A grouping of states in which each state retains its sovereignty. Hence, much looser than a federation.

Key term

Summit meetings, September 1959–May 1960

Between 1959 and 1961 there were more summits than at any time since the Second World War. When Khrushchev visited Eisenhower at Camp David, the holiday residence of the US President, in September 1959, the mood was friendly but, to quote the US historian John Gaddis, the two leaders 'got no further than an agreement to disagree'. Over the next two years Khrushchev alternated periods of *détente*, when he temporarily allowed the ultimatum to lapse again, with spells of acute crisis during which further threats were devised, to force the West into making concessions over the status of Berlin and the future of Germany.

Key question
Why was so little progress made in solving the Berlin Crisis in 1959–60?

Krushchev's actions were not without success. Behind the scenes in London and Washington, and at times even in Paris, various schemes for creating a nuclear-free zone in Central Europe, recognising Poland's western frontiers and the GDR, were considered quite seriously. Adenauer meanwhile was desperate to stop any of these plans from reducing the FRG to a neutral second-rate state, but by May 1960 when the Paris Summit was due to open, he had no idea what Eisenhower and Macmillan might be about to propose. Thus, for him at least, it was 'a gift from heaven', as the German historian Klessmann has called it, when Khrushchev used the shooting down of an US spy plane over the USSR as an excuse to cancel the Summit, and wait until a new US President was elected in the autumn.

Paris Summit breaks down: 16–17 May 1960

Key date

Key date

US U2 spy plane shot down over USSR: 1 May 1960

U2 spy planes and the arms race
In 1956 the US airforce bought 53 Lockheed U2 spy planes. Based in Japan, Turkey and Britain, they were able to fly over Soviet territory and photograph military bases, missile factories and launch pads. By 1961 Soviet technology caught up with the U2s, and on 5 May a Soviet anti-aircraft missile shot down a plane that had been sent to see whether there were missile bases in the Urals. These flights established that, for all Khrushchev's boasting, the Soviets possessed in the spring of 1961 very few ICBMs and no launching platforms for them. Indeed the USSR had only four ICBMs based on a site near Archangel.

The construction of the Berlin Wall
The growing crisis in East Germany

Key question
Why did Ulbricht want to seal East Berlin off from West Berlin?

Until the autumn of 1960 Khrushchev determined the course of the Berlin Crisis. Ulbricht, the East German leader, who certainly stood to benefit from a successful outcome, was little more than a spectator. Khrushchev still did not despair of using Berlin as a means to solve the German problem as a whole, and despite his bluster, he acted cautiously. He told Ulbricht in May 1960, for instance, that:

> Under present conditions, it is worthwhile to wait a little longer and try to find a solution for the long-since ripe question of a peace treaty with the two German states. This will not escape our hands. We had better wait, and the matter will get more mature.

However, in desperation, as the numbers of refugees to the West dramatically increased during the years 1960–1, Ulbricht pressed Khrushchev to sign a separate peace treaty with the GDR, at one juncture sarcastically observing: 'You only talk about a peace treaty, but don't do anything about it'. By this stage Ulbricht increasingly tried to use the very real threat of the collapse of the GDR to force Khrushchev to sign a separate peace treaty with it. Although the Soviet leader had indeed threatened the West with this, he was now reluctant to carry it out, because he feared that if the East Germans were given responsibility for controlling the links between West Berlin and the FRG without the West's agreement, they might provoke a major crisis, such as another blockade of West Berlin. Khrushchev was only using the threat of a separate peace to squeeze concessions from the West.

Khrushchev's consents to the Berlin Wall

Key question
Why did Khrushchev agree to the construction of the Berlin Wall?

Khrushchev's hopes that John Kennedy, the new US President, would make the concessions that Eisenhower had refused, proved unrealistic, but his response to Soviet threats to West Berlin hinted at a possible solution to the Berlin problem. While he dramatically built up US forces in Europe, Kennedy also urged

Building the Berlin Wall, August 1961.

negotiation on the whole German question and pointedly stressed in a television broadcast on 25 July 1961 that the USA was essentially interested in free access to West Berlin rather than to Berlin as a whole. Kennedy was in fact indicating where the West would draw the line and fight if necessary.

Up to this point Khrushchev had consistently rejected the option of closing off the East Berlin frontier. He had hoped rather to uncouple West Berlin from the FRG than to cut it off from East Germany. However, the growing unrest in the GDR caused by the forced collectivisation of agriculture and the ever increasing number of refugees to West Germany finally persuaded him that something had to be done to prevent an East German collapse. Somewhere between the end of July and the beginning of August Khrushchev decided that the East German border in Berlin would have to be closed. This decision was confirmed at a meeting of the Warsaw Pact states (see page 100) in Moscow on 3–5 August 1961, and in the early morning of 13 August the operation was efficiently and swiftly carried out. At first the border was sealed off with barbed wire, but when no Western countermeasures followed, a more permanent concrete wall was built.

Frontier between East and West Berlin closed: 13 August 1961

Key date

Profile: John Kennedy 1917–63

1917		– Born into a wealthy Irish American family in Massachusetts
1940–3		– Served in the US Navy; his boat was rammed and sunk by a Japanese destroyer
1953		– Elected to the Senate as a Democrat
1960		– Won presidential elections by a narrow margin, and became the first Roman Catholic President in the history of the USA
1961	April	– Allowed a disastrous invasion of Cuba by exiles – the Bay of Pigs incident
	June	– Met Khrushchev in Vienna and was told that the USA was on the 'wrong side of history'
	July	– Indicated that the USA would protect West Berlin with force if necessary
1962	October–November	– Successfully brought the Cuban Missile Crisis to an end
1963	November 22	– Assassinated in Dallas

After Kennedy had met Khrushchev for the first time in Vienna in June 1961, he remarked: 'He just beat the hell out of me. I've got a terrible problem. If he thinks I'm inexperienced and have no guts, until we remove those ideas, we won't get anywhere with him.' Kennedy was worried about the USA losing the Cold War and believed that the USSR was in a strong position to gain support in the **third world**. He built up the US armed forces and was determined that the USA should send a man to the moon by 1970.

In the Cuban Missile Crisis historians have traditionally seen him as a hard liner, who in the last resort was ready to risk war, but in fact secret tape recordings of his key advisory body, which were taken with the permission of Kennedy during the crisis, show that he took the lead in pressing for a compromise.

Key term

Third world
States that had for the most part been former colonies, but which were now free and independent of both the USSR and the West.

Key question
How important was the construction of the Berlin Wall for the Soviet bloc?

The importance of the Berlin Wall

The first Berlin crisis ended in complete failure for Stalin. Can it be argued that the second crisis was also a failure for Khrushchev? Like Stalin he had failed to force the Western allies to withdraw their troops from West Berlin or to compel them to negotiate peace treaties with the two German states. On the other hand, with the construction of the Berlin Wall he had achieved a limited but important success for Soviet policies. By tolerating it, the Western powers in effect recognised East Germany. The Wall both consolidated the GDR and ensured that the Soviet Union was still responsible for maintaining international access to West Berlin. In

1992 one former high-ranking Soviet official explained to a US historian that:

> After the building of the Wall, the signing of a separate treaty with the GDR was not necessary. All issues that needed to be resolved were resolved. Ulbricht saw in a peace treaty a way to receive international recognition. For us, international recognition was important, but not the most important [thing]. We saw this would happen no matter what; it was a question of time. After the borders were closed there would be no other choice than for the West to recognize the GDR. And that is what happened.

Learning to live with the Berlin Wall 1961–3

The prolonged crisis over Berlin effectively ended with the Wall, although this was not immediately obvious at the time. The Soviet Union renewed nuclear testing and on 30 October 1961 exploded an enormous bomb of over 50 megatons, which it was calculated could destroy a US state the size of Maryland. There was also continued tension along the Wall in Berlin. US troops were ostentatiously practising tearing down simulated walls, while on 27 October Soviet and US tanks stood almost muzzle to muzzle for several hours at **Checkpoint Charlie**. Khrushchev was determined to keep up the pressure on West Berlin. In October, for instance, he told the Soviet Foreign Minister, Gromyko, and the Polish leader, Gomulka, that 'we should … exploit the weakness of the enemy. We should strive to remove the official representatives from West Berlin'.

In a series of talks with the Soviet leaders over the next year Kennedy attempted to lower the tension by exploring the possibility of an agreement over Berlin, which would guarantee the rights of the Western allies, while recognising what he called the 'legitimate interests of others'. By this, of course, he meant the USSR and GDR. Inevitably Adenauer regarded these negotiations with great suspicion and dreaded that Kennedy would end up sacrificing West Berlin. Consequently he drew even closer to Gaullist France, signing in January 1963 the Franco-German Treaty of Friendship and supporting the French veto on Britain's application to join the EEC (see page 115).

In October 1962 the Cuban Crisis (see below) temporarily forced the Berlin question into second place and rallied the Western powers around Kennedy. After the crisis, discussions on Berlin continued, but the need to find a settlement was no longer so urgent. Having come so close to nuclear war in Cuba, Khrushchev shied away from another confrontation in Berlin and accepted that for the time being the Wall had consolidated the GDR. The Soviet government also began to reassess its policies and priorities in light of the lessons learnt in the Cuban missile Crisis. As far as they affected Europe these policies will be analysed in Chapter 7.

Key question
Why, despite the construction of the Berlin Wall, did tension remain high in Europe until 1963?

Checkpoint Charlie One of the few official crossing points between East and West Berlin. It is now a museum.

Key term

Summary diagram: Berlin Crisis 1958–61

Causes
- Berlin remained an unresolved issue
- East Germans could escape through Berlin to the West
- West vulnerable and could be put under pressure to make concessions

November 1958; Khrushchev issues Berlin Ultimatum:
- West Berlin to become a free city
- Peace treaty to be signed with both German states

Failure of Geneva and Paris Conferences 1959 and 1960

Threatened collapse of GDR persuaded Khrushchev to agree to sealing East Berlin frontier, August 1961

Key terms

Long peace
A period of international stability brought about by the nuclear balance between the USA and the USSR.

Guerrilla war
A war fought by small groups of irregular troops. The term comes from the Spanish resistance to Napoleon in the early nineteenth century.

4 | The Cuban Missile Crisis 1962

The US historian John Gaddis wrote in 1997 that the crisis over Cuba was:

> the only episode after World War II in which each of the major areas of Soviet–American competition intersected: the nuclear arms race to be sure, but also conflicting ideological aspirations, 'third world rivalries', relations with allies, the domestic political implications of foreign policy, the personalities of individual leaders. The crisis was a kind of funnel – a historical singularity if you like – into which everything suddenly tumbled and got mixed together. Fortunately no black hole lured at the other end....

Although the Cuban Missile Crisis was a direct confrontation between the USA and the USSR, involving neither NATO nor the Warsaw Pact, it had a profound impact on the Cold War in Europe. Both sides came to the brink of war but drew back from a nuclear conflict. After the crisis the Cold War changed, and gradually evolved into what some historians call the '**long peace**'.

The causes of the crisis

Key question
What were the origins of the Cuban Missile Crisis?

In the 1950s the Soviets had viewed South America as essentially a US sphere of interest. They had not protested when the CIA intervened in 1954 to topple the allegedly pro-Communist President Arbrenz in Guatamala. However, the USA's domination did cause a growing resentment among South American intellectuals and nationalists, and was one of the factors that influenced Fidel Castro to launch a **guerrilla war** against the government of Fulgencio Batista in Cuba in December 1956. By

January 1959, contrary to expectations, his forces were able to take over the government in Havana.

At this stage Castro was an anti-American nationalist but not a Communist. It was probably growing opposition from the Cuban middle classes to his economic policies and increasing US hostility to his attempt to adopt a policy of non-alignment in the Cold War that drove him into adopting Marxism–Leninism (see page 3). Friction with the USA was also caused by his seizure of property owned by the major US firms, particularly the United Fruit Company.

As relations with the USA deteriorated during the summer of 1959, Castro began to put out feelers towards Moscow, and in February 1960 he invited Anastas Mikoyan, Deputy Chairman of the Soviet Council of Ministers, to visit Havana. Mikoyan returned to Moscow with a glowing account of the Cuban revolution, which reminded him of the heroic early days of the Russian Revolution. In July, Khrushchev threatened the USA with a missile attack if it dared invade Cuba and suggested that Washington declare the end of the **Monroe Doctrine**.

Key date

Castro set up a revolutionary government in Cuba: January 1959

Key term

Monroe Doctrine
The doctrine formulated by President Monroe of the USA (1817–25) that the European powers should not intervene on the US continent.

Profile: Fidel Castro 1926–

1926		– Born into a wealthy farming family in Cuba
1945–50		– As a student, he became involved in anti-American nationalist politics
1955		– Exiled to Mexico where he founded the 26th July Movement
1956	December	– Landed in Cuba
1959	January	– Entered Havana
	February	– Became President
	May	– In response to US ban on Cuban sugar, Castro began to nationalise US property and businesses
1961	April	– Failure of the Bay of Pigs invasion
	December	– Declared that he was a Marxist–Leninist
1962	July	– Joint Cuban–Soviet agreement on deployment of missiles on Cuba
	October	– Cuban Missile Crisis came to a head
1975–7		– Deployed Cuban troops in Angola and Ethiopia
1989		– Critical of Gorbachev's economic reforms
1990–2008		– Remained in power despite collapse of Communism and the USSR

Castro's leadership was, to a great extent, unchallenged. His supporters naturally claimed that this was because he improved the living conditions of the population, while his opponents argued that he held power as a result of repression and the imprisonment of dissidents. In 2008 Castro's brother Raoul took over as President.

Key question
Why did the
US-backed invasion
of Cuba fail?

The Bay of Pigs incident

The growing links between Cuba and the USSR persuaded
Eisenhower to authorise the CIA to start planning Castro's
removal. In April 1961, four months after Kennedy came to
power, a force of about 1400 Cuban exiles landed south of
Havana at Playa Giron on the Bay of Pigs. It was hoped that this
would spark off a popular uprising against Castro, but Castro in
anticipation of such a move imprisoned thousands of suspects. At
the last moment Kennedy also cancelled both bombing raids by
the US airforce and a landing by US marines. Consequently,
Castro had no trouble in defeating the invasion. As John Gaddis
has observed, the Bay of Pigs incident was 'a monumental disaster
for the United States ... comparable only to the humiliation the
British and French had suffered at Suez five years earlier' (see
pages 111–13).

Although Khrushchev was delighted by this humiliation, he
nevertheless saw it as a warning that the Americans would
inevitably try again to topple Castro. In his memoirs he later
wrote:

> We welcomed Castro's victory of course, but at the same time we
> were quite certain that the invasion was only the beginning and that
> the Americans would not let Cuba alone ... There are infinite
> opportunities for invasion, especially if the invader has naval
> artillery and air support.

Khrushchev was certainly correct. The CIA continued to plan
Castro's assassination and large-scale military manoeuvres took
place in the Caribbean in the spring and summer of 1962.

The Soviet decision to place missiles on Cuba

Key question
Why did Khrushchev
decide to site
medium-range Soviet
missiles on Cuba?

In August 1962 Khrushchev negotiated the secret Soviet Cuban
Accord with Castro. Over the next few weeks the Soviets began
secretly to deploy medium-range nuclear missiles on Cuba. These
would be defended by 40,000 Soviet troops, anti-aircraft batteries,
short-range battlefield rockets and MIG-21 fighter planes.

There were two key reasons for this highly dangerous operation:

Missile gap
Where one side has
a temporary lead
over the other in
nuclear weapons.

Key term

- To gain a base from which the USA could be threatened by
medium-range Soviet missiles. This would correct the strategic
imbalance caused by the construction of US missile bases in
Turkey and Western Europe and go some way towards closing
the **missile gap** between the USSR and the USA.
- Castro also wanted to defend the revolution in Cuba. The
Soviets saw the revolution as a major success for
Marxism–Leninism, and its defeat would, as Mikoyan told
Castro, 'throw back the revolutionary movement in many
countries'.

On 4 October the Soviet ship *Indigirka* arrived at the port of Mariel in Cuba with enough nuclear warheads to equip at least 158 strategic and nuclear weapons.

The crisis comes to a head: 14–28 October 1962

On 14 October a US U2 spy plane discovered the missiles. President Kennedy was informed two days later and initially the news was kept quiet from the US public. The options open to the US government were explored by a small crisis committee, the **EXComm**:

Key question
Why did the Cuban Crisis not result in war between the USA and the USSR?

- Launching a surprise air attack was ruled out as too risky.
- An appeal to the United Nations was ruled out as it would take too long, especially as further reconnaissance flights indicated that the Soviets already had four medium-range missile sites operational.
- Plans were drawn up for a possible invasion of Cuba by US forces.
- An ultimatum was to be sent to Moscow demanding that the missiles be withdrawn.

Cuban Missile Crisis: October 1962

Key date

In the meantime the US navy set up a quarantine zone 800 miles from the Cuban coast. Once they entered this area Soviet ships would be stopped and searched for weapons due to be delivered to Cuba. On the advice of the British Ambassador this was reduced to 500 miles.

On 22 October Kennedy announced on US television the news of the existence of Soviet missiles on Cuba and that he had ordered the naval blockade of the island. He also made clear that if any nuclear missile was fired from Cuba, he would order a massive nuclear attack on the USSR. Khrushchev initially was determined to complete the missile sites in Cuba and ordered the Soviet ships to challenge the blockade. It looked as though a naval confrontation was inevitable.

Nevertheless on 26 October, in response to an appeal for negotiations from U. Thant, the Secretary-General of the United Nations, and fearing an imminent US air attack on Cuba, Khrushchev informed the Americans that he would withdraw the missiles. In return he demanded a guarantee that the US would not invade Cuba. However, once he realised that this made him look weak in the eyes of his political rivals, in a second message he insisted that the removal of missiles from Cuba was dependent on the dismantling of US **Jupiter missile** bases in Turkey. To appease US public opinion Kennedy responded to the first letter officially, but secretly he agreed to remove the 15 Jupiter missiles from Turkey once the Cuban Crisis was over. He stressed, however, that if the Soviets made this offer public, it would be withdrawn.

Effectively this ended the crisis, and all the Soviet missiles and troops were withdrawn from Cuba by 20 November.

EXComm
The Executive Committee of the US National Security Council.

Jupiter missile
A liquid-fuelled, surface-deployed missile, which was already out of date by 1962.

Key terms

Key question
What had Khrushchev achieved?

The consequences of the crisis

The Cuban Missile Crisis was a mixed success for the USSR:

- Khrushchev had achieved a US guarantee that it would not invade Cuba.
- He also received promises that the Jupiter missiles would be withdrawn from Turkey.
- But his ambition of achieving nuclear parity with the USA had failed.
- The world had witnessed Soviet ships turning back, apparently retreating before US power.

The confrontation emphasised how the Cold War had, for the time being at least, become bipolar. Britain, for instance, had given Washington advice, but otherwise had played no role in the crisis at all. Both the USA and the USSR were determined to avoid the repeat of such a confrontation with its attendant dangers of nuclear war and began to give priority to plans for controlling the proliferation of nuclear weapons and their testing (see page 137). In 1963, a **hotline** was established which linked by **telex** the Kremlin and the White House. The intention behind this was that both leaders could directly contact each other and stop misunderstandings that could lead to nuclear war.

Key terms

Hotline
A direct telegraphic link between Kennedy and Khrushchev, and their successors.

Telex
An international communications system with printed messages transmitted by teleprinters using the public telephone network.

Summary diagram: The Cuban Missile Crisis

Causes
- Castro's revolution in Cuba
- Deterioration in US–Cuba relations
- Failure of Bay of Pigs invasion
- August 1962: secret Soviet account signed: (a) medium-range missiles installed and (b) defended by Soviet troops, rockets and planes

US reaction when U2 plane discovers missile pads on 14 October

- Kennedy's ultimatum, 22 October
  - quarantine announced
  - massive nuclear retaliation by USA on USSR if missiles are fired from Cuba

Khrushchev's reaction – two conflicting messages

- Promises to withdraw from Cuba provided USA does not invade Cuba
- Withdrawal to depend on later dismantling of Jupiter missiles in Turkey

Consequences

Kennedy accepted first publicly, but privately agreed to the second message

5 | Assessment: The 'Second Cold War'

Deterioration in East–West relations

In 1955 it seemed that the Cold War in Europe, if not over, had at least stabilised. The Soviets had pulled out of Austria (see page 100) and there was much talk about the Geneva spirit. Yet over the next six years no progress was made towards *détente*, as relations between the Warsaw Pact states and the North Atlantic Alliance deteriorated to a level not seen since the Berlin Blockade of 1948–9. Do the reasons for this lie with Khrushchev or were there deeper causes?

A major cause of European instability was the failure of the USSR to set up in Eastern Europe what the Americans managed to create in Western Europe: 'an empire by invitation' (see page 103). The destalinisation policies of 1953–6 were attempts to create more popular regimes that did not depend on terror and the Red Army to survive, and to allow the peoples of Eastern Europe some input into influencing their own politics. Yet the Polish riots and the Hungarian revolt of 1956 showed how hard it was to get the balance between liberalisation and the maintenance of essential control. This was to remain one of the main dilemmas facing the Soviet leadership for the next 33 years.

To the brink and back?

Until 1961 the division of Germany and the unsolved problem of Berlin also remained a major destabilising factor in Europe. The root of the problem was the chronic economic weakness of East Germany, which could only be remedied by closing the inner Berlin frontier. This would prevent the flight of desperately needed skilled workers from East to West where they could earn more money. However, this measure would violate the Potsdam Agreement (see pages 38–41) and cause a major crisis involving the USA and its allies. Both German states depended for their existence on their superpower protector. As neither the USA nor the USSR could allow its part of Germany to collapse or be absorbed by the rival bloc, the two German leaders, Ulbricht and Adenauer, had at times immense influence over the foreign policy of Moscow and Washington, respectively. Thus, Adenauer did much to stop Eisenhower from effectively exploring the possibilities of a Berlin settlement in the period 1958–60, while recent research by Hope Harrison has shown that it was pressure from Ulbricht that finally propelled Khrushchev into building the Berlin Wall.

The crises of 1956 and 1958–61 were triggered by instabilities within the Soviet bloc and Central Europe, but they were made far more dangerous by Khrushchev's high-risk 'nuclear diplomacy'. In 1956, by threatening to bombard Britain, France and Israel with nuclear missiles, even when in reality the USSR had not yet developed the military capacity to do this, he was able to pose as the saviour of Egypt. He did not hesitate to use the ultimate threat of nuclear weapons as a bargaining counter in both the Berlin and Cuba crises. Yet, as we have seen, much of

Key question
How accurate is it to describe the whole period 1956–63 as the 'Second Cold War'?

Key question
How near to war did the USA and USSR come during the years 1958–62?

this was only 'bluff and bluster'. In that sense Khrushchev very much presided over a period of acute tension which perhaps could be called a Second Cold War.

In other ways, however, the Khrushchev years set the pattern for the next three decades in Europe. The Berlin Wall, however cruel in that it divided a city and so prevented families and friends from seeing each other, did at last stabilise the GDR and with it Central Europe. It also enabled both superpowers, as Gaddis has put it, to 'break loose' from their German allies and explore the possibility of *détente* in Europe. Paradoxically Khrushchev was also the father of *détente*. Despite his brinkmanship over Berlin and Cuba he aimed for peaceful economic and ideological competition with the West. After the Cuban crisis, Soviet policy settled down, as we shall see in the next chapter, to a dual policy of achieving *détente* in Europe and nuclear equality with the USA.

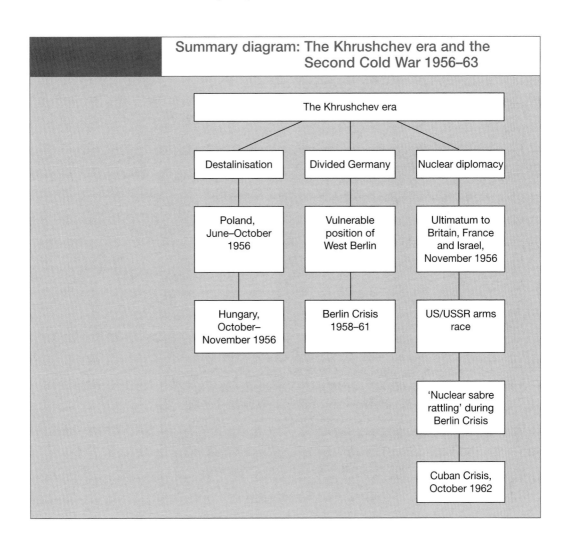

Summary diagram: The Khrushchev era and the Second Cold War 1956–63

Study Guide: AS Questions

In the style of OCR

1. If Khrushchev was really aiming at peaceful competition with the Western powers and destalinisation in Eastern Europe, why was his European policy often so aggressive? (50 marks)

2. Why did the Hungarian uprising of 1956 and the Berlin Crisis of 1958–61 not lead to war? (50 marks)

Exam tips

The cross-references are intended to take you straight to the material that will help you to answer the questions.

These are more wide-ranging essay questions, which require a considerable amount of planning before you write them out. In the introduction you should formulate clearly and briefly your main arguments and then develop each of them in separate paragraphs in the rest of your essay.

1. • First of all show what Khrushchev understood by peaceful competition: he did not want war but believed that the Soviet bloc would eventually overtake the West and also attract overwhelming support from the third world (page 109).

   • He was, however, often impulsive and opportunist and would take risks to strengthen the USSR's bargaining position. Here you will need to explain how he used 'nuclear diplomacy' to frighten the Western powers and to try to squeeze concessions from them (page 113).

   • The main part of the essay will be an analysis of the crisis of destalinisation in 1956 and the Berlin Crisis of 1958–61, which is essentially what the question means by 'aggressive policies' (pages 108–13 and 117–22).

   • You will also need to explain how Khrushchev's attempt to destalinise, win back Tito and reform the structure of control within the Soviet bloc led first to the Poznan riots and then to the Hungarian revolt, which he had little option but to crush (pages 108–13).

   • In the much more complicated Berlin Crisis his aims were also to a certain extent defensive, but they were dangerously open ended and pursued in a way that created great tension. He wished to use the status of West Berlin as a lever to gain major concessions from the Western powers, which would go far towards solving the German problem in the interests of the USSR. In the end he achieved little apart from building the Berlin Wall (pages 116–21).

   • In your conclusion you could, however, stress that this was a defensive action that stopped the GDR from collapsing (page 120).

2. The next question again refers to the two great crises of the Khrushchev period. It is simply put, but you need to plan your answer carefully before writing it out:
   - You need to show that the Western powers had no intention of intervening to help the Hungarians in 1956. It is true that the Suez Crisis complicated the issue, but Eisenhower was particularly careful not to provoke the Soviets over an issue that might lead to war. He accepted that Hungary and Poland were in the Soviet sphere of influence (pages 112–13).
   - Similarly, Britain and the USA had no desire to pull down the Berlin Wall in 1961, and were anxious to negotiate a settlement that would preserve the rights of the Western allies while recognising Soviet and GDR interests (page 122).
   - You must again explore how much of Khrushchev's 'nuclear diplomacy' was in fact based on bluff (page 113).

Study Guide: A2 Questions

In the style of AQA

To what extent was the Cuban Missile Crisis a conflict of
personalities?   (45 marks)

> ### *Exam tips*
>
> This question is asking you to consider the factors that created the
> Cuban Missile Crisis and a good starting point would be to make a
> list of these. You might include:
>
> *   ideological differences
> *   a clash of alliance systems
> *   the nuclear arms race
> *   personality clashes and pride
> *   domestic anxieties.
>
> From such a list you can see that the crisis was certainly more than
> a personality clash. Therefore, although you will need to focus on
> this issue in your answer, you may wish to stress an alternative
> factor as the 'main' cause and you will almost certainly want to show
> how the various factors interlinked to create the crisis. The order in
> which you address these and perhaps other points is your choice,
> but you will need to provide evidence to support your views.

In the style of Edexcel

How far was the nuclear arms race a threat to world peace in the years 1949–62? (40 marks)

Source: Edexcel specimen paper, 2007

Exam tips

The cross-references are intended to take you straight to the material that will help you to answer the question.

This essay question requires some knowledge of the nature and extent of the arms race, but not an extensive description of it. What is chiefly required is an assessment of its influence. Was it a threat? If so, how near did the powers come to open conflict because of it?

- For the build-up of nuclear weapons by the two blocs, the threat this posed and the reactions provoked by it, see pages 114–15.
- For Khrushchev's high-risk nuclear diplomacy in 1956 and 1958–61 and the extent to which this was bluff, see pages 113–15, 119 and 128–9.

But for occasions where crises and conflict developed see: tensions over Korea (pages 86–7); Hungary (page 111); Suez (page 111); and Berlin (page 116). These will need to be linked to the question if you decide to use them. Were they caused by the arms race; were they accompanied by the threat of the use of nuclear weapons?

The key crisis you will need to examine is that over Cuba (pages 123–7). How seriously was world peace threatened by this? And what is your conclusion consequently about the threat of nuclear arms race over the whole period 1949–62?

7 The 'Long Peace' in Europe 1963–91

POINTS TO CONSIDER
One of the most important consequences of the Cuban
Missile Crisis was the conviction in both Moscow and
Washington that there would be no winners in an all-out
nuclear war. Both sides were therefore ready to pursue a
policy of *détente* in Europe, but the Cold War still continued.
It was only in the late 1980s that economic pressures forced
the USSR to end the Cold War. These themes are studied in
this chapter under the following headings:

- The road to *détente* 1963–9
- *Ostpolitik*
- The Helsinki Accord
- The 'New Cold War' 1979–85
- The end of the Cold War in Europe 1983–91
- The reunification of Germany

Key dates

1963	August 5	Test Ban Treaty
1964	October 15	Fall of Khrushchev
1965	February 7	US bombing of North Vietnam began
1968	August 21–7	Invasion of Czechoslovakia
	July	Non-proliferation Treaty
1969	September 28	Brandt became Chancellor of FRG
1970	August 12	USSR–FRG Moscow Treaty
	December 7	Warsaw Treaty
1971	September 3	Four Power Treaty on Berlin
1972	May	SALT I
	December 21	Basic Treaty between FRG and GDR
1974	July	SALT II negotiations
1975	August 1	Helsinki Final Act
1979	December 27	Soviet invasion of Afghanistan
1980	December 13	Martial law declared in Poland
1982	November	Brezhnev succeeded by Andropov
1985	March 12	Gorbachev became USSR Party Leader
1986	October 2	USSR–USA summit at Reykjavik
1989	June	Elections in Poland
	September	Hungary allowed GDR citizens through frontier to Austria
	November 9	Berlin Wall breached
1990	October 3	Germany reunified
1991	December 26	USSR formally dissolved

1 | The Road to *Détente* 1963–9

After the Cuban missile crisis the nature of the Cold War in Europe changed. A new period of stability emerged, which has sometimes been called 'the long peace'. Both the two superpowers and the Western European states sought *détente* in Europe, although they all interpreted the meaning of *détente* differently. The Americans were heavily involved in the Vietnam War, and wanted *détente* to stabilise Europe and restrain the USSR, while the USSR was also facing a growing challenge from China. Consequently, it hoped that *détente* would lead Washington and its allies permanently to accept the postwar division of Europe, and to agree to something approaching nuclear parity between the USA and USSR. For the French *détente* was a way of undermining the influence of both superpowers in Europe so that the individual European states could regain their freedom, while for the West Germans it was an essential precondition for remaining in contact with and helping their fellow citizens in the GDR.

> ### The distracted superpowers
> *The USSR and China*
> Sino-Soviet relations had been deteriorating since the late 1950s. The Chinese were highly critical of Khrushchev's belief in peaceful competition between the USA and USSR and scornful of his apparent failure in Cuba. Fearing that China might risk a nuclear war against the USA, which would also involve the USSR, Khrushchev had refused to carry out his promises of supplying China with nuclear weapons. Throughout the 1960s Soviet–Chinese relations rapidly grew worse. In 1966 the Soviet and Chinese Communist parties, which should have had much in common, severed all **fraternal links**, and the USSR even began to target some of its missiles on China. In 1969 there were large-scale border clashes along the Sino-Soviet frontier.
>
> *The USA and Vietnam*
> At the same time the USA became ever more deeply involved in Vietnam. From 1945 to 1954 the French had been involved in a bitter war to re-establish their control over their former colony, Indo-China. In May 1954 the French were defeated at Dien Bien Phu and were forced to surrender. At the Geneva Conference in July of that year (see page 100) Vietnam was divided along the 17th Parallel. North Vietnam was Communist, while the south was under Dinh Diem, a Catholic and Vietnamese nationalist. To stop the Communists in the North from taking over South Vietnam the USA committed an increasing number of 'military advisers'. By 1966 there were 400,000 US troops in Vietnam. By 1968 it had become clear that the Americans were losing the war, but it was not until 1973 that the last soldiers finally left and President Nixon was able to negotiate a ceasefire. In 1975 the Communists took over South Vietnam, and both parts of the country were reunited.

Key question *(Key question)*
Why did the Americans and Soviets seek *détente*?

US bombing of North Vietnam began: 7 February 1965 *(Key date)*

Fraternal links *(Key term)*
'Brotherly' links between two Communist parties that should theoretically have much in common.

Controlling the development of nuclear weapons

Key question
How successful were the attempts to control the development of nuclear weapons?

Between 1963 and 1973 the following agreements were negotiated, which were aimed at stopping the spread of nuclear weapons and making the world a safer place:

Key dates
Test Ban Treaty: 5 August 1963

Non-proliferation Treaty: July 1968

SALT I: May 1972

Negotiations on SALT II Treaty started: July 1974

- The Test Ban Treaty of 1963, signed by Britain, the USSR and the USA banning nuclear tests in the atmosphere, under water and in outer space, was negotiated on the assumption that the only two nuclear powers who counted were the USSR and USA. It was, however, rejected by both France and China, whose leaders went on to develop their own nuclear weapons.
- In July 1968 Britain, the USA and USSR signed the Non-proliferation Treaty, in which they pledged themselves not to transfer nuclear weapons to other countries or to assist other states to manufacture them. In November 1969 they were joined by West Germany.
- In 1970 US and Soviet experts began the Strategic Arms Limitation Talks (SALT) in Vienna. In May 1972 President Nixon and the Soviet leader Leonid Brezhnev signed the SALT I agreement in Moscow. It consisted of two parts:
  - there was to be a five-year freeze on the construction of missile launchers and a freeze on intercontinental and submarine launched ballistic missiles and long-range bombers. President Nixon accepted that the Soviets should have a greater number of missiles than the USA as the Americans had had a superiority in MIRVs, multiple independently targetable re-entry vehicles (see page 11), which were capable of hitting more than one target at a time.
  - The second part of the treaty concerned defence against missiles. Both sides were allowed only two **anti-ballistic screens** one for their capital cities, Washington and Moscow, and one for their main missile sites. Both sides were left almost defenceless against attack. Hence MAD – mutually assured destruction (see page 11).

Key term
Anti-ballistic screens
Protection provided by rocket launching pads.

- In July 1974 the USA and USSR agreed that negotiations should start for a SALT II treaty, which would impose permanent limitations on nuclear weapons. It was eventually concluded in June 1979 when President Carter and Brezhnev signed the SALT II Treaty in Vienna. The numbers of missile launchers and MIRV rocket warheads for both sides were further limited. However, the treaty was never ratified by the US Senate as a result of the invasion of Afghanistan (see page 148).

Developments in Western Europe 1964–8

Key question
How did the West European states attempt to pursue a policy of *détente* with the USSR?

The Test Ban Treaty of 1963 and the Nuclear Non-proliferation Treaty in 1968 were the most significant achievements in the early period of *détente*. These agreements were welcome in Western Europe, but essentially they assumed a world divided into two blocs led by their respective superpower.

By 1968, however, the Vietnam War was causing a rising wave of anti-Americanism. The USA was both failing to win the war

Profile: Leonid Brezhnev 1906–82

1906	June 12	– Born in the Ukraine
1931		– Joined the Communist Party
1941–54		– Political Commissar attached to the Soviet army
1950		– Deputy of the Supreme Soviet
1952		– Joined the Politburo
1963		– Involved in plot to oust Khrushchev
1964		– After Khrushchev's fall, became First Secretary of the Russian Communist Party
1966		– Appointed General Secretary
1968	August	– Ordered occupation of Czechoslovakia by Warsaw Pact forces
1972		– Initiated *détente* with the USA
1975		– Signed Helsinki Pact
1979		– Decided to intervene in Afghanistan
1982	November 10	– Died

Brezhnev was a member of the first generation to grow up in Russia without having participated as an adult in the Russian Revolution. He gained his first experiences as a Communist official during the Stalinist era. He first met Khrushchev in 1931 and became one of his favourites. After Stalin's death he backed Khrushchev in his successful attempts to remove the Stalinist old guard from office. Up to the early 1960s he remained loyal to Khrushchev but after the Cuban Missile Crisis he helped to remove him from office in 1964. He had supported Khrushchev's more liberal policies but once in power he developed an increasingly conservative and repressive domestic policy. Abroad he pursued *détente* with the USA but also gave assistance to friendly regimes in Africa, Asia and the Middle East. In 1979 he committed Soviet troops to help prop up the socialist government in Afghanistan.

and, as a result of its ruthless but ineffective military tactics, losing its position as the moral leader of the West. Its European allies rejected President Johnston's argument that the war was a vital part of the **global confrontation** with Communism, and instead concentrated on easing tensions within Europe. This task was made easier by the fall of Khrushchev in October 1964 and his replacement by Brezhnev and Kosygin. Brezhnev, who rapidly emerged as the key figure in the USSR, was less erratic than Khrushchev and appeared to be more of a conciliator and **consensus** seeker, with whom the West European leaders thought they could negotiate.

Key question
Why did relations deteriorate between France and the USA?

Bloc mentality
A state of mind brought about by being a member of one of the two sides in the Cold War.

Trade missions
Organisations to promote trade between states.

Ostpolitik
West Germany's policy towards Eastern Europe, which involved recognition of the GDR and the postwar boundaries in Eastern Europe.

Key terms

Key question
What was the US reaction to the assertiveness of the Western European states?

France's withdrawal from NATO

Potentially the disagreements over the Vietnam War and the increasing assertiveness of the West European states could have destroyed NATO and led to a US withdrawal from Western Europe. De Gaulle, the French President, took the lead in the attack on US influence in Western Europe. In 1963 he vetoed Britain's application to join the EEC, on the grounds that Britain was still too pro-American, and three years later he both withdrew French forces from NATO and expelled its headquarters from Paris. He followed this up with a visit to the USSR, where he announced that the European states should liberate themselves from the '**bloc mentality**' of the Cold War. He also did all he could to weaken the dollar at a time when the USA was beginning to come under financial pressure as a result of the costs of the Vietnam War.

The beginnings of *Ostpolitik*

The West Germans were meanwhile cautiously beginning to put out feelers to Eastern Europe by setting up **trade missions** in Yugoslavia and Romania. *Ostpolitik* took on a more definite shape when the Social Democrat leader, Willy Brandt, became Foreign Minister in December 1966. The key to his policy was that German unification was a long-term goal that could only gradually be reached within the context of a European *détente*.

The US reaction

Given the prosperity of Western Europe and its refusal to assist the Americans in Vietnam, and the determination of its leading states to pursue their own ways to *détente*, it was not surprising that in 1967 a US Senator, Michael Mansfield, put forward a motion in Congress urging the withdrawal of the majority of US troops from Europe. This was defeated only by 49 votes. Both to persuade Congress to continue to support the US military involvement in Europe and to prevent his allies from following the French example and leaving NATO, President Johnson committed himself to negotiate mutual and balanced force reductions with Moscow. These negotiations eventually led to the SALT I treaty in 1972 (see page 137).

The Hamel Report

In December 1967 a high-powered NATO committee chaired by the Belgian Foreign Minister Pierre Hamel drew up a report, which committed NATO not only to defending Western Europe, but also to reaching a *détente* with the Warsaw Pact states. It stressed that:

Collective defence
The agreement of a group of nations to form an alliance such as NATO or the Warsaw Pact for mutual protection.

Key term

Collective defence is a stabilising factor in world politics. It is the necessary condition for effective policies directed towards a greater relaxation of tensions. The way to peace and stability in Europe rests in particular on the use of the Alliance constructively in the interests of *détente*. The participation of the USSR and USA will be necessary to achieve a settlement of the political problems in Europe.

The Hamel Report redefined NATO's role in the age of *détente* and prevented the political fall-out from the Vietnam War destroying the Western alliance.

Divisions within the Warsaw Pact

The Soviet retreat from Cuba, the growing atmosphere of *détente* and the Sino-Soviet split all combined to weaken Soviet control over Eastern Europe and provide some opportunities for the satellite states to pursue their own policies. Poland, for instance, wished to expand trade with the West, while Romania wanted to establish better relations with the FRG. In an attempt to stop these independent initiatives, the Warsaw Pact issued in 1966 the Bucharest Declaration, which tried to define what the whole Soviet bloc wanted to achieve through *détente*. This called for:

Key question
How divided was the Warsaw Pact during the period 1963–9?

- the recognition of postwar frontiers in Eastern Europe
- the creation of a new European security system
- a veto on nuclear weapons for West Germany
- a programme for economic, scientific and technical co-operation between East and West.

The Prague Spring

The Soviet government's efforts to consolidate its control over Eastern Europe and to co-ordinate the foreign and military policies of the Warsaw Pact suffered a serious setback when in January 1968 Alexander Dubcek became the First Secretary of the Czech Communist Party. Like Nagy in Hungary in 1956 (see page 111), he attempted to create a socialist system that would be based on the consent of the people, rather than forced on them by the USSR as had been the case in Eastern Europe since the late 1940s.

Key question
Why was the Prague Spring a threat to Soviet control of Eastern Europe?

Invasion of Czechoslovakia: 21–7 August 1968

Key date

In April 1968 he unveiled his programme for democratic change and modernisation of the economy, which marked the start of what was called the **Prague Spring**. In April the Czech Communists announced a new programme for 'a new profoundly democratic model of Czechoslovak socialism conforming to Czechoslovak conditions'. Like Gorbachev later in the USSR (see page 152) Dubcek wanted to preserve socialism, but increasingly public opinion began to press for the creation of a democracy based on the Western model. In June he abolished censorship, which led to a flood of anti-Soviet propaganda being published in Czechoslovakia.

Inevitably these developments began to worry Brezhnev and the other leaders of the Warsaw Pact, who after meeting on 15 July warned Dubcek that:

Prague Spring
The liberalisation process put into effect by Alexander Dubcek, the Czech Prime Minister. There were both economic reforms aimed at freeing the economy from unnecessary restrictions, and political reforms, which restored the freedom of speech and political pluralism (the existence of several political parties).

Key term

> We cannot reconcile ourselves … with the fact of hostile forces pushing your country off the road of socialism and creating a threat of tearing away Czechoslovakia from the socialist community. This is no longer only your concern. This is the common concern of all Communists and workers' parties and of states united by alliance co-operation and friendship. …

Although Dubcek reluctantly agreed to restore censorship, Brezhnev had no confidence that he would succeed and, during the night of 20–1 August, 20 divisions of Warsaw Pact troops provided by the USSR, Hungary, Poland, the GDR and Bulgaria invaded Czechoslovakia and terminated the Prague Spring. In November Brezhnev defended the invasion by again stressing that any threat to socialism in a Warsaw Pact country was also a threat to its allies. To counter this, collective intervention, as happened in Czechoslovakia, would be justified. This became known as the Brezhnev Doctrine and was only abandoned by Gorbachev in 1989.

Key question
Why was the Brezhnev Doctrine disastrous in the long term for the economy of the Soviet bloc?

Key terms

Centralised control of the economy
Control of a country's economy from the centre, as in Stalinist Russia.

Heavy industry
Coal, iron and steel production.

Gross national product
The total production of domestic industries combined with the earnings from exports, etc.

The economic consequences of the Brezhnev Doctrine

With the fall of Dubcek and the announcement of the Brezhnev Doctrine, economic experiments aimed at modernisation and increased economic competitiveness in the Soviet bloc were discouraged and gradually halted. There was, instead, a return to the Stalinist style of **centralised control of the economy** with its emphasis on **heavy industry**. For a time this did appear to work. *Détente* and *Ostpolitik* opened the way up for generous Western loans to the USSR and the satellite states, which helped to keep energy prices down and pay for massive industrial projects.

However, by the early 1980s the Eastern bloc economies were falling far behind the West. The total production of the USSR, for instance, was only 37 per cent of the **gross national product** of the USA. The Western European economies had been badly hit by the escalating rises in oil prices, which started in 1973, but they had responded to this challenge by modernising their economies and developing new industries and technologies. The USSR and its satellite states had failed to do this. They were therefore very vulnerable when faced with the triple crisis of inflation, rising oil prices and global economic depression in the early 1980s.

Soviet economic growth collapsed, just at the time when the USSR was trapped in a large-scale war in Afghanistan (see page 148) and the interest rates on US and West German loans increased significantly. This was the economic scenario that confronted Gorbachev when he came to power in 1985 and led to the collapse of Communism.

The invasion of Czechoslovakia was, as Michel Debré, the French Prime Minister, put it, 'a traffic accident on the road to *détente'*. It slowed down but did not halt progress. The elections of Richard Nixon to the US Presidency in November 1968 and of Willy Brandt to the West German Chancellorship in October 1969, with a mandate for his *Ostpolitik* policy, were soon to give it fresh impetus.

Summary diagram: The road to *détente*, 1963–9

The following factors made *détente* in Europe increasingly attractive:

After Cuba the desire by both the USA and USSR to control the spread of nuclear weapons

Both the USA and USSR wished for *détente* in Europe:
- The USA was involved in Vietnam
- The USSR faced the growth of Chinese power

The growing wish of the Western European states for *détente*

Increasing trade contacts between the Eastern and Western blocs

The acceptance by the West of the Brezhnev Doctrine after Warsaw Pact intervention in Czechoslovakia, August 1968

2 | *Ostpolitik*

Brandt negotiated a complex set of interlocking treaties which marked a major turning point in the Cold War. On one level his policy was primarily a matter of coming to terms with the postwar world. This, of course, involved the recognition of the GDR regime, although his whole strategy, by defusing the tense situation between the two Germanies, was also aimed at leaving the door ajar for future unification. *Ostpolitik* was not conducted in a vacuum. Brandt had gained the support of the USA and his NATO allies by emphasising that the FRG did not intend to quit NATO or the **European Community**. In the course of 1970–2, five sets of intricate and interdependent agreements were negotiated: the treaties between the FRG, USSR, Poland, Czechoslovakia and the GDR and then the Four Power Agreement on Berlin.

Key question
What were the aims of Brandt's *Ostpolitik* and how did he seek to achieve them?

Key date

Willy Brandt became Chancellor of the FRG: 28 September 1969

The Moscow Treaty 1970

No progress could be made in *Ostpolitik* until relations between the FRG and the USSR had improved. The FRG's signing of the Nuclear Non-proliferation Treaty in 1969, its readiness to increase technological and economic links with the USSR and willingness to agree to a European security conference, which Moscow hoped would confirm its postwar control over Eastern Europe, were all preliminary concessions that helped to pave the way for a treaty with Moscow.

   After prolonged and difficult negotiations the 'foundation stone of *Ostpolitik*', as the British historian A.J. Nicholls calls the

Key question
Why was the Moscow Treaty the key to Brandt's *Ostpolitik*?

Key date

USSR–FRG Treaty: 12 August 1970

Key terms

European Community
The European Economic Community (EEC) had changed its name to the European Community (EC).

Inviolable
Not to be attacked or violated.

Immutable
Unchangeable.

Ethnic Germans
German people who still lived in Poland. In 1945 much former German territory was given to Poland.

Moscow Treaty, was eventually signed on 12 August 1970 by Brandt and Brezhnev. In this the USSR and FRG declared that they had no territorial claims against any other state. The FRG recognised the 'non-violability' of both Poland's western frontier and the inner German frontier. In a second part of the treaty the FRG committed itself to negotiating treaties with Poland, the GDR and Czechoslovakia. While the FRG still did not officially recognise the GDR, it agreed to abandon the Hallstein Doctrine (see page 100) and accept that both Germanies would eventually become members of the United Nations.

The Soviets had in effect gained West German recognition of their European empire, yet this recognition was not unconditional. The West Germans also presented Brezhnev with a 'letter on German unity'. This stressed the FRG's right to work towards a state of peace in Europe in which 'the German people regains its unity in free self-determination'. Similarly, the term '**inviolable**' as applied to the Oder–Neisse line and the inner German frontier, rather than the preferred Soviet word '**immutable**', arguably kept the door open for a later peaceful revision of the frontier. Finally the ratification of the treaty was made dependent on a Four Power Agreement over Berlin.

The Warsaw and Prague Treaties

Negotiations with Poland ran parallel with the Moscow talks and were completed in December 1970. Both states recognised that they had no territorial demands on each other and that the Oder–Neisse line was 'inviolable'. Trade and financial assistance from the FRG were to be increased, while the **ethnic Germans** still within Poland were to be allowed to emigrate to West Germany.

In June 1973 a similar agreement was signed with Czechoslovakia, which specifically revoked the Munich Treaty of 1938.

Four power negotiations over Berlin

In March 1970, four power discussions began on the thorny problem of access to West Berlin. The involvement of Britain, France and the USA in these negotiations sent signals to both NATO and the Warsaw Pact that *Ostpolitik* would not lead to a weakening of the FRG's links with the West. The Western allies wanted a settlement underwritten by the USSR that would finally confirm West Berlin's links with the FRG and guarantee its freedom of access to the West.

At first the Soviets were anxious to avoid making too many concessions, but both their desire for a general European security conference and their reluctance to annoy President Nixon at a time when he was planning to improve relations with China made them more responsive to Western demands. When relations deteriorated between China and the USSR in 1969–70 (see page 136), President Nixon had sought to exploit the situation to the advantage of the West, and in 1972 he became the first US President to visit China.

Key date

Warsaw Treaty: 7 December 1970

Key question
To what extent did the Four Power Treaty on Berlin solve the Berlin problem?

Key date

Four Power Treaty on Berlin: 3 September 1971

The Berlin Wall in the 1970s.

The Four Power Treaty on Berlin, signed on 3 September 1971, was a 'milestone in the history of divided Berlin and divided Germany'. The Soviets conceded three vital principles:

- unimpeded traffic between West Berlin and the FRG
- recognition of West Berlin's ties with the FRG
- finally, the right for West Berliners to visit East Berlin.

In return Britain, France and the USA agreed that the Western sectors of Berlin were not legally part of the FRG, even if in practice they had been so ever since West Berlin adopted the FRG's constitution in 1950.

The Basic Treaty

Once the Moscow Treaty and the agreement on Berlin had been signed, the way was open for direct negotiations between the GDR and FRG. For the GDR an agreement with the FRG was not without risk. If successful, it would undoubtedly secure the GDR international recognition, but at the continued risk of closer

Key question
To what extent was the Basic Treaty a victory for the GDR and USSR?

Basic Treaty signed: 21 December 1972

Key date

Key terms

Magnetic social and economic forces of the West Brandt believed that the economy and way of life in West Germany was so strong that ultimately it would exert a magnet-like attraction on the GDR.

Social Democratisation Converting the Communist SED into a more moderate Western-style Social Democratic Party like the SPD in the FRG.

Rapprochement Establishing close relations between two states.

Transit traffic Traffic crossing through another state.

contact with the **magnetic social and economic forces of the West**. In July Brezhnev stressed to the somewhat sceptical Honecker, who had just replaced Ulbricht as the GDR leader, the solid advantages of the treaty for the GDR in that '[i]ts frontiers, its existence will be confirmed for all the world to see ... '. However, he also warned him that Brandt was aiming ultimately at the '**Social Democratisation**' of the GDR, and added: 'It ... must not come to a process of *rapprochement* between the FRG and the GDR. ... Concentrate everything on the all-sided strengthening of the GDR, as you call it'.

First of all a series of technical agreements on **transit traffic**, the rights of West Berliners to visit East Berlin, and on postal communications were concluded. Then the two states moved on to negotiate the more crucial Basic Treaty, which was signed in December 1972. In it the FRG recognised the GDR as an equal and sovereign state and also accepted that both states should be represented at the United Nations. The FRG did, however, stress that it still considered the people of the GDR to have a common German citizenship, and in a 'Letter Concerning German Unity', which it presented to East Berlin, it repeated its determination to work peacefully for German reunification.

The existence of the two Germanies now seemed to be a permanent fact confirmed by treaty. The two German states joined the United Nations in 1973. Within their respective blocs both the FRG and the GDR played increasingly important economic, military and political roles. Nothing, however, had changed the essential vulnerability of the GDR, whose very existence in the last resort still depended on Soviet bayonets, as the events of 1989–90 were to show (see pages 154–5).

Summary diagram: *Ostpolitik*

Willy Brandt needed to secure approval from the USA, USSR and NATO

Moscow Treaty, August 1970: FRG committed itself to recognising post-1945 frontiers

Berlin Treaty signed by the four occupying powers, September 1971: unimpeded transit rights to West Berlin recognised

Treaties with Poland, December 1970, and with Czechoslovakia, June 1973, confirmed 1945 borders

The Basic Treaty, December 1972: FRG gives up Hallstein Doctrine

3 | The Helsinki Accord

In July 1973 the conference on security and co-operation opened in Helsinki. A journalist, Robert Hutchings, has called it the 'centrepiece of Soviet and East European diplomacy' in the 1970s. Essentially the USSR wanted to persuade the West to recognise as permanent the territorial and political division of Europe made at Yalta (see pages 28–30), while stepping up economic, scientific and technological co-operation. It was anxious to exploit Western know-how and technology to modernise its economy.

The USA initially consented to holding the conference in return for a Soviet agreement on Berlin and the opening of negotiations at Vienna on mutual reductions of troops and armaments in Central Europe (see page 137). It also used the conference as a means to extract from the USSR concessions on **human rights**, which in time could bring about fundamental changes in the Soviet bloc and lead to a loosening of Soviet control over the satellites. The subsequent Helsinki Agreement marked the high point of *détente* and was signed on 1 August 1975 by 33 European states, Canada and the USA.

It was divided into three sections or 'baskets' as they were called:

- The first dealt with 'questions relating to security in Europe' and laid down a set of principles to guide the participating states in their relations with each other. These included peaceful settlement of disputes, non-interference in internal affairs of other states and the 'inviolability' of frontiers. Brezhnev had hoped initially that he would be able to negotiate a peace treaty permanently guaranteeing the new postwar frontiers, but under West German pressure, Henry Kissinger, the US Secretary of State, managed to persuade the Soviets to accept the eventual possibility of a 'peaceful change to frontiers'.
- 'Basket two' concerned co-operation in 'the field of economics, of science and technology and the environment'.
- 'Basket three' called for 'co-operation in humanitarian and other fields'. This meant expanding trade, tourism and cultural contacts between the two blocs, as well as promoting the reunion of families split by the Iron Curtain.
- Finally there was to be a follow-up conference two years later to work out further measures for European security and co-operation.

Who gained most from Helsinki?

At first glance perhaps it could be argued that Brezhnev had achieved Western recognition of the Soviet Empire and an end to all attempts to undermine it. Right-wing politicians, such as British Prime Minister Margaret Thatcher and US President

Key question
What were the terms of the Helsinki Accord?

Key date
Helsinki Final Act (or agreement): 1 August 1975

Human rights
Basic rights such as personal liberty and freedom from repression.

Key question
Did the East or West benefit more from the terms of the Helsinki Accord?

REP. DEM. ALLEMANDE

DANEMA

REP. FED. D'ALLEMAGNE

The two German leaders talking to each other during the Helsinki Conference, 30 July 1975. On the right is FRG Chancellor Helmut Schmidt, on the left the GDR leader Erich Honecker.

Key term

New Yalta
At the Yalta Conference in 1945 the USSR was given much of eastern Poland. A 'New Yalta' would merely confirm this.

Key question
How justified are historians in referring to the period 1979–85 as the 'New Cold War'?

Key term

Dissident
Critical of the official line taken by the state.

Ronald Reagan, saw it, to quote the latter, as a **'new Yalta'** placing 'the American seal of approval on the Soviet Empire in Eastern Europe'. While there was some truth in this, Helsinki's stress on human rights and fundamental freedoms, as well as the increased East–West contact it encouraged, did in the medium term contain the potential for undermining the unpopular Soviet-dominated regimes in Eastern Europe. The Helsinki Treaties have been called 'a time bomb planted in the heart of the Soviet Empire'.

4 | The 'Third' or 'New Cold War' 1979–85

The weakening of *détente*

International developments over the next decade were to confirm Nixon's comment that '*détente* does not mean the end of danger … *détente* is not the same as lasting peace'. The USSR intensified its efforts to intervene and support sympathetic regimes in the Middle East, Africa and Asia, while the new US President, Jimmy Carter, partly to deflect criticism of the Helsinki Treaty, made human rights in Eastern Europe one of the priorities of his foreign policy. In February 1977, much to the annoyance of Brezhnev, he championed the rights of the **dissident** Soviet physicist, Andrei Sakharov.

However, the first major blow to the new Helsinki spirit came when Moscow placed in 1976 SS-20 medium-range missiles in Eastern Europe. This led NATO to adopt in 1979 the controversial two-track policy, whereby the USA would deploy its own medium-range Pershing and Cruise missiles in Western Europe by 1983 if no agreement could first be reached with the USSR. In the face of the threat posed by the Soviet SS-20s and the events in Poland and Afghanistan (see below), Britain and West Germany agreed in 1983, despite mounting public protest from the **Greens** and the **political left**, to deploy the Pershing and Cruise missiles in West Germany.

The invasion of Afghanistan

The historian S.R. Ashton has observed that 'if a date has to be fixed for the onset of a New Cold War, it would be late 1979 when Soviet troops invaded Afghanistan'. Between 24 and 27 December 50,000 troops were airlifted to Kabul, the capital of Afghanistan, and within the next few weeks this number was increased by 85,000.

It can be argued that the Soviets were acting defensively as they had done in East Germany in 1953, Hungary in 1956 and Czechoslovakia in 1968 (see pages 96–8, 111 and 140–1). In April 1978 a *coup*, mounted independently of the USSR, by the local Afghan Communist Party had overthrown the monarchy. This regime then embarked on a radical reforming programme that provoked widespread opposition from the conservative Islamic forces in the countryside, threatening the existence of the new regime. Moscow became increasingly worried about the impact that this revolt would have on **Islamic fundamentalism** in the Muslim republics of southern Russia. If successful, it also feared that it would be another link in the **global encirclement** of the USSR at a time when China had just signed a peace treaty with the USSR and established diplomatic relations with the USA.

To the West, the invasion was seen as a new and highly threatening development in Soviet foreign policy, which would open up the possibility of further expansion southwards to the Indian Ocean and the Persian Gulf. The invasion was condemned in the United Nations by 104 countries. President Carter banned the export of grain and high-technology equipment to the USSR and the Senate refused to ratify the SALT II Treaty (see page 137). As a protest US athletes also boycotted the 1980 Olympic games.

The Solidarity crisis in Poland 1980–2

Poland was, in many ways, the key country in the Soviet bloc:

- militarily it provided the main route to the West
- it provided about one-third of the combined forces of the Warsaw Pact
- it had the largest population of the satellite states – 36 million.

Key terms

Greens
Those supporting the Green Party, whose stated aim is to protect the environment.

Political left
Left-wing parties such as the Labour Party in Britain or the Social Democrats in Germany.

Key question
What impact did the invasion of Afghanistan have on the outbreak of the 'New Cold War'?

Key date

Soviet invasion of Afghanistan: 27 December 1979

Key terms

Islamic fundamentalism
A very literal and traditional version of Islam that is hostile to Western civilisation, be it Marxist or Christian.

Global encirclement
Surrounded on a global scale.

Key question
What was the significance of the Solidarity crisis for East–West relations?

Key date

Martial law declared
in Poland:
13 December 1980

Key terms

**Solidarity
movement**
A movement that
originated in
support of the
strikes in the
Gdansk shipyards.

Martial law
Military rule
involving the
suspension of
normal civilian
government.

Consequently, any instability in Poland inevitably threatened the whole cohesion of the Soviet bloc. By the summer of 1980 Poland was facing a major economic crisis. The rising cost of oil forced up prices and the economic recession in the West meant that Poland had no market for its exports. The government had also failed to modernise the economy and make it more competitive.

In 1980 strikes broke out in the shipyards in Gdansk over the question of price increases. The government made far-reaching economic and political concessions, and in August recognised the **Solidarity movement** as an independent trade union. At first it tried to claim that this concession only applied to Gdansk, but this provoked a wave of labour unrest culminating in the threat of a national strike. Membership of Solidarity rose to nearly eight million, and it was supported by both Polish intellectuals and the Roman Catholic Church, which had been greatly strengthened by the election of a Polish Pope in 1978.

Both Brezhnev and the other Warsaw Pact leaders urged the Polish Prime Minister, Stanislaw Kania, to crush the 'anti-Socialist opposition forces'. Honecker, the East German leader, wanted Brezhnev to send in troops. In a letter dated 28 November 1980 he wrote:

> According to information we have received through various channels, counter-revolutionary forces in the People's Republic of Poland are on constant offensive, any delay in acting against them would mean death – the death of socialist Poland.

Warsaw Pact forces were mobilised in early December, but at the last moment intervention was cancelled as Kania convinced Brezhnev that he could restore order himself. US warnings against the use of force were probably also a powerful deterrent.

In 1981 Solidarity began to call for further drastic political changes. At the ninth Congress of the Polish Communist Party, delegates attacked the party leaders and even began to dismantle the party organisation. Once more the question of Soviet intervention arose, but eventually Moscow agreed in December to a declaration of **martial law** by General Jaruzelski, Kania's successor. The Americans had again called on the USSR to allow Poland to solve the crisis itself. Arguably this indicated to Jaruzelski that Washington would tolerate the declaration of martial law provided Soviet troops did not cross the frontier.

Key question
Why did the events in
Poland threaten
Ostpolitik?

Ostpolitik under threat

Ostpolitik, which was a product of *détente*, was inevitably threatened by the 'New Cold War'. Both the German Chancellor Helmut Schmidt (1974–83), who had played a leading role in alerting the Western alliance to the dangers of the SS-20s, and his successor, Helmut Kohl, tried to protect it from the consequences of the sharply deteriorating East–West relations. At Tito's funeral in Belgrade in May 1980 Schmidt observed to Honecker that the European states must ensure that 'the really big brothers don't get nervous'. A month later he visited Moscow where he managed to persuade Brezhnev in principle to negotiate with the USA on the crucial question of intermediate nuclear missiles, although little was achieved in subsequent talks in Madrid, 1980–3.

It is arguable that *Ostpolitik* by 1980 was beginning to degenerate into an open appeasement of Moscow and the Eastern European regimes. While the West German and French governments did condemn the Soviet invasion of Afghanistan and pointedly remarked that *détente* 'could not withstand another shock' like that, they did not join London and Washington in criticising the Soviet invasion of Afghanistan or the Polish government's reaction to Solidarity. Indeed no less a person than the former West German Chancellor Willy Brandt actually condemned Solidarity for threatening the stability of the Polish regime! When martial law was declared by the Polish government in Poland in December 1981, Schmidt went out of his way to avoid criticising it. He was unwilling to sacrifice what had already been achieved by *Ostpolitik*, in improving relations between the two Germanies, for the sake of Poland. By the time the Pershing and Cruise missiles were deployed in the FRG in November 1983 Schmidt had been replaced by Kohl, who also took great care to minimise the impact of this action on *Ostpolitik*.

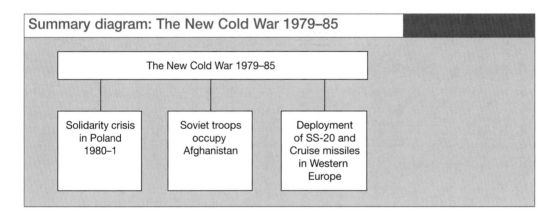

Summary diagram: The New Cold War 1979–85

Key date
On Brezhnev's death, Yuri Andropov became leader of USSR: November 1982

5 | The End of the Cold War in Europe 1983–91

Détente and economic reform in the USSR 1983–5

After Brezhnev's death in 1982, there were already signs that the Soviet leadership wished to resume its policy of *détente* with the USA and start the difficult task of making the Soviet economy more competitive with the West. Although his successor, Yuri Andropov, died in February 1984 from kidney failure, he initiated the process of economic reform in the USSR. He began, to quote the British historian S.R. Ashton, to contrast:

> the fiction of a Soviet system capable of generating growth and technological progress with the reality of an economy, which was still relatively backward, of workers who lacked discipline, of bureaucrats who were corrupt and of party managers who were complacent.

When Andropov died in February 1984, at a time of deepening tensions with the USA, the Soviet Politburo chose Konstantin Chernenko, a cautious and elderly conservative. Shortly before his death he did, however, re-open arms negotiations at Geneva in March 1985.

The problems facing Mikhail Gorbachev

Key question
Why did Gorbachev inherit a difficult situation in 1985?

Chernenko's successor, Mikhail Gorbachev, inherited a difficult situation:

Key date
Gorbachev became leader of the USSR: 12 March 1985

- The collapse of *détente* in the late 1970s between the USA and USSR had led to a new and expensive arms race. In 1983 President Reagan announced the development of 'Star Wars' or SDI, the strategic defence initiative, which was a plan for setting up nuclear and laser-armed satellites. These would be able to destroy ballistic missiles in the atmosphere and therefore make the USA safe from a Soviet attack. Moscow lacked both the financial means and the technology to build a rival system and feared that SDI might tempt the USA to launch a pre-emptive nuclear strike on the USSR.

Key term
Global over-stretch
The situation when great powers take on more global responsibilities than they can afford or manage easily.

- The USSR, like the USA in the 1960s, was increasingly suffering from '**global over-stretch**'. It was fighting an unwinnable war in Afghanistan and was giving financial and military aid to left-wing regimes which had seized power in Angola and the Horn of Africa. All of this cost a great deal of money.
- The Soviet economy was stagnating and desperately needed both technological and financial input from the West. Since 1975 its industrial production rate had been dropping and it was far behind the West in developing the new technologies.

Profile: Mikhail Gorbachev 1931–

1931	March 2	– Born into a peasant family in Stravropol
1952		– Joined the Communist Party
1966		– Graduated from Agricultural Institute as an agronomist–economist
1970		– Appointed First Secretary for Agriculture
1979		– Joined the Politburo
1985	March 11	– Elected General Secretary of the USSR
1986	February	– Launched the policies of **glasnost** and **perestroika**
1987	January	– Called for multi-candidate elections in the USSR
1988		– Announced the withdrawal of Soviet forces from Afghanistan and the abandonment of the Brezhnev Doctrine
1989		– A string of mostly peaceful revolutions in Eastern Europe
1990		– Received Nobel Peace Prize for ending the Cold War
1991	August	– Soviet hardliners launched unsuccessful *coups* against him
	August 25	– Resigned

Key terms

Glasnost
Openness.

Perestroika
Reconstruction, reform of the political and economic system.

When Gorbachev became General-Secretary, compared to his elderly and sick predecessors, he appeared a youthful and dynamic leader. His great aim was to modernise the USSR, and the two key words *glasnost* and *perestroika* set the tone for his period in power.

The ultimate survival of the USSR depended on *perestroika*. The historian S.R. Ashton, paraphrasing Henry Kissinger, observed that 'the Soviet Union found itself in the unenviable position of being threatened simultaneously by two crises – an economic crisis if it did nothing to change its system, and a political crisis if it did anything'. He was convinced that the USSR could no longer afford Cold War confrontation, and he renounced the idea of inevitable world conflict. Arguably, Gorbachev was therefore the single biggest force in ending the Cold War. The US historian Raymond Garthoff argues that 'his avowed acceptance of the interdependence of the world, of the priority of all human values over class values, and of the indivisibility of common security marked a revolutionary ideological change'.

It was clearly therefore in the USSR's interests to restore the Soviet–Western *détente* and resume negotiations on the reduction of armaments, but Gorbachev wished to go further than that. He was determined to end the Cold War because waging it was too costly and stopped him from implementing his policies of *perestroika* and *glasnost*, that is fundamentally reforming the Soviet economy and liberalising the Soviet political system. Unlike

Stalin, Khrushchev and Brezhnev, he did not conduct Soviet foreign policy according to the Marxist–Leninist revolutionary ideology. He no longer believed that Communism would eventually triumph over the West. Instead he worked towards achieving international co-operation and a real co-existence between the two hitherto rival systems, whose values and principles would in time converge rather than conflict. In 1994, R.L. Garthoff, described the new Gorbachev doctrine as representing:

> a shift of policy and performance, disengaging by choice from a whole global confrontation with the United States, to a policy predicated [based] on co-operative security and normalised relations with other countries.

Key question
What steps did Gorbachev take to restore the policy of *détente*?

Key date
Reagan–Gorbachev summit meeting at Reykjavik: 2 October 1986

Détente renegotiated 1985–8

Although the decision had been taken to renew arms talks only months before Gorbachev came to power, he quickly showed that he was determined to negotiate major reductions in nuclear weapons. In April 1985 he stopped increasing the number of SS-20s being installed in Eastern Europe, and in October started to reduce the total number deployed. He failed at the Reykjavik Conference in 1986 to persuade Reagan to give up the SDI plan in return for the negotiation of arms control treaties. However, such was his wish to end the arms race that he accepted unconditionally the NATO plan for a total withdrawal of medium-range missiles by both sides in Europe at the Washington summit in December 1987.

For the next two years Gorbachev showed a determination not just to restore *détente* but to end the Cold War. In February 1988 Soviet troops began to pull out of Afghanistan, and at the United Nations in December he publicly conceded that Marxism–Leninism was not the key to ultimate truth. According to one US Senator, this was 'the most astounding statement of surrender in the history of ideological struggle'.

Key question
To what extent did Gorbachev's policy in Eastern Europe contradict the Brezhnev Doctrine?

Key date
Free elections in Poland: June 1989

Gorbachev and Eastern Europe

By withdrawing from Afghanistan and Africa Gorbachev re-focused Soviet policy on Europe. Again here he hoped to safeguard Soviet security through a policy of political co-operation and negotiation. On 6 July he told the Council of Europe in a famous speech that:

> the common European home … excludes all possibility of armed confrontation, all possibility of resorting to threat or use of force, and notably military force employed by one alliance against another, within an alliance, or whatever it might be.

It is hard to imagine a more complete rejection of the Brezhnev doctrine (see page 141).

Gorbachev encouraged the former satellite states to reform and to liberalise. In the USSR in March 1989 there were for the first time multicandidate elections which led to reformers and dissidents sitting in the **Congress of People's Deputies**. In Poland Solidarity was legalised, elections took place in June and a non-Communist Prime Minister took power in August, while in Hungary the Communists agreed to multiparty elections – the very demand that had led to Soviet intervention in 1956 (see page 111). It is not surprising that US observers were beginning to come to the conclusion that 'we are quite literally in the early phases of what might be called the **post-Communist era**'.

At first the other satellite states – Bulgaria, Czechoslovakia, the GDR and Romania – attempted to insulate themselves from the consequences of Gorbachev's policies, but in September the GDR was confronted with a major crisis that led not only to the downfall of Communism in Eastern Europe but to the unification of Germany and the end of the Cold War.

The collapse of the GDR

The GDR was a product of the Cold War, and to survive into the Gorbachev era it needed to win the loyalty of its population, as it could no longer appeal to Soviet power to maintain law and order. By the summer of 1989 it seemed unlikely that it would be able to achieve this. Its economy, like the USSR's, suffered from centralised planning and a top-heavy system of bureaucratic control. Ironically only massive West German loans in 1983–4 had saved it from bankruptcy.

The GDR faced a major challenge when the Hungarian government decided in August to open its frontiers with Austria and some 150,000 East Germans poured across the border on their way to the FRG. Under pressure from the West German Chancellor, Helmut Kohl, Honecker also granted exit visas to the thousands of East Germans who had travelled to Poland and Prague, and who were quite literally besieging the West German embassies there in a desperate attempt to flee the GDR.

Honecker was now facing a crisis potentially every bit as grave as Ulbricht had in 1961 (see page 119). His belated grants of exit visas did nothing to restore confidence in the GDR. On the contrary, it merely made his handling of the crisis look unsure. In Leipzig a series of large but peaceful demonstrations took place in late September and early October, which the regime reluctantly tolerated because it knew that Gorbachev would not support a hard-line policy. Indeed when Gorbachev visited Berlin on 5 October to attend the celebrations marking the fortieth anniversary of the GDR (page 75), he advised Honecker to follow the example of the Poles and Hungarians and pointedly warned him that 'life punishes latecomers'.

In an effort to stabilise the situation Honecker was sacked by the GDR Politburo, and on 9 November the Berlin Wall was opened. More than anything else this highly symbolic event marked the end of the Cold War. Under the leadership of Hans Modorow, the GDR then rapidly followed the example of Poland

By February 1990 GDR troops had already started to demolish the Berlin Wall.

and agreed to free elections, which were held in March 1990. The 'Alliance for Germany' coalition, which supported reunification, won a majority of seats, and on 12 April the new government announced that it wished to join the FRG.

The other Eastern European states: Bulgaria, Czechoslovakia and Romania

In Bulgaria and Czechoslovakia events followed very much the same pattern as in the GDR. Peaceful demonstrations forced the replacement of the Communist government by new **multiparty regimes**. As the old Soviet bloc disintegrated, Gorbachev resolutely refused to intervene. His spokesman, Gennadii Gerasimov, startled the West when he said that the Brezhnev doctrine had been replaced by the 'Frank Sinatra doctrine'. By this he was referring to the singer's signature ballad, 'I did it my way', implying that the Eastern European states should be allowed to determine their own future. Only in Romania was there any attempt to resist the tide of *glasnost* sweeping over Eastern Europe. Here Nicolae Ceausescu, the Communist dictator, made several attempts to break up demonstrations, which led to escalating violence. In December after a violent clash between the army, which had come out against the regime, and the security forces, he was arrested and executed together with his wife.

Given these dramatic events in the second half of 1989, it is not surprising that the US President George Bush and Gorbachev agreed, when they met at Malta in December, that the Cold War was over.

Key question
How did Communism collapse in Bulgaria, Czechoslovakia and Romania?

Multiparty regimes
Democratic states where genuinely different parties exist, fight elections and form governments.

Key term

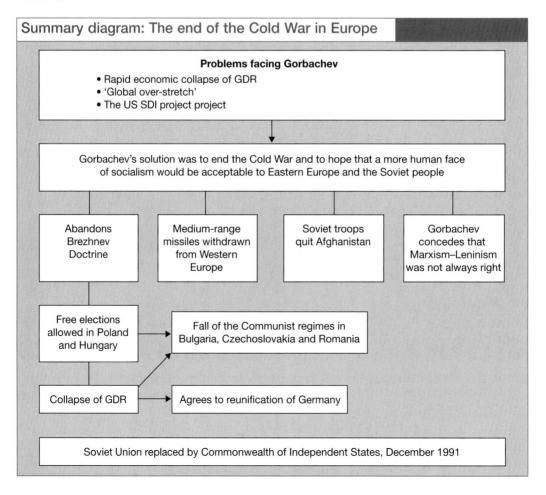

Summary diagram: The end of the Cold War in Europe

Problems facing Gorbachev
- Rapid economic collapse of GDR
- 'Global over-stretch'
- The US SDI project project

Gorbachev's solution was to end the Cold War and to hope that a more human face of socialism would be acceptable to Eastern Europe and the Soviet people

| Abandons Brezhnev Doctrine | Medium-range missiles withdrawn from Western Europe | Soviet troops quit Afghanistan | Gorbachev concedes that Marxism–Leninism was not always right |

Free elections allowed in Poland and Hungary → Fall of the Communist regimes in Bulgaria, Czechoslovakia and Romania

Collapse of GDR → Agrees to reunification of Germany

Soviet Union replaced by Commonwealth of Independent States, December 1991

6 | Reunification of Germany

Key question
How was Germany reunified?

The end of the Cold War still left the future of Germany undecided. At first neither the USSR nor Britain nor France wanted a united Germany, and Chancellor Kohl himself was thinking only of forming a very loose confederation which would very slowly grow into a political union, or federation. Nevertheless the strength of East German public opinion in the winter of 1989–90 convinced him that unity was the only option. The division of Germany had marked the beginning of the Cold War; its reunification marked the end.

Key date

Germany reunified:
3 October 1990

Kohl could not reunify Germany without the agreement of the USSR, the USA and Germany's main Western European allies, Britain and France. However, only the USSR and the USA had the power to stop it. Thus, the real negotiations were between Bonn, Moscow and Washington. At first Gorbachev was opposed to the liquidation of the GDR, and in December 1989 promised that he would 'see to it that no harm comes to the GDR'. Yet by the end of January his support for it was ebbing rapidly. On 10 February he told Kohl in Moscow that the Germans themselves should decide on the question of German unity, and at Ottawa four days later President Bush also gave the green light and outlined a formula for proceeding with the negotiations, the 'two-plus-four talks', which would bring together both the two Germanies and the four former occupying powers which still had **residual rights** in Berlin.

Key term

Residual rights
The remaining privileges, going right back to 1945, which the four occupying powers of Britain, France the USA and USSR still enjoyed.

In a series of negotiations in Bonn, Berlin, Paris and Moscow in the summer of 1990 German unity was brokered. Any lingering Russian opposition to German unity and the membership of a united Germany in NATO was overcome by generous West German loans, which Gorbachev hoped would facilitate the modernisation of the Soviet economy. Opposition in the West, particularly in London and Paris, was stilled by Kohl's insistence on a united Germany's continued membership of NATO and on the incorporation of East Germany into the European Community.

On 12 September the Two-Plus-Four Treaty was signed in Moscow. It was in effect a peace treaty ending the partition of Germany, as it terminated the residual rights of the former occupying powers in Germany and committed the new Germany to recognising the Oder–Neisse border with Poland. At midnight on 2 October 1990 the GDR was integrated into the FRG and a reunited Germany came into existence. The West, albeit with Gorbachev's blessing, had indeed won a spectacular victory.

7 | Conclusion

Key question
Why was Cold War
Europe so stable for
so long and why did
this stability break
down by 1989?

Writing in 1987, John Gaddis argued that the Cold War had
brought a 'long peace' to Europe. Certainly from 1963 onwards
Europe was, with the exception of Czechoslovakia in 1968 and
Poland in 1980–1, a stable and peaceful, although divided,
continent. Even the 'New Cold War' of the early 1980s did
not really see a return to the tensions of the Stalinist and
Khrushchev eras.

Stability during this period rested on two main foundations:

- mutually agreed nuclear arms control between the two
  superpowers at a level where each could deter the other from
  risking war
- and in Europe the *Ostpolitik* pursued by the FRG since 1969,
  which for the foreseeable future appeared to have regulated the
  German question.

What brought this 'long' peace to a close was essentially the
collapse of the centralised command economy of the Soviet
Union, which had squandered enormous sums on nuclear
armaments and failed to restructure itself to face the economic
challenges of the 1970s and 1980s. The USSR, weakened by the
renewed arms race and the flare up of ethnic conflicts within its
borders and virtually bankrupt, was no longer in the position to
enforce the Brezhnev doctrine. Gorbachev thus had little option
but to wind up the Cold War, seek **Western credits** and try to
modernise the Soviet economy by the partial introduction of **free
market principles**. He hoped that a reformed and economically
strengthened USSR would be able to forge new links of genuine
friendship with the Eastern European states. He did not foresee
that by December 1991 real political power in Moscow would lie
with an elected president and that the USSR would be replaced
by the establishment of a Commonwealth of Independent states.
His resignation on 25 December marked the end of the USSR.

Key date
USSR formally
dissolved: 21
December 1991

Key terms
Western credits
Loans of money
from Western
banks.

**Free market
principles**
Rules determining
the running of a
capitalist economy.

Summary diagram: The 'long peace' in Europe 1963–91

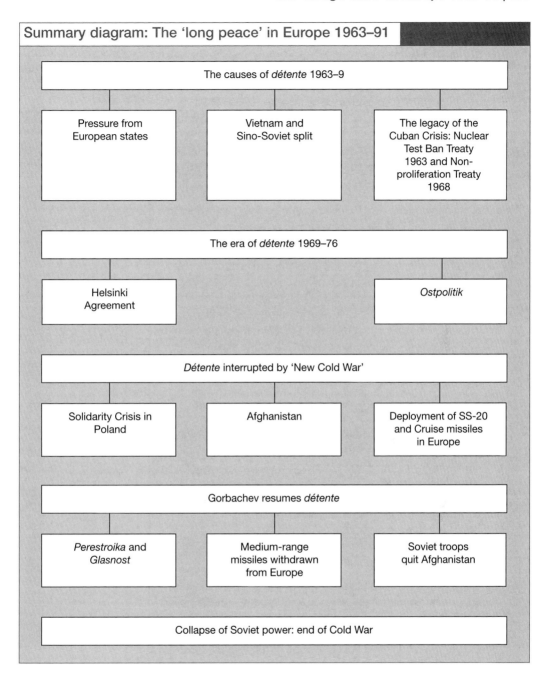

The causes of *détente* 1963–9

- Pressure from European states
- Vietnam and Sino-Soviet split
- The legacy of the Cuban Crisis: Nuclear Test Ban Treaty 1963 and Non-proliferation Treaty 1968

The era of *détente* 1969–76

- Helsinki Agreement
- *Ostpolitik*

Détente interrupted by 'New Cold War'

- Solidarity Crisis in Poland
- Afghanistan
- Deployment of SS-20 and Cruise missiles in Europe

Gorbachev resumes *détente*

- *Perestroika* and *Glasnost*
- Medium-range missiles withdrawn from Europe
- Soviet troops quit Afghanistan

Collapse of Soviet power: end of Cold War

Study Guide: AS Questions

In the style of OCR

1. Explain why the Cold War in Europe between 1963 and 1989 has been called the 'long peace'. (50 marks)
2. Why do historians sometimes call the years 1979–85, a 'new' Cold War? (50 marks)

Exam tips

The cross-references are intended to take you straight to the material that will help you to answer the questions.

Before planning your answers to these, make sure you are aware of the relevant facts and problems of the period covered by the question. Look, too, at the advice on essay writing on page 58.

1. Question **1** is a complex question covering a sweep of 26 years. Its defining words are 'long peace'. It would help you to plan your answer if you remembered that John Gaddis used this term in 1987 to explain how the Cold War in Europe had settled down after the Cuban crisis into a relatively stable international system. Do you agree with Gaddis' assessment? Was the situation really stable or was Nixon more perceptive about its dangers when he remarked that '*détente* is not the same as lasting peace'. Bearing this observation in mind, ask yourself the following questions:

   - Did *détente* lead to the stabilisation of nuclear weapons in Europe (pages 137 and 148)?
   - How was the long peace enforced in Eastern Europe (page 136)?
   - Did both powers feel free outside Europe to intervene to prop up friendly regimes (pages 136 and 147)?
   - What were the aims of *Ostpolitik* (page 142)?
   - What did the USA, Western Europe and USSR hope to gain from the Helsinki Agreement (pages 146–7)?

2. By the time you come to plan question **2** you will have already thought about the increasing tension in Europe during the period 1978–85. Was this a 'new' Cold War or simply a phase in the old one? To answer this you will need to look at these years in the context of the whole Cold War in Europe. What was the Cold War really about? Were those issues still alive in the early 1980s? Was the new Cold War perhaps just a flare-up of old tensions?

Study Guide: Advanced Level Questions

In the style of AQA

How far was the policy of *Ostpolitik* responsible for the collapse of the GDR in 1989? (45 marks)

Exam tips

The cross-references are intended to take you straight to the material that will help you to answer the question.

You will need to refresh your memory on the policy of *Ostpolitik* and its implications (pages 142–5), and the collapse of the GDR (pages 154–5). Clearly, *Ostpolitik* had an important effect in that recognition of the GDR opened the way for that state to greater communication with the West. Note also that it paved the way for West German loans to the East that helped prop it up, but also increased its dependence. Nevertheless, the collapse of the GDR was the result of a collection of factors rather than simply one. You will need to look at:

- the implications of Gorbachev's *perestroika* and *glasnost* policies
- activities in other Eastern European countries, particularly Poland and Hungary
- the implications of the opening of the Hungarian border
- the behaviour of Honeker.

Try to decide the factor or factors you consider to be most significant and argue accordingly. You should support your ideas with references to factual detail and should arrive at a substantiated conclusion.

In the style of Edexcel
Study Sources 1–3 below.

Source 1
From Martin Walker, The Cold War, *published in 1994.*

By the mid-1980s, both sides were hoping to achieve a new *détente*: the uneasy slackening of confrontation, an increase in trade and diplomacy, and the acceptance of one another's spheres of influence. But for the extraordinary coincidence of two extraordinary men, Reagan and Gorbachev, that might well have been what the world got, a replay of the *détente* era of the 1970s. Neither the diplomats nor the arms-control experts were prepared for the quantum leap in the nuclear relationship that Reagan and Gorbachev were about to make.

Source 2
From John Lewis Gaddis, The Cold War, *published in 2005.*

The upheavals of 1989 caught everyone by surprise. What no one understood, at the beginning of 1989, was that the Soviet Union, its empire, its ideology – and therefore the Cold War itself – was a sand pile ready to slide. All it took to make that happen were a few more grains of sand. The people who dropped them were not in charge of superpowers or movements: they were ordinary people with simple priorities who saw, seized, and sometimes stumbled into opportunities. In doing so, they caused a collapse no one could stop. Their leaders had little choice but to follow.

One particular leader did so in a distinctive way. He ensured that the great 1989 revolution was the first one in which almost no blood was shed. This revolution became a triumph of hope. It did so chiefly because Mikhail Gorbachev chose not to act, but rather to be acted upon by ordinary people.

Source 3
From Niall Ferguson, Colossus: The Rise and Fall of the American Empire, *published in 2004.*

After the East German revolution of 9 November 1989, it was suddenly apparent that Mikhail Gorbachev would not or could not maintain the Russian empire by sending tanks into East European cities. Germany was crucial to Soviet interests. A Western-led reunification of Germany had been the stuff of previous Soviet leaders' darkest nightmares. It now followed that the United States had a free hand more or less everywhere.

Source: Edexcel Specimen Paper, 2007

How far do you agree with the view that the Cold War came to an end because of popular protests in Eastern Europe which the USSR was powerless to resist?

Explain your answer using Sources 1, 2 and 3 and your own knowledge of this controversy. (40 marks)

Exam tips

The cross-references are intended to take you straight to the material that will help you to answer the question.

Source 1 suggests that political leaders rather than popular protests were significant in ending the Cold War, referring to Reagan and Gorbachev as 'extraordinary men'. It also suggests an era of declining hostility between the superpowers. You could expand on *détente* renegotiation and Gorbachev's radically different approach to his predecessors (page 152) both in terms of ideology (page 153) and in withdrawal from Afghanistan (page 153). Reagan's policy of developing the SDI (page 167) is also relevant.

Sources 3 and 4 both focus on protests in the East. They lend support to the statement in the question. Source 3 concentrates on the 'upheavals' of 1989 and the challenge to the Soviet Union. It offers a 'sand pile' interpretation, shows the significance of the actions of 'ordinary people' and offers support for the contention that 'the USSR was powerless to resist'. However, it is also important to note the comments on the decisions of Mikhail Gorbachev – and this provides an opportunity for you to cross-refer with Source 1 and also with Source 3 that comments on Gorbachev's reaction to popular protest in East Germany; that he 'could not or would not' send in the tanks.

For Ferguson in Source 3, it is not so apparent that the USSR was powerless to resist, but it is certainly made clear that the USSR does not attempt to impose its own military solution on a satellite state. Since this is different from earlier Soviet reactions, this will help you to raise the issue of how far it indicates 'powerlessness' and how far it reflects changed policies. You can explore the issue of the collapse of the GDR in more depth using pages 154–5. Your own knowledge could be used to show that Gorbachev attempted to manage diplomacy in a different way from his predecessors, criticising the Brezhnev years. You should also examine how far events in Poland (pages 148–50 and 153–4) suggest changed circumstances or changed policies and how far, after the collapse of GDR, events in Bulgaria, Czechoslovakia and Romania (page 156) lend support to the sand-pile theory.

The sources set up a clear debate for you, and a very interesting one. Organise your material – both from the sources and your own knowledge – to address both elements in the debate: 'ordinary people' or 'extraordinary personalities' of political leaders. Which of these appears to have been more significant in the sudden ending of the Cold War at the end of the 1980s?

8 Interpreting the Cold War

POINTS TO CONSIDER
This chapter is a general survey of the Cold War
concentrating on the main issues that need to be
considered if the Cold War is to be understood:

- Could the Cold War have been avoided?
- When did the Cold War actually start?
- Why did the Cold War in Europe last for so long?
- Why did the Cold War end?

The Cold War in Europe lasted for over four decades and by the
mid-1960s the divisions that had grown out of the immediate
postwar years were accepted as a permanent fact of international
life. Twenty years later, as we have seen, the US historian, John
Gaddis, was able to describe the uneasy stability that it had
created as the 'long peace'. It was, however, more a truce than a
peace. Even at the height of *détente* during the 1970s, tension,
hostility and competition still characterised the relations between
the Warsaw Pact and NATO states.

1 | Could the Cold War Have Been Avoided?

Revisionist historians such as Daniel Yergin and Willy Loth argue
that it was the USA that provoked the Cold War by refusing to
recognise the Soviet sphere of interest in Eastern Europe or to
make concessions over reparations in Germany. Could the Cold
War really have been avoided if Stalin had been treated more
diplomatically and greater sympathy shown to the appalling
postwar problems in the USSR? It is possible to make out a case
that Stalin did in fact act with greater restraint in Eastern Europe
than his later Cold War critics in the West gave him credit for. He
stopped Tito from intervening in Greece and, until 1948, allowed
semi-democratic regimes to function in Hungary and
Czechoslovakia. Loth argues that initially he also tried to restrain
his own **military government officials** in the Soviet zone of
Germany from applying too rigidly the Soviet Communist model.
Indeed it is arguable that up to the summer of 1947 Stalin gave
precedence to trying to maintain the wartime Grand Alliance and
failed to exploit favourable opportunities for establishing Soviet
influence in such areas as Iran and Greece.

Key question
What caused the Cold
War?

Key term
**Military
government
officials**
Officials who
worked on Soviet
military
governments in
Eastern Europe.

Was it then British and US policy that caused the Cold War? Can Stalin really be regarded as an innocent party pushed into waging the Cold War by the manoeuverings of the Anglo-Americans? Revisionist historians point to the determination of the Americans to deny the Soviets access to raw materials in the Western hemisphere and of British attempts to force a decision on the future of Germany, which would almost inevitably lead to its division. There is no doubt that initially Stalin's policy was 'moderate' in that he did not want a third world war, as the USSR was hardly in the position to wage it. Yet what in retrospection can be called moderation did not necessarily seem to be so at the time. The British and Americans were alarmed by Soviet requests for control of the Black Sea Straits and of the former Italian colony of Libya. Even though Stalin withdrew these, they were seen as evidence of expansionist tendencies. Similarly the exclusion of Western influence from Poland and most of Eastern Europe seemed to be an aggressive act and fed suspicions in London and Washington of Soviet actions. There was an ambiguity about Soviet policy. Stalin's ruthless suppression of all opposition in Poland and the '**shotgun marriage**' of the SPD and SED in the Soviet zone in Germany in 1946 alienated politicians in London and Washington even when he still hoped to work closely with them. On the other hand London and Washington also gave out conflicting signals. They resented being excluded from Eastern Europe, but in their turn excluded the USSR from Western Europe and the Mediterranean.

Key term
Shotgun marriage
A forced union.

Great power rivalry, mutual fears about security and rival ideologies were all causes of the Cold War. Stalin's personality, too, is relevant, and it is arguable that the Cold War was an extension of the same distrust and suspicion which characterised his domestic policy. According to Gaddis, 'he functioned in much the same manner whether operating within the international system, within his alliances, within his country … or party. [He] waged war on all these fronts. The Cold War we came to know was only one of many from his point of view.'

Key question
Why is there a debate about when the Cold War started?

2 | When Did the Cold War Actually Start?

As we have seen in Chapter 1, historians disagree about when to date the beginning of the Cold War. Relations between the Allied powers, particularly the USA and the USSR, had been deteriorating ever since the defeat of Hitler, which had been the main cement holding together the Grand Alliance. The Cold War has been dated variously from the dropping of the atom bombs on Hiroshima and Nagasaki, Churchill's famous Iron Curtain speech in March 1946 or the launching of the Truman Doctrine in March 1947. Although the beginnings of the Cold War are hard to pinpoint, it was certainly well under way by the end of 1947. The withdrawal of the USSR from the Paris talks on Marshall Plan aid, the creation of the Cominform and the breakdown of the London Conference were important stages in the escalation of the Cold War in that year.

The Cold War in Europe

Europe was the main, although not the only, theatre of the Cold War. It was there that it both began and ended. For the USSR it was essential to keep Eastern Europe under its control as a protective barrier against any possible attack from the West. It was this fact that led to Soviet intervention in Hungary in 1956 and to the formulation of the Brezhnev Doctrine 12 years later. The prize that both sides struggled for was Germany. In this the Western powers had the advantage as they controlled two-thirds of the country, which included the great industrial centre of the Ruhr. The military and economic integration of the Western two-thirds of Germany into Western Europe was what Stalin most dreaded. The Berlin Blockade was an attempt to stop this from happening, but it merely intensified Western efforts to create an independent West German state in 1949. Again, to prevent West Germany from joining NATO and/or the planned European Defence Community (EDC), Stalin orchestrated a massive peace movement, and finally, as a last desperate try, he proposed in March 1952 a plan for creating a neutral and apparently free Germany. In 1953 Lavrentii Beria, one of the key politicians in the USSR just after Stalin's death, very briefly played with the possibility of 'selling' the GDR to West Germany subject to certain restrictions on its armaments, but after the East German uprising of 1953, this idea was quickly dropped and until 1989 Soviet policy was to build up the weak and vulnerable East German state.

The division of Germany mirrored the division of Europe. The construction of the Berlin Wall confirmed the division of Germany for another 28 years, and in time brought a certain stability to Central Europe. The only problem was that in the long term the division was unstable or **asymmetrical**. As President Eisenhower's National Security Council pointed out, the FRG 'had nearly three times the population, about five times the industrial output and almost twice the size' of the GDR. Similarly Western Europe and the USA together represented infinitely more economic power than the Soviet bloc could command.

The same lack of symmetry can be seen in the way the two superpowers influenced their respective blocs. On balance it is true to say that the USA initially set up in Western Europe an 'empire by invitation'. The Western Europeans in the late 1940s were desperate for US military and financial aid. On the other hand in Eastern Europe, with the partial exceptions of Hungary and Czechoslovakia until 1947, the USSR established an empire by conquest.

In the Soviet zone of Germany the behaviour of the Red Army and the mass raping carried out by its soldiers in 1945 created an atmosphere of hate and fear, which reinforced West Germany's determination to remain within the US sphere of influence at all costs. Essentially, the Americans helped to create an independent, prosperous, economically and increasingly politically integrated Western Europe functioning within a capitalist global system. The Soviets had little to offer Eastern Europe that could rival this.

Asymmetrical
Having a lack of symmetry or balance.

Key term

Hence, the economic strength of Western Europe exerted a magnetic attraction on the peoples of Eastern Europe.

Key question
Why did the West overestimate the power of the USSR?

3 | Why Did the Cold War in Europe Last For So Long?

If the West had such a significant advantage over the Soviet bloc, why did the Cold War last for so long? It is possible to argue that its eventual outcome should have been predicted as early as 1968 when the crushing of the Prague Spring forced the Czech government and the other satellite states to abandon their attempts to liberalise their economies and to return instead to a system of more rigid centralised control, which made them less flexible and responsive to change. Yet it still seemed inconceivable that the USSR and its Eastern European satellites would eventually collapse like a row of dominoes. The USSR seemed to be a superpower at least as strong as the USA. This overestimation of its power was caused by assessing its strength solely in terms of its nuclear weapons. This was the one area where it could effectively compete with the West. The long period of *détente* preserved the Soviet nuclear deterrent, but only slowed down its economic decline, despite massive loans from the West.

Key question
Could the Cold War have ended before 1989?

4 | Why Did the Cold War End?

Behind the nuclear facade the whole Soviet bloc was suffering a steady economic, ideological, moral and cultural decline. This was primarily caused by its own economic inefficiencies and inability to match the West's economic growth. *Détente*, the Helsinki Agreement and *Ostpolitik* increasingly exposed the Soviet empire to Western influences. As Gaddis has put it:

> To visualise what happened, imagine a troubled triceratops [a plant-eating dinosaur]. From the outside, as rivals contemplated its sheer size, tough skin, bristling armament and aggressive posturing, the beast looked sufficiently formidable that none dared tangle with it. Appearances deceived, though, for within, its digestive, circulatory and respiratory systems were slowly clogging up, and then shutting down. There were few external signs of this until the day the creature was found with all four feet in the air still awesome but now bloated stiff, and quite dead. The moral of the fable is that armaments make impressive **exoskeletons**, but a shell alone ensures the survival of no animal and no state.

Key term

Exoskeletons
Rigid external coverings or shells for the body.

Until the Reagan presidency no statesman in the West dared call the USSR's bluff. After all, even if the USA had a greater nuclear arsenal, the USSR had the capacity to land, at the very least, a few missiles on the USA, and that was still a formidable deterrent. By developing the SDI Reagan challenged the USSR in a way that had not happened since the late 1940s. The USSR simply could not keep pace. This was the context in which Gorbachev came to the conclusion that the only chance the USSR had of surviving was to modernise its economy and society along Western lines. He thus embarked on an ambitious but ultimately unsuccessful attempt to base the USSR's links with its satellite states on consent rather than coercion. This approach, however, came too late. In 1968 many East Europeans could perhaps still have been won over by the prospect of 'Socialism with a human face', but 20 years later all socialist idealism had evaporated. After the grey, corrupt and repressive years of the Brezhnev era, the sudden freedom offered by Gorbachev was used by the Eastern Europeans to reject socialism and look to the US and Western European economic models.

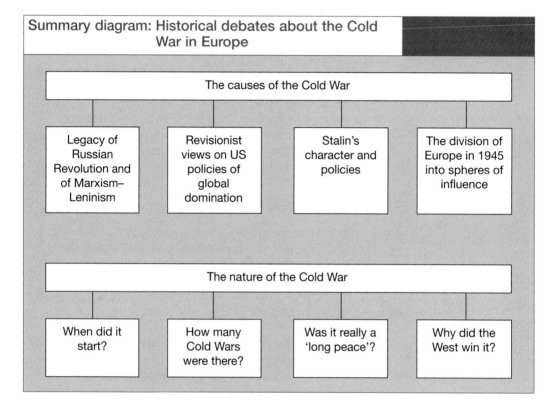

Summary diagram: Historical debates about the Cold War in Europe

The causes of the Cold War

- Legacy of Russian Revolution and of Marxism–Leninism
- Revisionist views on US policies of global domination
- Stalin's character and policies
- The division of Europe in 1945 into spheres of influence

The nature of the Cold War

- When did it start?
- How many Cold Wars were there?
- Was it really a 'long peace'?
- Why did the West win it?

Study Guide
Answering Essay Questions on the Cold War

The following are examples of essay questions covering the whole of the Cold War in Europe:

1. Why did the Cold War in Europe last for so long?
2. Why did the USA and its Western allies win the Cold War in Europe?
3. Why was the German question such an important issue in the Cold War?

Exam tips

The cross-references are intended to take you straight to the material that will help you to answer the questions.

Ideally you should never be surprised by an essay question in an exam. When you revise, always try to understand what the underlying issues of a particular topic are, before beginning to master the mass of factual detail. If you have done that with the Cold War, the above questions should not surprise you. Once you have thought through one leading question very carefully, you will find that the next question will not be so difficult as there will be some factual and thematic overlap.

1. Obviously the first essay title is a leading question about the Cold War. The key words here are 'so long'. To answer it you need discuss briefly:

    - how the Soviet and Western blocs reflected the balance of forces in 1945 (pages 18–19)
    - how the USSR was determined never again to allow an attack to be launched on it through Eastern Europe (page 14).

    It was therefore in the strategic interests of the USSR to dominate the Eastern European states for as long as it could. This can be seen in Khrushchev's reaction to the Hungarian revolt in 1956 and the formulation of the Brezhnev Doctrine in 1968. The USSR had sufficient force to do this. Its land forces vastly outnumbered the Western armies, and after 1949, when it exploded its first nuclear bomb, war against the USSR was too great a risk for the West to undertake (see page 84). Hence there was little real alternative to an armed truce. Yet we have seen that increasingly the USSR was like a triceratops with a tough skin but decaying internal organs. Why then did the Cold War not end in the mid-1950s or 1960s? In answering this you need to bear in mind the following factors:

    - The Western alliance believed that the USSR would rather go to war than see its vital interests in Eastern Europe suffer (see pages 112–13).
    - The long period of *détente* was particularly advantageous to the USSR, as it preserved its status as a great power (see pages 146–7).
    - Willy Brandt's *Ostpolitik* brought recognition of the GDR and the postwar frontiers of Poland and Czechoslovakia (see pages 142–5).
    - The Cold War was also an ideological struggle. Both sides were determined to defend their core beliefs in the areas of Europe they influenced.

2. In this question the key word is 'win'. To answer this you need to explain:

    - How the West controlled, or had access to, the most prosperous and dynamic areas of the world. The most wealthy two-thirds of Germany was, for example, economically, politically and militarily integrated into Western Europe. The magnetism that this could exert on the East can be seen in the way millions of East Germans fled the GDR to the FRG until the construction of the Wall in 1961 (see page 119).

- How, after the collapse of the Prague Spring, the states of the Soviet bloc virtually gave up attempts to modernise and liberalise their economies. They returned, instead, to the old-fashioned and rigid neo-Stalinist system where all economic decisions were controlled from the centre by the government. By the end of the 1970s their economies were facing major crises. The GDR, for example, was by this stage only kept solvent by huge loans from the FRG (see page 154).

- The USSR also had to pay for its massive intervention into Afghanistan and then was faced with Reagan's SDI challenge (see pages 148 and 153).

- Gorbachev therefore took a daring but ultimately unsuccessful gamble in his efforts to modernise the USSR and reform its relations with East Europe (see page 152).

On the other hand in 1989 Gorbachev alone took the initiative to end the Cold War without any discussions within the Warsaw Pact. The consent of the USA and USSR was also crucial for the reunification of Germany in 1990.

3. The third question targets the pivotal role of Germany in the Cold War. Here you need to stress the position of Germany in the middle of Europe, its enormous economic potential and large population. Essentially, whichever bloc possessed it was in a powerful position to win the Cold War. That was why Stalin tried to prevent the Western zones, in which most of Germany's heavy industry was located, from being formed into the FRG in 1948–9 by launching the Berlin Blockade. By the same token it was also why Britain and the USA wanted West Germany included in NATO. To stop this from happening Stalin proposed in March 1952 a neutral but reunified Germany. Even when Khrushchev recognised the GDR in 1955, the German question remained one of the flash points of the Cold War. West Berlin was an Allied outpost in the middle of the GDR, in which hundreds of thousands of East Germans could find refuge and be flown to the West. By 1961 this labour drain threatened to destabilise the GDR and bring about its collapse. Hence, Khrushchev had little option but to sanction the construction of the Berlin Wall to preserve the existence of the GDR. After 1961 the German question was less acute, but it nevertheless remained of great importance. Willy Brandt attempted to normalise relations between the two Germanies with his *Ostpolitik*, but the future of Germany still remained open, as the FRG did not ultimately give up its aim of uniting the two states. Then with the collapse of Communism in 1989–90, the reunification of Germany was one of the most urgent questions facing the USSR and the Western states.

Study Guide: A2 Question

In the style of AQA

To what extent was the Cold War in Europe a 'bipolar struggle' dominated by the USSR and USA? (45 marks)

Exam tips

The cross-references are intended to take you straight to the material that will help you to answer the question.

In this question the key words are 'to what extent' and 'bipolar'. This is a difficult question that spans the whole period of the Cold War. Obviously in the crucial area of nuclear missiles and bombs there was an overwhelming bipolarity, although both France and Britain possessed small nuclear deterrents. The USSR and the USA were, of course, the 'really big brothers', as Chancellor Schmidt said (see page 149), but right through the whole Cold War there were other players on the stage.

- In the early period Britain and France played key roles, the former in NATO, the latter in launching European integration through the ECSC and, later, the doomed EDC (see pages 84–5 and 87).
- In the 1960s the West European states, particularly France, distanced themselves from the USA, which suffered defeat in Vietnam with subsequent serious economic difficulties (see pages 136 and 139).
- The FRG also seized the initiative in launching its highly successful *Ostpolitik* in 1970–2 (see pages 142–5).
- In the Soviet bloc there was also more diversity than initially appeared. Tito went his own way in 1948 and was a considerable influence on Khrushchev in 1956 (see page 108).
- Gomulka carved out an element of independence for himself and Ulbricht was able to bring a certain amount of pressure to bear on Khrushchev during the period 1960–1 (see pages 110–11 and 119).

Further Reading

There is a growing number of specialised books and articles dealing with all aspects of the Cold War in Europe, as archive material in the USSR and the former satellite states becomes available to historians. Before you read these it is important that you should familiarise yourself with the general accounts of the period.

Textbooks Covering the Whole Period

All the books recommended below are worth reading, but for different reasons:

J. Laver, C. Rowe and D. Williamson, *Years of Division Since 1945* (Hodder & Stoughton, 1999) has some very useful introductory chapters on the Cold War, Germany, the USSR and Eastern Europe.

J.W. Mason, *The Cold War, 1945–91* (Routledge, 1996) is an excellent introductory survey of just 75 pages.

G. Roberts, *The Soviet Union in World Politics: Coexistence, Revolution and Cold War, 1945–91* (Routledge, 1999) is a brief but comprehensive survey of Soviet foreign policy during this period.

M. Walker, *The Cold War* (Vintage, 1994) is a readable, journalistic study of the whole Cold War. It covers all aspects of this struggle and contains much useful information.

J.W. Young, *Cold War Europe, 1945–91* (Arnold, 1996, 2nd edn) has an informative chapter on the Cold War and *détente* and then further useful chapters on European integration, Eastern Europe, the USSR and the main Western European states.

S.R. Ashton, *In Search of* Détente: *The Politics of East–West Relations since 1945* (Macmillan, 1989) was published just before the Cold War ended, but it is nevertheless a very useful survey, particularly on *détente*.

Historiography and Problems of the Cold War

D. Reynolds, ed., *The Origins of the Cold War in Europe: International Perspectives* (Yale UP, 1994) is an excellent survey of the historiography and the international historical debates on the Cold War covering the period 1945–55.

K. Larres and A. Lane, *The Cold War: The Essential Readings* (Blackwell, Oxford, 2001) contains some interesting articles and extracts from leading Cold War historians.

J.L. Gaddis, *We Know Now: Rethinking Cold War History* (OUP, 1997) is an important and readable book, which puts the

European Cold War into its global context. It is based as far as possible on recent research.

The Cold War *International History Project Bulletin* (CWIHP, Woodrow Wilson International Center for Scholars, Washington DC) has published hundreds of articles and documents from Eastern European and Soviet archives. Its aim is 'to disseminate new information and perspectives on Cold War history emerging from previously inaccessible archives'. What makes it a particularly usable source for A-level students is that it can be accessed on the internet at cwihp.si.edu.

Specialist Studies

The specialised literature on the Cold War is often complex and written primarily for historians and political scientists. However, the following are some suggested starting points for further study, which are not too difficult to read and understand:

(a) The origins of the Cold War up to 1953

M. McCauley, *The Origins of the Cold War, 1941–49* (Longman, 1995, 2nd edn) is a clear and well-explained introduction to the causes and early stages of the Cold War.

M. Leffler and D.S. Painter, *Origins of the Cold War* (Routledge, 1994) contains a number of interesting essays on different aspects of the early Cold War, which represent various conflicting interpretations.

C.M. Maier ed., *The Cold War in Europe* (Markus Wiener, 1996, 3rd edn) again has a collection of essays representing contradictory views on the Cold War.

D. Yergin, *Shattered Peace: The Origins of the Cold War and the National Security State* (Houghton Mifflin, 1977) is a revisionist study of the US's involvement in the Cold War in Europe.

(b) The Khrushchev years 1953–64

M. McCauley, *The Khrushchev Era* (Longman, 1995) is a clear, concise study of this dramatic period.

(c) *Détente* and *Ostpolitik*

M. Bowker and P. Williams, *Superpower* Détente: *A Reappraisal* (Sage, 1988) gives a full account of *détente* in the 1970s.

T. Garton Ash, *In Europe's Name: Germany and the Divided Continent* (Jonathan Cape, 1993) is a very useful guide to *Ostpolitik* and the reunification of Germany.

(d) Eastern Europe

J. Laver, *The Eastern and Central European States, 1945–92* (Hodder & Stoughton, 1999) provides a clear guide to the Eastern European states.

G. Swain and N. Swain, *Eastern Europe since 1945* (Macmillan, 1993) is a fuller study of the same subject.

(e) The end of the Cold War

T. Garton Ash, *We the People – The Revolution of 1990* (Penguin, 1990) is a journalist's account of the collapse of Communism in Eastern Europe.

M. Hogan, ed., *The End of the Cold War, its Meanings and Implications* (CUP, 1992) contains some excellent but difficult essays on the reasons for the end of the Cold War.

R. Garthoff, *The Great Transition: American–Soviet Relations and the End of the Cold War* (Brookings Institution, Washington, 1994) is a difficult but important book on the end of the Cold War.

Glossary

Advisory Steering Committee A committee that would advise on priorities and the key decisions to be taken.

Airlift The transport of food and supplies by air to a besieged area.

Allied Control Commissions These were set up in each occupied territory, including Germany. They initially administered a particular territory in the name of the Allies.

Anti-ballistic screens Protection provided by rocket launching pads.

Appease To conciliate a potential aggressor by making concessions. In the 1950s appeasement was a 'dirty word' associated with Britain's and France's appeasement of Nazi Germany in the 1930s.

Archives Government records which are deposited in a repository and later open to historians.

Arms race A competition or race between nations to arm themselves with the most deadly and effective weapons available.

Asymmetrical Having a lack of symmetry or balance.

Atlantic Charter A statement of fundamental principles for the postwar world. The most important of these were: free trade, no more territorial annexation by Britain or the USA, and the right of people to choose their own governments.

Austria In 1945 Austria, like Germany, had been divided into four zones. At Geneva, the USSR agreed to independence provided it remained neutral and did not join NATO.

Autarchic economy An economy that is self-sufficient and protected from outside competition.

Axis powers The major powers opposing the Allies: Germany, Japan and Italy.

Benelux states Belgium, the Netherlands and Luxemburg.

Big Three The major powers who formed the Grand Alliance: Britain, the USA and the USSR.

Bizonia In 1945, war-defeated Germany was divided into four zones occupied by the Americans, British, French and Soviets. In January 1947 the British and American zones were amalgamated and called Bizonia.

Bloc A group of allies or closely linked states.

Bloc mentality A state of mind brought about by being a member of one of the two sides in the Cold War.

Bolsheviks Russian Communists. The term, which means majority, was originally given to Lenin's group within the Russian Social Democrat Party in 1903.

C54s Large US transport planes.

Capitalism An economic system in which the production of goods and their distribution depend on the investment of private capital.

Central Executive Central organising committee.

Centralised control of the economy Control of a country's economy from the centre, as in Stalinist Russia.

Checkpoint Charlie One of the few official crossing points between East and West Berlin. It is now a museum.

Chief of Staff The head of military planning.

Collective defence The agreement of a group of nations to form an alliance such as NATO or the Warsaw Pact for mutual protection.

Collective security Security gained through joining an alliance where the security of each state is guaranteed by the others.

Collectivising agriculture Abolishing private farms in favour of large units run collectively by the peasantry along the lines of Soviet agriculture.

Comintern The Communist International was formed in 1919. Theoretically, in the words of its chairman, Zinoviev, it was 'a single foreign Communist Party with sections in different countries', but in reality it was controlled from Moscow.

Commonwealth Made up of the states that originally formed part of the British Empire.

Confederation A grouping of states in which each state retains its sovereignty. Hence, much looser than a federation.

Congress of People's Deputies The assembly to which representatives of the Communist Party were elected.

Congress The US parliament.

Congressional leaders Influential political leaders in the US Congress (parliament).

Consensus General agreement.

Consultative Council A council on which the member states of the Brussels Pact were represented and where they could discuss mutual problems.

Conventional forces Military forces that do not rely on nuclear weapons.

Council of Foreign Ministers Composed of the foreign ministers of Britain, France, the USA and the USSR. Its role was to sort out the German problems and prepare the peace treaties.

Customs union An area of free trade unhindered by national tariffs.

Defeat in Indo-China From 1945 to 1954 France attempted to hold on to its colony, Indo-China, and fought a bitter war against the Communists led by Ho Chi Minh. In March 1954 French troops surrendered at Dien Bien Phu.

Democratic local governments Town and regional councils that were elected democratically.

Destalinisation The attempts to liberalise the USSR after the death of Stalin in 1953.

Destalinisation and liberalisation A policy aimed at reversing Stalin's repressive policies and replacing them with a more democratic policy.

Détente A state of lessened tension or growing relaxation between two states.

Devalued Reichsmarks The original German currency had been destroyed by wartime and early postwar inflation and was almost valueless by 1948.

'Differentiated' policy Stalin's policy to treat each Soviet-occupied country differently.

Doctrine of containment A policy of halting the USSR's advance into Western Europe. It did not envisage actually 'rolling back' Soviet power from Eastern Europe.

Economic nationalism An economy in which every effort is made to keep out foreign goods.

EDC The European Defence Community, the aim of which was to set up a West-European army jointly controlled by the Western European states.

Electoral bloc An electoral alliance by a group of parties.

Embryonic state Organisation that has some of the powers of a proper state, and is likely to grow into a fully fledged state.

Empire by invitation The Western Europeans were in effect asking to be put under US protection and so become a part of a US 'empire' or a US-dominated region.

Ethnic Germans German people who still lived in Poland. In 1945 much former German territory was given to Poland.

European Community The European Economic Community (EEC) had changed its name to the European Community (EC).

EXComm The Executive Committee of the US National Security Council.

Exoskeletons Rigid external coverings or shells for the body.

Four power control In 1945 it was agreed that Berlin should be divided into four zones and be administered jointly by the four occupying powers.

Fraternal links 'Brotherly' links between two Communist parties that should theoretically have much in common.

Free city A city that enjoys self-government and is not part of a state.

Free French The French who supported de Gaulle after the fall of France in June 1940, when he set up his headquarters in London.

Free market principles Rules determining the running of a capitalist economy.

Free trade area A region where states can trade freely with each other.

Glasnost Openness.

Global confrontation The attempt to stand up to the enemy anywhere or everywhere in the world.

Global encirclement Surrounded on a global scale.

Global over-stretch The situation when Great Powers take on more global responsibilities than they can afford or manage easily.

Grand Alliance In 1941 Britain, the USSR and the USA allied to combat the Axis powers led by Germany, Japan and Italy.

Greens Those supporting the Green Party, whose stated aim is to protect the environment.

Gross national product The total production of domestic industries combined with the earnings from exports, etc.

Guerrilla war A war fought by small groups of irregular troops. The term comes from the Spanish resistance to Napoleon in the early nineteenth century.

Guns and butter A country's economy can finance both rearmament and a rising standard of living for its inhabitants.

Heavy industry Coal, iron and steel production.

High Commission A civilian body charged with the task of defending the interests of the Western allies in Germany.

Hotline A direct telegraphic link between Kennedy and Khrushchev, and their successors.

Human rights Basic rights such as personal liberty and freedom from repression.

Hydroelectric sources Power stations that generate electricity through water power.

Hydrogen bombs Thermonuclear devices, which explode at a very high temperature. Each one is capable of devastating 150 square miles by the blast and 800 square miles with radioactive fall out.

Immutable Unchangeable.

Imperialists Britain and France, who both still had extensive colonial empires. The Soviets also regularly called the Americans imperialists.

Independence Front A political bloc or alliance of parties.

Industrial and military complex The powerful combination of the armed forces and the defence industries.

Intercontinental ballistic missile A long-range missile that is powered initially, but falls on its target as a result of gravity and which can, for example, reach the USA from the USSR.

International Ruhr authority   Laid down how much coal and steel the Germans should produce and ensured that a percentage of its production should be made available to its Western neighbours. It was replaced in 1951 by the European Coal and Steel Community.

Inviolable   Not to be attacked or violated.

Iron Curtain   A term used by Churchill to describe how Stalin had separated Eastern Europe from the West.

Islamic fundamentalism   A very literal and traditional version of Islam that is hostile to Western civilisation, be it Marxist or Christian.

Isolation   A situation in which a state has no alliances or contacts with other friendly states.

Jupiter missiles   A liquid-fuelled, surface-deployed missile, which was already out of date by 1962.

Lackey   An uncritical follower, a servant, who cannot answer back.

Land corridors   Roads, railways and canals, which the Soviets had agreed in 1945 could be used to supply West Berlin.

Latent fear   Concealed (latent) or indirect terror and pressure.

Legal and mutually agreed framework A legal agreement freely negotiated that would, for instance, allow the USSR to maintain bases in Hungary.

Lend–lease aid programme   In March 1941 Roosevelt approved the Lend–Lease Act which enabled any country, whose defences were judged to be vital for the USA, to obtain war supplies. These would, however, have to be paid for later on. By 1945 over $50 billion had been spent on this scheme.

Liberation   The freeing of a country from foreign occupation.

Long peace   A period of international stability brought about by the nuclear balance between the USA and the USSR.

Magnetic social and economic forces of the West   Willy Brandt believed that the economy and way of life in West Germany was so strong that ultimately it would exert a magnet-like attraction on the GDR.

Make-believe constitution   A constitution that was not genuine and merely hid a dictatorship by one party: the SED.

Martial law   Military rule involving the suspension of normal civilian government.

Marxist–Leninist   A combination of the doctrines of Marx and Lenin. Lenin adapted Karl Marx's teaching to the situation in Russia. Unlike Marx he advocated the creation of a party dictatorship, which would have absolute powers, even over the workers.

Military government officials   Officials who worked on Soviet military governments in Eastern Europe.

Military Governor   The head of a zone of occupation in Germany.

Minister President   Prime Minister.

MIRVs   Multiple independently targeted re-entry vehicles. These were rockets that could fire well over 12 nuclear missiles on different targets.

Missile gap   Where one side has a temporary lead over the other in nuclear weapons.

Monroe Doctrine   The doctrine formulated by President Monroe of the USA (1817–25) that the European powers should not intervene on the US continent.

Multiparty regimes   Democratic states where genuinely different parties exist, fight elections and form governments.

Munich Agreement   In September 1938 this handed over the German-speaking Sudetenland, which had become part of the new Czech state in 1919, to Hitler's Germany.

National federation of trade unions A national organisation representing all the trade unions.

National roads to Socialism Khrushchev meant by this that the Eastern European states would have the freedom to work out their own 'brand' of socialism, rather than having it imposed on them by the USSR.

Nationalise To take over ownership of privately owned industries, banks, etc., by the state.

Nationalists Those who champion their nation or country.

NATO The North Atlantic Treaty Organisation was a military alliance which linked the USA and Canada to Western Europe. It became the cornerstone of the defence of Western Europe against Soviet threats.

NATO Council NATO's decision-making committee on which each member state was represented.

New Yalta At the Yalta Conference in 1945 the USSR was given much of eastern Poland. A 'New Yalta' would merely confirm this.

Non-aligned movement Not allied with either the USSR or the West.

Nuclear diplomacy Diplomacy backed up by the threat of nuclear weapons.

Nuclear-free zone An area, such as Central Europe, in which nuclear weapons would be neither used nor based.

Nuclear sabre rattling Threatening or hinting at the possibility of nuclear war in order to intimidate the Western powers.

Occupation Statute Treaty defining the rights of Britain, France and the USA in Western Germany.

October Revolution The second Russian revolution in October 1917, in which the Bolsheviks seized power.

Oder–Neisse line The line formed by the Oder and Neisse rivers. The Neisse had both a western and an eastern branch.

Ostpolitik West Germany's policy towards Eastern Europe, which involved recognition of the GDR and the postwar boundaries in Eastern Europe.

Paramilitary police force A police force that is armed with machine guns and armoured cars.

Paranoia Literally a mental condition characterised by an exaggerated fear of persecution. Here it means obsessive distrust.

Partisan groups These were resistance fighters or guerrillas, in German- and Italian-occupied Europe.

Peasant parties Parties representing the small farmers or peasants.

Perestroika Reconstruction, reform of the political and economic system.

Polarised Divided into extremes (polar opposites).

Political left Left-wing parties such as the Labour Party in Britain or the Social Democrats in Germany.

Post-Communist era A new historical period in which Communism is no longer a dominant force in Russia and Eastern Europe.

Pragmatic Practical, guided by events rather than by an ideology.

Prague Spring The liberalisation process put into effect by Alexander Dubcek, the Czech Prime Minister. There were both economic reforms aimed at freeing the economy from unnecessary restrictions, and political reforms, which restored the freedom of speech and political pluralism (the existence of several political parties).

Preventive war A limited war fought to prevent the later outbreak of a much larger war.

Provisional government A temporary government, in office until an election can take place.

Rapprochement Establishing close relations between two states.

Ratified When an international treaty has been signed, it can come into effect only after the parliaments of the signatory states have approved, or ratified, it.

Red Army The army of the USSR.

Referendum The referring of a political question to the electorate for a vote.

Reparations Materials, equipment or money taken from a defeated power to make good the damage of war.

Residual rights The remaining privileges, going right back to 1945, which the four occupying powers of Britain, France the USA and USSR still enjoyed.

Revisionist In the sense of historians, someone who revises the traditional or orthodox interpretation of events and often contradicts it.

Ruhr The centre of the German coal and steel industries and at that time the greatest industrial region in Europe.

Second front The 'first' front was in the USSR, where there was large-scale fighting between Soviet and German troops. A 'second' would be elsewhere, for example, in Western Europe, where the Germans could be directly engaged by the British and US allies.

Secretary of State The US Foreign Minister.

Shotgun marriage A forced union.

Social Democratisation Converting the Communist SED into a more moderate Western-style Social Democratic Party like the SPD in the FRG.

Socialisation of the economy Conversion of the economy from a capitalist to a socialist economy where industries are owned by the state, not individuals.

Socialist A believer in socialism: the belief that the community as a whole, rather than individuals, should control the means of production, the exchange of goods and banking.

Solidarity movement A movement that originated in support of the strikes in the Gdansk shipyards.

Sovereignty Independence. A sovereign state possesses the power to make its own decisions.

Spheres of interest Areas where one power is able to exercise the dominant influence and to influence local politics.

Splitters The SED accused the West Germans and the Western allies of splitting or dividing Germany.

Sputnik This satellite weighed 84 kg and was able to orbit the earth. In Russian the word means 'fellow traveller', or supporter of the USSR.

Stalin cult The propaganda campaign vaunting Stalin as the great ruler of the USSR.

Summits Conferences attended by the top political leaders.

Supranational Transcending national limits.

Tactical nuclear weapons Small-scale nuclear weapons that can be used in the battlefield.

Tariffs Taxes placed on imported goods to protect the home economy.

Telex An international communications system with printed messages transmitted by teleprinters using the public telephone network.

Test Ban Treaty This prohibited the testing of nuclear weapons in the atmosphere, outer space and under water, but allowed them to be tested underground.

Thaw A period of improved relations between East and West: a 'thaw' in the 'Cold War'.

Third world States that had for the most part been former colonies, but which were now free and independent of both the USSR and the West.

Totalitarian regimes Regimes such as those in Soviet Russia or Nazi Germany, which sought to control every aspect of their people's lives.

Trade missions Organisations to promote trade between states.

Trade surplus A surplus of exports over imports.

Traditionalist In the sense of historians, someone who has a traditional view of historical events.

Transit traffic Traffic crossing through another state.

Vienna Settlement of 1815 Re-drew the map of Europe after Napoleon had finally been defeated.

Western bloc An alliance of Western European states and the USA.

Western credits Loans of money from Western banks.

Western European integration The process of creating a Western Europe that was united politically, economically and militarily.

Western intelligence Information gained by Western spies in Eastern Europe.

Yugoslavia In 1918 the kingdom of Serbs, Croats and Slovenes was formed. In 1929 it officially became Yugoslavia. The Serbs were the strongest nationality within this state. In 1991 Yugoslavia ceased to exist when Croatia and Slovenia left the union.

Index